Emigration in a South Italian Town

Emigration in a South Italian Town

An Anthropological History

William A. Douglass

RUTGERS UNIVERSITY PRESS
New Brunswick, New Jersey

Library of Congress Cataloging in Publication Data

Douglass, William A.
Emigration in a south Italian town.

Bibliography: p.
Includes index.
1. Agnone (Italy)—History.   2. Italy—Emigration and
immigration.   3. Italians—Foreign countries—Emigration
and immigration.   4. Agnone (Italy)—Economic conditions.
5. Agnone (Italy)—Social conditions.   I. Title.
DG975.A2229D68 1983   945′.719   82–21626
ISBN 0–8135–0984–X

Copyright © 1984 by Rutgers, the State University

Manufactured in the United States of America

To my mother,
Barbara Josephine Douglass

To study history one must know in advance that one is attempting something fundamentally impossible, yet necessary and highly important. To study history means submitting to chaos and nevertheless retaining faith in order and meaning.

   . . . the writing of history—however dryly it is done and however sincere the desire for objectivity—remains literature. History's third dimension is always fiction.

—Hermann Hesse, *Magister Ludi*

Contents

Contents

Illustrations

Figures

Maps

Tables

Tables

Preface

A word is in order on my methodological and theoretical approach to this work. Until recently, anthropologists (and other social scientists) were prone to downplay history in their work. This was, no doubt, in part a function of the discipline's traditional focus on preliterate societies. To the extent that history was incorporated at all, it was gleaned from oral traditions and the recollections of tribal elders.

As anthropologists turned their attention to Europe, few were prepared to address the plethora of available written records on even one small community. I recall the trepidation with which I approached the municipal archive of Echalar, Navarra, upon initiating a comparative study of depopulation in two Spanish Basque villages.[1] The wall of the council chambers was lined with a chaotic mass of parchment and paper, some dating back to the fifteenth and sixteenth centuries. I made the rather arbitrary decision to use the earliest available (mid-nineteenth-century) household census as a base line so that I could ignore all of the earlier documentation. While this eased my task, it did not improve the analysis.

In initiating the Agnone study, I was determined to effect a more meaningful marriage of anthropological and historical methods. In some respects the decision was costly, for it added years to my original time-table. Once having made such a commitment, however, I can no longer conceive of any other satisfactory approach to the study of my main research concern: the causes and consequences of emigration. Furthermore, only by casting the historical net broadly was it possible to address the more challenging question of why transatlantic emigration from the Molise essentially began in the town of Agnone, province of Isernia.

Having framed the research question in such terms, I believe that my current study highlights as much as any to date both the strengths and weaknesses, the platforms and pitfalls of anthropological history. Anthropologists concerned with social change, yet wary or devoid of historical methodology, have long evoked an oftentimes ludicrous and ill-defined contrast between "modern" and "traditional" times for a particular society or community. Such a distinction is of little use for understanding the interplay of historical forces and processes in Agnone's evolution and devolution as an urban place. It is in the context of detailed microanalytical studies of social processes viewed over considerable time spans that current theories of the nature of social change must be tested and refined. Any criticism that an explanation is "merely historical" and that history is simply the recounting of "one damn thing after another" is a weak metaphysical defense of ill-developed theory spawned in frustration at the failure to meet the demanding challenge of conducting the relevant data collection and analysis.[2]

Conversely, when entering the tangle of documentary evidence, there is the ever-present danger of slipping into an anecdotal rather than analytical treatment. The more one learns about historical events in even one small human community, the more reticent one becomes about generalizing. Historians and social scientists have long posed different kinds of questions and hence elicited different information from the same record of human activity. Carried to an extreme, this difference in approach has led some anthropologists to upbraid historians for being atheoretical chroniclers,[3] while some historians have, in turn, leveled the charge that anthropology violates historical reality in the mindless, reductionist search for general laws.[4]

There are encouraging signs that the distinction between historians and other social scientists is finally breaking down. Anthropologists, sociologists, economists, and historians alike are finding considerable common ground in such areas as historical demography and what has come to be called the "new social history."[5] The recent spate of interdisciplinary journals and associations is testimony to the vigor of the consensus. With respect to the emerging anthropological history (the use of meaningful historical perspective by anthropologists), there is Macfarlane's analysis of the life of a seventeenth-century clergyman, Blok's treatment of a century of *mafioso* activity in one Sicilian community, the Halperns' diachronic analysis of their Serbian data, and Horwitz's use of ethnoscience to delineate the occupational domains and life cycles of a nineteenth-century Maine community. Conversely, Ladurie's works on peasant life in the Langedoc may be regarded as historical anthropology (i.e., employment of an anthropological perspective by an historian).[6] To the extent that this work merits its subtitle, it is meant to be a contribution to his convergence of historical and social scientific methodologies and perspectives.

Between October of 1972 and August of 1973, and again in the summer of 1974, I conducted standard anthropological field research in the south Italian hill town of Agnone. At the same time, I was impressed with the wealth of historical documentation available for study. The Archivio Comunale of Agnone's town hall contains considerable information on the past two centuries. The records in the magnificent private libraries in the town (Biblioteca Emidiana and Biblioteca La Banca) are rich in manuscript material dating from even earlier periods. Each of Agnone's seven parishes possesses its own archive. Then, too, Agnone documents are to be found in the Archivii di Stato of Isernia, Campobasso, Chieti, Lucera, Foggia, and Naples as well as in the Archivo de Simancas and the Biblioteca Nacional in Spain (a result of Spanish domination of the kingdom of Naples). Private collections, such as that of the Monastery of Montecassino and the papers of the Principe di Santo Buono, could be searched profitably. Agnone has had one or more newspapers for most of the period from 1886 to the present, all of which provide much detail about local life.

Furthermore, unlike most small communities, Agnone has a written history, indeed a tradition of local historiography. Unfortunately, it is one that is given to excesses of filiopietistic zeal. Much is claimed and disputed, but little is documented, a state of affairs that often makes it difficult to unravel fact from myth in Agnone's history. It is not that there is a dearth of information but rather, that so little of it has been incorporated into the interpretations.

Therefore, I have tried, whenever possible, to rely on primary sources. At the same time, I have felt frustrated by the many lacunae that appear in the existing documentation: the missing items, the paleographic enigmas, the parchments too mildewed and brittle to be read without extensive restoration. In some cases, I am aware of documents only through the citations of chroniclers such as Biondo, Antinori, Ughelli, Orlandi, Ciarlanti, and the local Agnone historian Ascenso Marinelli, for the originals either have been destroyed or have simply disappeared. I have accepted on faith some of these chroniclers' crucial points, largely on the strength of their plausibility viewed in context with other evidence.

The many people who graciously assisted me as I was researching the present work are far too numerous to mention by name. The staff members of the archives and public and private libraries that I consulted in both Italy and Spain were unanimously cordial and helpful. In the town of Agnone, several hundred people provided me with information. I am particularly grateful to the staff of the Comune di Agnone for their ready facilitation of my access to materials without which this study would have been impossible. Certain people were so important to my work as to deserve special mention. These include my assistant Angelo de Vita, Antonio Arduino (director of the Biblioteca La Banca of Agnone), Don Filippo la Gamba (director of the Biblioteca Emidiana), and Remo de Ciocchis (local historian). Alma Smith provided invaluable assistance with computations, tables, and editorial matters. All translations from the Italian are my own. Generous support for both the field research and the preparation of the manuscript came from a National Institute of Health Research Scientists Career Development Award 5 K02 MH 24303. The interpretations contained herein are, of course, my own.

Emigration in a South Italian Town

1

Introduction

This is the story of a community whose locus is the south Italian Appenines but whose focus presently embraces five continents. For it is a history of emigration and the common thread that runs through the lives of people residing in many different parts of the world but whose orientation and behavior are in at least some respects conditioned by a continued loyalty to birthplace. The town in question, Agnone, is in the region of the Molise. But today, after a century of emigration, "Agnone" is as much an idea as a place.

In the special world of south Italy, community loyalties assume special form and are identified by a special term: *campanilismo*.[1] There is a sense in which community boundaries set off a distinctive moral and social universe. In the case of Agnone and its district, the Alto Molise, community differences assume tangible form. Agnone, or Agneun in local parlance, has its own dialect, its dietary peculiarities, its oral traditions, and formerly, its dress style. It is distinguished by its inhabitants and, in the view of its neighbors, by a peculiar history and role as a regional servicing and cultural center. The Agnonesi are prone to view their past with pride, a pride often expressed in hyperbolic fashion. They cite the fact that the town has many schools and churches and a history of producing several secondary figures in Italian letters to support their claim to social superiority. The inhabitants of the surrounding commu-

1

nities concur that the Agnonesi are a proud people, but they apply the term in a negative and derisive sense. What the Agnonese regards as legitimate *orgoglio* is, for his neighbor, unwarranted *superbia*.

There is, then, marked local particularism in the makeup of Agnone and the world view of the Agnonesi. Such abstractions as Italy (the nation), the Mezzogiorno (south Italy), the Molise (the region), Isernia (the province), or even the Alto Molise (the district) are all objects of secondary loyalty that pale beside that of community.

At the same time, there is a cosmopolitan element in Agnone's history. For more than one hundred years the town has provided candidates for emigration. Their destinations have been varied, embracing North and South America, Africa, Europe, and Australia. Here, too, however, such terms as Argentina, Brazil, Australia, Libya, the United States, Switzerland, and Canada are too abstract. Rather, the destinies of the Agnonesi are rooted in such places as Buenos Aires and Belleville in Argentina; São Paolo, Brazil; Melbourne and Adelaide, Australia; Neuchâtel, Switzerland; Montreal, Quebec; Columbus, Ohio; Pueblo, Colorado; and Trail, British Columbia. Indeed, there is a sense in which at present the realities of Agnone and Trail are interwoven. Neither community would have exactly its present form without their shared history. A piece of Trail survives in the minds of some Agnonesi, just as a piece of Agnone persists in the thoughts of many a Canadian.

It is thus that a community like Agnone must be examined and understood more as a concept than as a place. Rather than a relatively isolated regional center of circa six thousand inhabitants (down from twelve thousand) speared upon a number of twentieth-century dilemmas, Agnone today is a community of possibly twenty to thirty thousand people scattered widely throughout Italy, Europe, and the world and aware of their collective past while shaping their individual futures.

I have never been to Trail, British Columbia. Consequently, I must portray this intricate interplay of personnel, capital, and ideas as viewed from Agnone—a weakness, no doubt, but one that is alleviated somewhat by a wealth of local sources. For an overriding characteristic of the last century of Agnone's history has been the conscious attempt of those who remained behind to influence, indeed manipulate, the destinies of the emigrants. To this end, the nonemigrants founded newspapers for, and dispatched emissaries to, the town's New World colonies. Their initial success and subsequent failure to orchestrate the loyalties of the *emigranti* are perhaps the two most salient themes in the last one hundred years of Agnone's history.

It is my purpose in this study, however, to go beyond a general treatment of the causes and consequences of emigration in one south Italian town. Rather, I address a unique historical fact, namely, that emigration from the Molise apparently began in Agnone. The town was therefore in the forefront of the movement both chronologically and in magnitude. It is in addressing the question Why Agnone? that an extensive analysis of local history becomes indispensable.

It is necessary to delve into the nature of Agnone's feudal social structure, whose features were both general within the south Italian framework and peculiar to the local context. Considering the special characteristics of Agnone's feudal heritage makes it possible to understand why, in the early nineteenth century, the town emerged as one of the strongest bastions of liberalism in all of south Italy. The impact of liberal thought and social institutions on local life in turn provides the background with which to explain why, beginning in the late 1860s, some Agnonesi were among the first south Italians to respond to the opportunities and incur the risks of overseas emigration.

At the same time, I am concerned with the effects of emigration on Agnone itself. Initially, the feedback of men, money, and ideas from the New World was instrumental in providing the town with a period of progress and prosperity. Ultimately, however, emigration became the prime factor in Agnone's decline as a regional center. The emigration issue is therefore inextricably intertwined with the question of the evolution and devolution of Agnone as an urban place.

There is a sense, then, in which Agnone's emigration is but a symptom of a larger malady. For this is the story of an aristocracy that relinquished its land and hence its privileges; of a peasantry that gained the land but at a time when peasant agriculture was itself becoming anachronistic; of a clergy that lost its hold on its congregation; of an artisan class driven to despair by industrial manufacturers. To demonstrate the magnitude of Agnone's decline, I begin with a contemporary description of the community.

2

Contemporary Impressions

There are many Agnones, the sources of which are varied. They include the town's ecology, settlement pattern, and situation within its region and vis-à-vis the outside world. There are marked social class distinctions, which are in turn cross-cut by political and economic factionalism. The population is further differentiated internally according to birthplace. Agnone society is age graded, with generational distinctions acquiring considerable importance, and segregated along sex lines. Within the rhythm of local life there are several distinct temporal sequences, each of which gives particular and distinctive flavor to the lives of only a part of the town's inhabitants.

The Ecological Setting

The municipality of Agnone is large by south Italian standards, encompassing 9,630 hectares.[1] It occupies a large, bowl-shaped valley that constitutes the headwaters of the Verrino river. Agnone's waters flow to the Adriatic; those of Carovilli, its contiguous neighbor to the southwest, reach the Mediterranean.

There are marked altitudinal differences within the municipality that range from approximately 475 meters where the Verrino leaves the valley to 1,746 meters on Mount Capraro. The urban center (*cittadina*) is located at 830 meters above sea level. The topography is extremely broken, and even relatively flat land is at a premium. Agnone's climate is rigorous to an extreme, with cold winters and cool summers. Winter snowfalls are frequent and heavy, with accumulations of 2 or 3 feet common in the urban center, and considerably greater accumulations at the higher elevations.

The combination of uneven topography, high altitude, and harsh climate place Agnone as a whole at the upper margins of the growing zone for the Mediterranean crop trilogy of wheat, olives, and grapes. The jumbled terrain, variety of soil types, and differential exposures of each field to the sun and the wind currents create within the municipality a wide variety of microecologies. For my purposes here, however, three broad ecological zones may be distinguished, each with its attendant agricultural potentialities and life style.

Between 475 meters and about 700 meters above sea level, the Mediterranean crop trilogy produces considerable and rather reliable yields. Agnone's most productive agriculture is concentrated in this zone. From 700 meters to about 900 meters, it is still possible to raise wheat, olives, and grapes, but the yields decline and become less predictable. The Mediterranean crops in this altitude range are clearly vulnerable. Locally, these farming operations are regarded as precarious at best. Above 900 meters the Mediterranean crops may not be expected to ripen. Plow agriculture gives way to pastoralism (sheep, goats, and cattle) and silviculture. In some cases, the peasants seed hardier grains and potatoes, but the emphasis remains on fodder production.

On balance, nature in Agnone conspires against the agriculturalist. In 1970, of the 9,630 hectares in the municipality, 2,139.74 hectares were under cultivation, 1,660.31 hectares were in pasturage, and 2,567.56 hectares were forested.[2] The remainder was either barren, abandoned, or in urban use. These figures for agriculture represent a decline from the past century, when population pressure and a smaller range of alternatives to agriculture prompted the inhabitants to cultivate the most marginal of fields. Even in the nineteenth century, however, much of the municipality was nonproductive from an agricultural standpoint.

Its ecological variations provide Agnone with a multifaceted rural economy. Each of the different cropping zones has its own characteris-

5

tics, potentialities, and individual histories of out-migration. Consequently, even within the peasant sector of local society, it is possible to distinguish more than one Agnone.

The Settlement Pattern

There are three distinct residential arrangements within the community. There is the town nucleus, or *cittadina*, which is located on a rocky outcrop roughly in the center of the municipality. There are two hamlets, or *borgate*, Fontesambuco and Villacanale. The latter is practically a village in its own right with post office, school, church, and several businesses. Finally, there are the disseminated farmsteads (*case sparse*, or in local parlance, *massarie*). Scattered throughout the rural district, or *agro*, are a number of small, one-room schools. Some parts of the *agro* also have a church, used only once annually on the feast day of its patron saint.

Almost everyone residing in either the hamlets or the farmsteads are *contadini*, or peasants. In some cases the householders combine agriculture with other activities. Many young male *contadini* commute daily to do manual labor in the municipal center while also engaging in agriculture after hours and on weekends. In these households the wife, the elderly, and the very young assume a considerable part of the burden of agriculture. Current residential arrangements among the *contadini* are heavily influenced by a century of extensive emigration. There are many households in which an elderly couple resides alone. In other cases, grandparents care for grandchildren while both parents are away for most of the year working in northern Italy or other Common Market countries. There are also the *vedove bianche*, or "white widows," who raise their children alone in Agnone while their husbands work abroad.

The *contadini* are not restricted residentially to the rural areas alone. Many live in the town nucleus and travel to their fields daily. Also, most families residing in the rural areas have a small house (or at least access to a room) in town. There are whole streets of modest dwellings in the town that are practically vacant during the week but bustling with activity on Saturday (for market day), Sunday (for mass attendance) or a *festa*.

The residential continuum, ranging from farmstead to town residence, is not without its social significance. Physical isolation is felt to co-vary with *civiltà*, or civility. Life within the confines of the town nucleus is seen to be of a different order than that outside its bounds. This distinction between town and countryside may well be generic in south Italian society and has been noted in central Italy as well.[3]

The town nucleus has its own residential divisions and peculiarities. One's overall impression is that it might house comfortably twenty thousand people rather than the approximately four thousand who reside there today. In part, its overbuilt appearance derives from the many town residences maintained by the rural *contadini*. It is partly due to the plethora of small business establishments, for commerce is small scale and organized into single-family enterprises. It is also a reflection of a particularly ironic fact of life in contemporary south Italy, namely, the conscious government attempts (through the Cassa per il Mezzogiorno) to staunch the emigratory hemorrhage with bricks and mortar. New schools, health agencies, government offices, recreation centers, roads, bridges, and subsidized private dwellings dot the landscape.

Then there is the private initiative of many of the emigrants themselves. When a family leaves, it may hold on to its house or even remodel it for use during infrequent return visits to Agnone. July, and especially August, are times when the town suffers a veritable traffic jam of automobiles bearing licenses from Rome, Turin, Milan, Switzerland, Germany, and the tourist plate of the overseas visitor. The house in Agnone remains the tangible symbol of the emigrant's *campanilismo*. It is also his tie to a part of himself. That this tie is felt profoundly is seen in the fact that such houses, standing vacant for much of the year, number literally in the hundreds, and few are offered for rent. The 1971 census lists 504 uninhabited residences in the town center alone.[4]

There is another factor in Agnone's expansion. Unlike the physical setting of many south Italian communities, which are perched on rocky redoubts, Agnone's center has room to expand. The town's perch resembles more a peninsula than a peak, as the area to the northeast of the older, walled sections is almost-level farmland. In recent years the town has burst its former bounds. Families desirous of improving their circumstances have frequently preferred building a house or buying an apartment in "new Agnone" to remodeling a residence in "old Agnone."

Thus, during this century, and for a variety of reasons, old Agnone has become semiabandoned. An area of narrow, twisting streets, crumbling residences, remnants of city walls and medieval gates, abandoned convents and churches, and flanked by sheer cliffs that have claimed the lives of more than one frolicsome child and reveling adult, the old city stands in stark contrast to the straight, tree-lined boulevards and five-story apartment houses of new Agnone. The ancient Piazza del Popolo, once flanked by the town hall and court of justice, no longer serves as the hub of the town's civil life. In times past, the piazza was the focus of commerce in Agnone, housing the *tomolo*,[5] or hollowed-out stone of three compartments used to measure grain. It was there that peasants paid their annual rents to the landowners and tithes to the church. It was also there, according to local tradition, that a man might come to publicly declare bankruptcy by lowering his pants and placing his bare posterior on the *tomolo* stone.

At the same time, old Agnone has experienced social class impoverishment. With the exception of two or three residential pockets where a few of the better homes are still occupied by prominent families, the old section is inhabited by the *contadini*, day laborers, artisans, and a few families of minor public officials. There is now a feeling that it is more prestigious to live in the newer section of town.

So Agnone is changing. Dwellings are abandoned; others become ghost residences for people living elsewhere; new four- or five-story apartment buildings are built with potential tenants queued up to take occupancy. The town nucleus is now more than a kilometer in length, too great a distance to cover comfortably on foot. Consequently, within the town there are many neighborhoods, and few if any residents penetrate all of them with regularity. Services are duplicated almost from block to block; the young people at one end of town form one social club, those at the other, another. Old people talk about how the people who live outside their immediate neighborhood are strangers, not just in terms of acquaintanceship but in personal habits, character, and even general physical appearance. The spatial distance may be but a few hundred meters; the social distance is considerable.

Parish lines provide another dimension along which life in the center is fragmented into smaller, circumscribed spheres of activity. Historically, Agnone had seven parishes: San Marco, San Emidio, San Pietro, San Amico, San Nicola, San Antonio, and San Biase, each with its imposing church and clerical retinue of a parish priest and several assistant priests. Recently, Villacanale became a parish apart, and a new parish, serviced by Capuchin friars, has been created in the newer section of town. Despite considerable secularization of life in Agnone over the past one hundred years, these parish divisions still constitute important boundaries on the mental map of the individual Agnonese.

Both ecologically and residentially, then, there is a broad distinction in Agnone between rural and town life. The differences are most clearly expressed in terms of economic activities and *civiltà*. Within both contexts there are further refinements to be made. In the rural areas, location is a prime conditioner of the type of agriculture engaged in and the quality of one's social relations as measured in the frequency of contact with one's fellows. In this latter respect, life in the hamlet of Villacanale differs from life on the isolated farmstead. Similarly, within the town proper there is a distinction to be made between old and new Agnone as well as a sense of fragmentation into official parishes and de facto neighborhoods. In terms of internal residential organization alone, then, there are many Agnones. All of this residential heterogeneity actually transpires within a town center whose total population is scarcely four thousand people at present and declining. Finally, it is a present irony that the residences of Agnone are multiplying at a time when the number of residents is declining.

The Situational Factors

In the 1970 census the total population of Agnone was 6,481 inhabitants, which made it the fifth-largest community in the region. Insernia, the provincial capital, had 15,575 residents, and Campobasso, the seat of regional government, 41,889.[6] Today, after a century of extensive out-migration from the Alto Molise (Map 2.1), Agnone is a small servicing center with a hinterland that, if extensive in territory, is bereft of human resources. The extent of the decline of Agnone's importance may be appreciated by comparing the above statistics with those of a century ago. In 1871 Agnone, with its 11,073 people, was the second largest town in the entire region of the Molise. The population of Isernia stood at 9,193 inhabitants, while Campobasso, with 14,360 residents, was only a little larger than Agnone.[7]

Much of the local history is dominated by the fact that Agnone is centrally located in what would otherwise be an enormous jurisdictional vacuum (Map 2.2). Sixty-eight kilometers separate the town from Isernia, the closest large community. It is 97 kilometers from Agnone to Campobasso. Chieti, in the region of the Abruzzo, is 107 kilometers distant. Naples is 160 kilometers away.

Even with modern means of transport, until recently Agnone remained

Map 2.1. *Region of the Alto Molise*

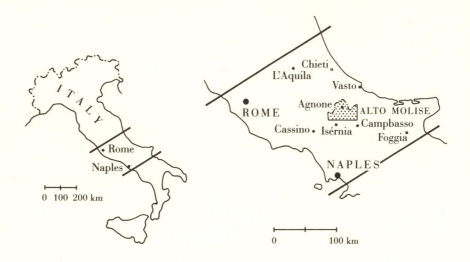

relatively isolated. The road system linking it to the outside world traversed a series of tortuous curves. Most of the highways in the Alto Molise are broken and warped by the harsh climate and frequent landslides. During the winter months the region is prone to paralysis by heavy snowfalls. If a certain sense of isolation is characteristic of Agnone today, the situation in the past was extreme. Distances and lack of roads conspired to make Agnone a regional servicing and administrative center for the smaller communities of much of the Alto Molise and a part of the Abruzzo.

Physical isolation colored Agnone's relations with the external sources of power. The town pertained, until the emergence of the modern Italian state, to the kingdom of Naples; but the city of Naples was distant, and its administrative rays refracted through many prisms before reaching Agnone. Similarly, Agnone successfully maintained considerable local autonomy vis-à-vis the smaller administrative centers to which it was accountable. Before 1809 the town was administered from Chieti. From

Map 2.2. *Agnone and Its Hinterland*

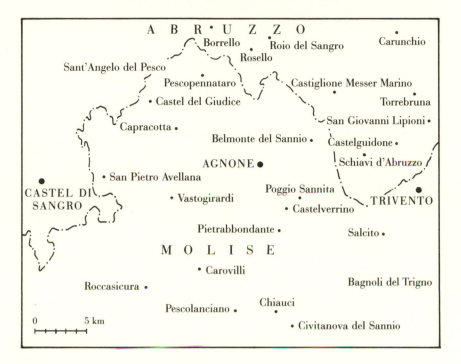

1809 to 1970 Agnone was dependent on Campobasso. Since 1970 its provincial capital is Isernia. The ease with which the needle of Agnone's compass of subordination and superordination changed direction historically is itself eloquent testimony to the town's marginality with respect to external sources of authority.

The historical consequences of this flexibility transcend simple administrative arrangements, for Agnone's autonomy, as interpreted and implemented in different periods by local community leaders, provided a unique quality to its collective life. In the remote feudal past, whether orders emanated from absent princes and nobles or from the officials of the kingdom of Naples, Agnone reacted as a mountain enclave tied only tenuously to wider political purposes and easily given to challenging central authority. The local representatives of outside authority risked insubordination and even personal injury. Popular revolts and brigandage were constant themes in the history of the town.

On occasion, Agnone actively sought redefinition of political arrange-

11

ments that would provide it with both a maximum of local autonomy and a greater degree of hegemony over its own natural hinterland of nearby villages. During the 1860s, as the details of the unification of Italy were under parliamentary debate, representatives of Agnone sought provincial recognition for the Alto Molise and capital status for the town.[8] It is said today that some officials participating in local government during Benito Mussolini's rule did so in order to agitate for creation of an autonomous province of the Alto Molise. The creation of the new province of Isernia in 1970 required Agnone's approval and was viewed by many Agnonesi as desirable decentralization of political power.

There is, then, a theme that emerges from Agnone's situational reality that may best be expressed in a maxim: Exert influence over the nearby smaller communities; resist the influence of distant larger ones.

It is at this point that once again Agnone fragments into many Agnones, the description of any one of which is time and place specific. For if Agnone has served as a regional administrative, juridical, electoral, religious, educational, and economic center, the definition of its hinterland changes accordingly. Today there are still many regionally significant services concentrated in Agnone. These include the offices of the INAM (health insurance service), the *finanze* and *imposte* offices (for registry of taxation and land tenure), the *carabinieri*, the highway patrol, the court system, the forestry division, and a hospital that services a large area. Agnone's fairs, markets, and festivals are attended by inhabitants of nearby communities. Agnone's schools attract students from outside the community. In several cases people residing elsewhere commute to jobs in the town. In the past, Agnone served as a religious center. Its monasteries and convents accepted novitiates from near and distant communities and sometimes held property in them. There is also a complicated local tradition of itinerant marketing that took Agnone's artisans and middlemen as much as 200 kilometers afield to peddle handicrafts. Each of these dimensions has its own particular history, and the hinterland of each changes over time. Just as there are many Agnones, Agnone has many hinterlands.

Social Class

There is an elaborate and rigid social hierarchy in Agnone society. Social relations in the town are characterized by considerable deference and by a demeanor played out within the framework of narrowly prescribed forms of courtesy and address. These generalizations, while more descriptive of the past, may be applied to the contemporary scene as well. Any statement concerning the precise nature of the social class hierarchy is necessarily time specific, and such historical detail is the subject of some of my subsequent analysis. My present purpose is to provide an overview of class distinctions and interclass relations.

Agnone society may be depicted in pyramidal form in which the apex contains what are both the socially most prominent and the numerically fewest families (Figure 2.1).[9] Conversely, the peasantry and day laborers (frequently overlapping categories) together constitute the socially least prominent families and numerically largest group in the town.

The peasants. There is a sense in which the social gulf (as expressed by the double line in Figure 2.1) between the peasants and everyone else is greater than that between any two of the other social classes. In fact, the chasm is so great in the minds of so many that it practically assumes caste-like overtones. The denigration of the *contadini* by the other Agnonesi is blatant. Peasants are ignored, ridiculed, or patronized, depending on the situation. When the nonpeasant Agnonese enters the peasant's realm, it is more as a superior intruder or visitor than as a fellow citizen. There is a furtiveness and deference in the *contadino*'s dealings with others. He is distinguished as much by his uneasiness as by the cut of this clothes, his speech, his etched physical features and gnarled hands. He waits in line patiently as others are served before him. He never frequents the town's bars, preferring the more rustic *cantine* that specialize in the peasant trade. He does not join voluntary associations; if he subscribes to a political party, he assumes a passive role. He is particularly deferential and ill at ease when dealing with officials. His children receive less attention in the schools and have less chance of advancement and less of a future if they conclude their education.

Even contacts with the supernatural are class particular. Although the *agro* of Agnone is divided among the seven parish churches, the parish priests, with one exception, rarely visit the peasants, preferring to deal with them exclusively within the confines of the *cittadina*. When a priest is seen in the *agro* the common question is Who is dying? Not surprisingly, the peasantry constitutes a strong repository of folk religious beliefs.

The artisans. Agnone has long been famed for its artisan traditions.

13

Figure 2.1. *Social Class Pyramid of Agnone*

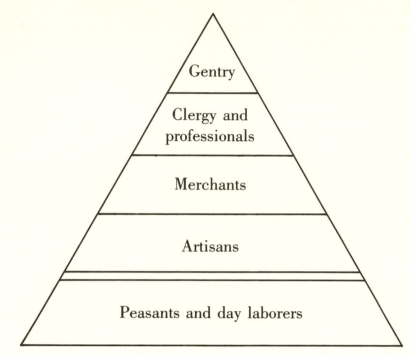

The town's charters, or *statuti*, contain ordinances regulating the artisans of fifteenth-century Agnone. A 1753 census for the town lists a remarkable variety of artisan occupations: potters, shoemakers, key makers, clockmakers, tinkers, tanners, cane makers, saddlemakers, rope makers, ironsmiths, coppersmiths, silversmiths, goldsmiths, gunsmiths, wood-carvers, stonemasons, hatters, tailors, organ makers, and bell makers. Each of these crafts had its own hinterland of nearby and, in some cases, distant communities.

In social class terms, the artisans reflect considerable internal differentiation. The several artisan trades were ranked in prestige. Goldsmiths enjoyed the greatest social standing, whereas stonemasons were practically treated as day laborers. Coppersmiths were regarded as better than shoemakers. At the same time, within each artisan category there was a differential ordering of prestige. The social distance obtaining between a master artisan and his employees (even if they were kinsmen) was considerable. The master used first names and the familiar form of speech with his employees and in return was addressed formally and by his title.

Within the broader spectrum of Agnone's social classes, artisans were viewed as social superiors to the *contadini*; yet they were still men engaged in manual, at times dirty, endeavors. This fact demeaned them in the eyes of the town's social elite.

The merchants. As the largest and most centrally located town in the Alto Molise, Agnone has a history of commerce and administration. The town's markets and fairs date from medieval times. In the 1753 census there were sixteen merchants, some with permanent store locations in the town and others ambulatory and presumably visiting surrounding communities.

More recently, improved transportation facilities have undercut Agnone's commerce. Both the Agnonesi and other Alto Molisani can now shop in the larger centers with relative ease. Conversely, there is a fleet of traveling merchants who penetrate Agnone's market on a regular basis. Every Sunday the main boulevard is lined with trucks selling foodstuffs, dry goods, furniture, yard goods, household wares, and linens. These merchants specialize in large discounts, to the chagrin of Agnone's storekeepers.

There is a sense in which the commercial life of Agnone is today overdeveloped. The increase in local consumerism that characterized the turn of the present century was predicated on a population of circa ten thousand people in the town and the regular feedback of emigrant savings from abroad. Agnone's population has been halved since 1871, and that of the communities that make up the town's hinterlands (see Table 2.1) has declined by 40 percent. Yet today there are more businesses in Agnone than at any time in its history.

In part this is due to the tendency for returnee peasant emigrants to establish a business. There is also a strong predilection for children to continue their father's enterprise. Then, there is the possibility of combining economic strategies. That is, one or two members tend the family store while the others work at different trades. By combining a little bit of agriculture, a small income from commerce, and possibly a salary or two, they retain the family business. They may also have savings from a stint abroad and possibly a foreign pension (such as U.S. social security benefits) to supplement their store income.

The clergy. Throughout Agnone's history the clergy has played a prominent role in local affairs. During the Middle Ages many churches and monasteries were founded in the town, some by private endowment, others through the initiative of religious orders.

15

Table 2.1. *Population Decline in Agnone's Hinterland, 1871–1970*

Town	Population in 1871	Population in 1970	Total net change	Percentage of difference
Bagnoli del Trigno	4,210	1,987	−2,223	52.80
Belmonte del Sannio	1,879	1,389	−490	26.08
Capracotta	4,264	2,384	−1,880	44.09
Carovilli	3,093	1,935	−1,158	37.44
Castel del Giudice	1,590	636	−954	60.00
Castelverrino	866	321	−545	62.93
Castiglione Messer Marino	4,347	3,477	−870	20.01
Chiauci	1,269	526	−743	58.55
Pescolanciano	1,898	1,424	−474	24.97
Pescopennataro	1,394	725	−669	47.99
Pietrabbondante	4,067	1,715	−2,352	57.83
Poggio Sannita	2,907	1,939	−968	33.30
Roccasicura	1,889	869	−1,020	54.00
Rosello	1,673	677	−996	59.53
San Pietro Avellana	2,250	1,154	−1,096	48.71
Sant'Angelo del Pesco	1,246	901	−345	27.69
Schiavi d'Abruzzo	3,861	3,876	+15	0.39
Vastogirardi	2,427	1,450	−977	40.26
Totals	45,130	27,385	−17,745	39.32

Sources: ISTAT, *Popolazione e movimento anagrafico dei comuni*; idem, *Popolazione residente e presente dei comuni ai censimenti dal 1861 al 1961.*

Note: Agnone's hinterland is determined by including all communities listed in the "Zona Omogenea di Agnone" in *Il Molise altissimo e i suoi problemi*, p. 94, and including the nearby towns of Schiavi d'Abruzzo, Castiglione Messer Marino, and Rosello of the province of Chieti and Bagnoli del Trigno in the province of Isernia.

Over time, the religious institutions of Agnone acquired considerable land and wealth. Furthermore, church wealth enjoyed continuity; unlike that of individual households, whose accumulations were likely to be dissipated through sales, partible inheritance, and dowering practices. In the case of church property, the endowment of one generation was simply added to those of previous generations. By the eighteenth century the religious establishment was the single largest landowner in the town.

With the abolition of feudalism in the early nineteenth century, the religious establishment came under attack. This culminated in the suppression of the monasteries and certain religious sodalities, whose holdings passed to the local municipal government. The unification of Italy, which destroyed papal political authority over the former Vatican State, triggered a protracted battle between church and state that was not resolved until the years of Mussolini's rule. During the many decades of confrontation, Italian attitudes underwent considerable secularization, and the power of the local clergy waned accordingly.

At present Agnone's clergy retains little of its former influence and importance. Two of the parishes no longer have priests; the others are serviced by a single pastor. The monasteries are gone or converted to other uses. The majority of churches and chapels are in a state of disrepair. The few remaining priests support themselves by teaching catechism in the local school system. Attendance at mass is sporadic, and with few exceptions, religious *feste* no longer attract their former followings.

The professionals. As a servicing center with a significant and a diversified economic life, Agnone has long had a considerable number of professionals. The town served as a medical center for its hinterland from an early period. Even in 1753, when the total population of Agnone was less than five thousand, it had seven physicians and four pharmacists.[10]

By the mid-nineteenth century, when the population of Agnone was in the neighborhood of ten thousand inhabitants, there were fourteen physicians and five pharmacists.[11] In 1928 there were thirteen physicians and three pharmacies.[12] By 1971, despite the sharp decline in the population, there were twelve physicians and two pharmacies in Agnone.[13] This reflects both increased emphasis on medical care and the founding in Agnone of a hospital for the entire Alto Molise and a part of Chieti.

Given Agnone's role as administrative center, it is not surprising that the legal profession flourished in the town. Since the fifteenth century both the district court and prison have been located in Agnone, providing a considerable demand for the services of advocates. In 1753 there were four lawyers and two judges in the town's population.[14] By the mid-nineteenth century the legal profession in Agnone had seemingly exploded. Forty-one men listed their occupation as lawyer, and seven were notary publics.[15] By 1928 the number of lawyers had declined to thirteen,[16] and the 1971 census lists only three.[17]

Another major profession in Agnone is teaching. The historical roots of the local educational system are deep. The earliest records I have found of a local pedagogical institution refer to the founding of the Convent of Santa Chiara. Established in 1434 by private endowment, its goal was to provide educations for the daughters of the well-to-do.

It was during the nineteenth century that Agnone became an academic center of regional importance. Between 1848 and 1900 several private and state schools were founded in the town. Agnone developed an educational hinterland of students from distant towns who attended its schools. A smaller proportion of the boarding-student population was drawn from abroad, as emigrants sent their sons back to be educated.

In the post–World War II period, Agnone, despite its declining population, retained and even enlarged upon is role as an educational center. A number of state institutions have been established in the town since the war. These include the Scuolo Media Unificata, the Istituto Tecnico Industriale Maschile, the Istituto Tecnico Femminile, the Istituto Professionale and the Liceo Scientifico. The first is a kind of junior high school, and the last is a prep school for students who intend to apply to a university. The others are trade schools that teach mechanics and electronics to the boys and tailoring to the girls. Many of the students come from nearby communities. The hinterland of the Liceo Scientifico is considerably more extensive, including a few students from as far afield as central and northern Italy. One official of the school attributed such attendance to the fact that Agnone is an isolated, conservative community and hence largely uninfluenced by the political ferment that permeates the school systems of large urban areas. Some parents prefer such an atmosphere for their children. Today the schools are Agnone's only healthy "industry."

Another aspect of the present educational climate in Agnone deserves mention. Since World War II there has been a dramatic upsurge in the number of Agnonesi pursuing university careers. Furthermore, the Italian educational system has become so democratized that a university degree is not beyond the reach of even the sons and daughters of the *contadini*. Consequently, there is now an army of *laureati*, a glut of specialized people in almost every conceivable profession. At the same time, by attaining a degree in any subject, one qualifies for a primary school teaching credential.

In 1971 Agnone, with its total population of 6,838, had 148 school teachers. Despite the poor wages (in 1972 $250 monthly for full-time teaching), many accept part-time positions in the local schools. Others commute to jobs in the surrounding communities. There are people in

Agnone who drive as many as 40 kilometers to teach part time in some village school. In one extreme case a woman teacher commutes to Venafro (91 kilometers each way). Agnone's relations with its educational hinterland are therefore two directional. Students come to the town to be educated; Agnone's educators travel out to smaller villages.

The gentry. During the feudal period Agnone was the home of a few aristocratic families, or *baroni*. Local life was also affected by other *baroni* who resided elsewhere but held property in the town. In the sixteenth century Agnone had at least sixteen *baroni*. By the beginning of the eighteenth century, there were still fourteen feudal estates in the town.[18]

The abolition of feudalism in the early nineteenth century removed the *baroni* as a factor in local life. During the ensuing years the emerging middle-class merchants, professionals, and more successful artisans effectively monopolized the land. In the process, they assumed the airs of a new gentry, referring to themselvess as *galantuomini*, or "gallant men." This new self-proclaimed aristocracy never achieved the wealth or the social standing of the feudal gentry. Most still had to work for a living, and their landholdings never reached the magnitude of true estates. Their control over local agriculture and their social pretensions were, however, prime elements in a class confrontation with the manual laborers and *contadini* that was ultimately to trigger mass emigration from the town.

Today, Agnone is almost entirely devoid of its former artistocratic heritage. The last names of many a former illustrious family have disappeared from the local scene. There are even few direct descendants of the nineteenth-century *galantuomini*, and many of those who remain are economically strapped. In some cases the ancestral home, practically a palace, is inhabited by a single person or an elderly couple, grown eccentric while mingling little with the citizenry and meddling little in local affairs.

There are signs that Agnone's social hierarchy is presently undergoing realignment. The demise of peasant agriculture and the artisan trades, coupled with the increased importance of Agnone as an educational and administrative center, have served to place added emphasis on government employment as the major underpinning of the new economy. The uneducated vie for jobs as doorman, janitor, and errand boy, while the educated seek administrative posts and teaching positions.

The new elite is constituted by the political power brokers, who use influence to retain a retinue of "clients" who then perpetuate them in office. In return, the political patron dispenses the *raccomandazione*, or reference, that is the requisite for obtaining everything from entry into one of the universities to a coveted state-salaried job.

Until the twentieth-century there was only a minimum of socioeconomic mobility within Agnone's social hierarchy. People were born to their status in life, and their social affiliations were reinforced by a strong tendency for class endogamy. Artisans married artisans' daughters; *contadini* wed *contadine*. The children of these unions were automatically assigned their fathers' occupations in the birth registry. There were, to be sure, peasant households whose wealth surpassed considerably the net worth of many artisan and merchant households. But this in itself was testimony to the fact that, in traditional Agnonese society, wealth alone did not determine status. There existed social chasms that few, if any, could expect to cross within a lifetime. To aspire to social mobility was at best to undertake a project requiring generations of a family's efforts.

During the late nineteenth and twentieth centuries, this social class rigidity eased somewhat. Both the gentry and the *galantuomini* simply disappeared from the local scene, creating a vacuum at the pinnacle of the traditional class pyramid. Emigration and its feedback created a new cosmopolitanism among the lower classes. The emerging interest in modern consumerism among all Agnonesi placed new emphasis on wealth, and many emigrants possessed considerable savings. Finally, since World War II there has been considerable democratization of Italian institutions. Education and health services are available to all. The rhetoric (if not necessarily the reality) of political life has become more egalitarian.

This is not to say that today Agnone is a classless society. Indeed one is struck by the degree to which class perspectives and considerations still dominate local life. In this respect Agnone is still a traditionalist town within Italian society. If parents no longer dictate whom one marries, they still may determine whom one will not marry. The present generation of young adults differs considerably from its elders in interpreting and applying class distinctions; yet few sons of professionals, merchants, or artisans socialize with their age peers among the *contadini*. Even the politically active leftist youth who expresses concern for the peasant's lot is prone to view the problem paternalistically.

To this day Agnone retains the traditional practice of the *passeggiata*. Each evening and on Sundays and holidays, hundreds of people walk interminably up and down the central boulevard. The *passeggiata* speaks volumes about the persistence of class distinctions in Agnone society. Absent are the *contadini* on the one hand and the most socially prominent on the other. People of similar professional standing and family background walk together. Those of inferior social status initiate greetings in a formal fashion that involves the use of titles: "*Buona sera dottore.*" "*Buona sera professore.*" There is an accompanying smile that must be learned. It is assumed with feigned spontaneity and must be fixed upon the face for a moment that is neither too fleeting nor too lasting. Subtleties in the accompanying gestures convey proper doses of deference depending on one's status. This performance is apt to be repeated dozens of times in the course of an evening stroll, and more than once with the same person.

Factionalism

Political alignments provide another source of differentiation in Agnone society. There is a sense in which political interests in the town are class specific and hence a feature of the social hierarchy considered above. Viewed in this fashion, it is possible to analyze local politics in the classical Marxist framework of class conflict. Both during the feudal period and the capitalistic era of the nineteenth century, Agnone possessed a peasant and manual-laborer population with many of the characteristics of both a rural and an urban proletariat. It is clear that, by any standard, these people experienced extreme poverty and were subject to exploitation. One symptom of the situation was the extent to which brigandage was a problem in the Alto Molise. Another possible barometer was a high crime rate, generally constituted by robberies and crimes of violence. On occasion the resentment of the lower classes broke the bonds of local control, resulting in bread riots and short-lived peasant revolts.

To view Agnone's political life exclusively in terms of class conflict is, however, to ignore a salient feature of the local structuring of power: the political factionalism present throughout Agnone's history, cutting cross class lines and based on alignments cemented together by patron–client relations. While the leaders of such factions were generally of the elite,

21

their effectiveness depended on their ability to obtain clients in the other social classes who could, in turn, activate kinship and friendship ties to secure for the patron a significant political following.

Local politics during the twentieth century continued to be characterized by clientelism. The exception was the period of Mussolini's rule, when political opposition was not tolerated and hence local affairs were dominated by the Fascists (although contending groups existed within their ranks). While there were dissenters, few braved the consequences of open hositility, and those who did could scarcely be said to have constituted a viable political faction.

During the postwar period, Italian political life has been dominated by by the middle-of-the-road Christian Democrats (DC) and their coalitions. There exists, however, a multitude of political parties that embrace the entire ideological spectrum from the Italian Communist party (PCI) to the Italian Socialist movement (MSI), or neofascists. Agnone is today conservative in its politics, while possessing political clout far out of proportion to the size of its electorate. During the 1970s the town has had a senator and a deputy in the Italian Parliament. Both are of the DC, although of different tendencies (*correnti*) within it. There is considerable local sentiment for the MSI, and in fact, during the days of Mussolini, Agnone was regarded as a Fascist stronghold. Many of today's DC activists were officials or members of the Fascist youth group under Mussolini.

The left in Agnone is considerably weaker. Although the Italian Socialist party (PSI) and the PCI maintain local offices in the town, they do not appear to constitute a serious threat to the control of the DC. There is an activist young people's group that challenges the authorities in debate and publishes an opposition newspaper, but their political clout is minimal.

The May 7, 1972 local election results for the Italian House of Deputies give an indication of the relative strength of the several political parties (see Table 2.2). Relative electoral strength as reflected in the results in Table 2.2 should not be confused in every case with ideological conviction, for a combination of campanilism and clientelism dominate the electoral process. Candidates for national office are expected to devote their energies to protecting and promoting local interests. The senator and deputy are discussed locally less for their stands on national issues than for their ability to acquire new governmental offices, schools, and health facilities for Agnone. When, in 1973, it was announced that two

Table 2.2. *Electoral Results in Agnone for the Italian House of Deputies, May 7, 1972*

Leftist						Centrist	Rightist		
PCI	Socialismo	PSIUP	MPL	PSI	Partito Agricolo	DC	PLI	MSI	Total
419	34	40	1	139	42	2,321	190	749	3,935

Source: Electoral records, Archivio Comunale di Agnone.

governmental offices were to be transferred from Agnone to Isernia, the senator and deputy had to face a hostile town meeting to explain the situation and plead for understanding. The blunt and open question they confronted was How could a town with both a senator and a deputy be stripped of its agencies?

The extent to which politics are clientelistic is well symbolized in the mechanics of the electoral process. While the PCI, DC, PSI, and MSI all maintain offices in Agnone, they stand vacant except during an election campaign. Little attempt is made to use these locales to either educate or proselytize. Once the campaign begins, however, there is a flurry of activity as each becomes a dispensary of political favors, promises, and, it is said, kilos of pasta and rolls to banknotes to purchase votes. Many comment with irony that it is during political campaigns that road construction and public works flourish, as incumbents seek to retain their offices.

There is, then, considerable cynicism about the electoral process and politicians in general. Few confuse power with ideology, and fewer still are willing to risk their personal security for political ideals. The brute fact is that the leftists and rightists depend on the centrists for the political influence required to get ahead. A common expression in Agnone is *Chi fa politica, fa schifo* ("He who engages in politics, engages in dirt").

Birthplace

While during the past century the total population of Agnone has been almost halved by emigration, the movement is not entirely unidirectional. As a regional center with a multifaceted economy and occupational structure, Agnone receives in-migration. Some of the new arrivals come from distant places and are sojourners rather than permanent residents. Examples include orphaned children of the Italian navy placed by the state in Agnone's boarding schools and the *carabinieri* and other officials subject to frequent transfer. There is also a more permanent recent migration into the town. Many of the businesses in the town nucleus are owned by people born elsewhere, and a sizeable contingent of the resident day laborers are originally from the smaller surrounding villages. It is one of the many ironies in Agnone's recent history that the same local economic conditions that prompt the Agnonesi to emigrate in large numbers prove attractive to residents of more impoverished nearby communities.

Therefore, during the twentieth century Agnone has undergone not only a marked decline in overall population but modification in its makeup. In south Italian society, where loyalties to birthplace are strong, this fact has important implications. It may be argued that shared common origins made the residents of Agnone at the turn of the century a considerably more cohesive social unit, and one more capable of collective action, than the more heterogeneous population that inhabits the town at present. Today the organizers of the local festivals complain that collecting funds on a house-to-house basis is less productive than formerly because the *forestieri*, or outsiders, are less inclined to donate. This is viewed as symptomatic of a deteriorating sense of community.

Age and Sex

Agnone society is both age graded and segregated along sex lines for certain purposes. The ideal social unit of Agnonese society was the patrilineal joint family in which married sons co-resided with their father.[19] Authority relations within the family were rigidly patriarchal. As long as they lived, the patriarch and his wife wielded nearly absolute power over the other household members. Until recently it was assumed that every man would adopt his father's occupation and serve him as an apprentice. Sons who resided in their father's household while working elsewhere were expected to turn over their wages to him. There are stories of men stealing grain from the common family store in order to purchase items for their wives and children. Middle-aged men had to outwit their elderly parents to obtain spending money for tobacco.

In recent years the patriarchal structuring of authority has mellowed considerably. A century of emigration has relieved both the economic and psychological dependencies that underpinned the joint family household. Modernistic, twentieth-century pressures also conspired to modify family living arrangements. The twin traditional economic activities of Agnone were artisanship and peasant agriculture. Both have become anachronistic in the modern world, and fathers are now loath to encourage sons to follow in their footsteps. The broadened educational opportunities in contemporary Italy, with the increased likelihood of both physical and socioeconomic mobility for the younger generation, have all but destroyed the joint family household as a viable social form.

Nonetheless, even today a large measure of paternal demand and filial compliance characterizes father–son relations in Agnone. Young men still experience postponed adulthood. It is not uncommon for a twenty-five-year-old unmarried "student" to live at home with his parents and depend on them for spending money. Social adulthood in Agnone is not conferred automatically at marriage. Young married men are likely to continue to socialize and recreate with their unmarried bachelor peers. They frequent the taverns and belong to the social clubs preferred by the young precisely because they do not have access to the circles of middle-aged and elderly men who really run local affairs. Thus, Agnone remains today gerontocratic to an extreme, and this aspect of its collective life provides one more axis along which the community fragments into more than one Agnone.

South Italian society is notorious for its sharp segregation of community life along sex lines. A strong correlation between a family's honor and the virtue of its female members made brothers custodians of sisters and husbands of wives. Fear of becoming a cuckold still makes the term *cornuto* the most explosive insult in south Italian society. Consequently, there was a time when the movements of women were circumscribed, producing a sharp distinction between the male and female worlds.

Several comments are in order on sex segregation in Agnone. Certainly in the recent past the town manifested the general south Italian pattern in all of its aspects. Local newspapers from the late nineteenth and early twentieth centuries report maimings and killings that grew out of the suspected sexual indiscretion of a wife, sister, or daughter. The fact that many men emigrated to the New World during this period, absenting themselves for years at a time, exacerbated the problem. More than one emigrant returned to discover an extra infant in his home.

Elderly Agnonesi note that, in the past, arranged marriages were common and courtships zealously chaperoned. Formal schooling was largely reserved for males; the handful of female students were trained in the convent or by private tutors. Women were not expected to participate or opine in political matters. The majority of voluntary associations were exclusively male. The division of labor between the sexes was rather extreme. Only among the peasantry were women expected and permitted to engage in the household's economic activities. Indeed, to this day it is a part of the peasant woman's social denigration that she uses the *zappa* (a type of hoe) alongside her menfolk.

In the past, then, Agnone society was clearly divided along sex lines into distinct spheres of activity. The details might vary from one social class to another, but the general theme was familiar to all. It should be noted, however, that in recent years, and particularly since World War II, there have been many modifications in this pattern. Today daughters are as likely as sons to receive schooling. With the exception of a few families, girls are no longer chaperoned. Few still make a formal declaration of engagement as prelude to overt courtship. Girls and their families no longer place the former emphasis on preparing dowries and trousseaus. Dowryless unions are now commonplace, whereas a generation ago marriages could be postponed or canceled altogether if dowry negotiations between the fathers of the affianced proved unsatisfactory.

Today there is considerably more sexual egalitarianism manifest among the younger generation of Agnonesi. Girls are expected to be informed on current events; many take political stands. In public meetings that I witnessed during my stay, fewer women than men expressed their opinion, and they were blatantly patronized for doing so; but in the recent past it would have been inconceivable for them to attend at all. Similarly, women now enter the bars, travel alone outside of the town, and join formerly all male voluntary associations. Few girls have their movements monitored by their male kinsmen to any significant degree.

Yet there is still a sense in which men and women in Agnone inhabit separate worlds. Despite liberated dress styles, a greater willingness to express opinion, and such acts of independence as the purchase of an automobile, young women in Agnone are still subjected to the double standard of south Italian male–female relations. When a politically oriented young people's organization in Agnone recently challenged the local power structure, the town newspaper denounced it by impugning the virtue of its female members.

Temporal Sequence

Agnone's diversified social structure and multifaceted ecology and settlement pattern produce a variety of discernible temporal sequences within local life. The activities of certain sectors of the populace are regularly distributed throughout the year; the bureaucrats and shopkeepers are cases in point. There are other life styles in which activities are cycled unevenly. The educators respond to the academic year. The artisans formerly spent the winter and spring in their workshops producing their wares and then traveled widely during the summer and fall marketing them.

Two traditional activities in Agnone, charcoal making and herding, were also highly subject to seasonal cycling. Charcoal making was concentrated in the autumn months. Herding at one time (though no longer) meant transhumance. Sheep, goats, cattle, and horses were pastured in the highest reaches of the municipality during the spring and summer months, then trailed to the Apulian plain for the fall and winter. This temporal sequence and physical isolation made the life of the transhumant herder unlike that of the other Agnonesi.

The peasantry is prone to peak and slack periods of activity. Early and late summer and fall are particularly busy times. There is a lull in agriculture during midsummer and throughout much of the winter. For those peasants engaged primarily in raising the Mediterranean crop trilogy, agricultural activity is divided somewhat evenly throughout the year. Even in winter there are tasks to be done such as the pruning of vines and trees, although for those involved in animal husbandry and grain cropping in the higher elevations, the winter months provide a slack season of near paralysis.

The Totality

In conclusion, despite the several sources of internal differentiation, the Agnonesi do share a sense of common purpose, a loyalty to community, and a capability for collective action. The many differing interpretations of social reality in Agnone are not entirely atomistic and random; yet this does not mean that an overview of the society should be regarded as a jigsaw puzzle in which a single image emerges from the proper juxta-

27

posing of the individual pieces. Rather, a more useful metaphor is the kaleidoscope. With each twist of the hand, each modification of perspective, the composite image changes, though the constituent pieces remain the same. It is in this sense that there are many Agnones, which is to say, myriad local social and temporal realities. To paraphrase Durkheim, "Agnone" is *less* than the sum of its parts.

3

Origins and the Feudal Order

The Molise forms a part of the region of Samnium, homeland in antiquity of Rome's most formidable Italic foes. Between 343 and 290 B.C. Samnites linked their destiny with that of other enemies of Rome, such as King Pyrrhus and Hannibal. In the words of the historian Salmon:

> Of all the tribes and nations with whom the Romans found themselves obliged to dispute the supremacy of Italy none were more formidable that the Samnites of Samnium. They were the stalwart possessors of a larger territory and of a more determined temperament than any other people in the peninsula.[1]

The Samnites were a rugged mountain group, a league of Oscan (rather than Latin) speakers divided into several tribes known as the Sabellians. As the population of these tribesmen increased beyond the carrying capacity of their harsh mountain environment, they became feared raiders of adjacent lowland areas.[2] They were for the most part of a hardy people with the life style of peasants and herdsmen. They had few cities, although they posssessed a sufficiently evolved civilization to include a privileged class and an indigenous artistic heritage.[3] The major surviving examples of Samnite architecture are massive fortifications dominating key access routes into their territory.[4] The Samnites relished spectacle and probably initiated what were later regarded as the Roman gladiatorial and comic-theater traditions.[5]

Agnone is in the very heartland of Samnium, in the area inhabited by the Sabellian tribe called the Caraceni; and one of the most important pieces of evidence concerning Samnite civilization was unearthed there: a bronze tablet with Oscan inscriptions discovered in the nineteenth century. Salmon remarks:

> Most Oscan inscriptions belong to the period when the native Samnite had been long exposed to Greek, Etruscan and Roman influences. Fortunately one of them, the Agnone tablet, deals with Samnite cults and it happens to be not only the longest, but probably also the oldest, inscription from Samnium proper. Its value can hardly be overestimated.[6]

Agnone has another claim to Samnite fame, although one of less demonstrable merit than the Oscan tablet. There is a local tradition that the town was the site of the ancient city of Aquilonia, the Roman destruction of which, in the year 293 B.C., proved to be the decisive victory in the third and last Samnite war. Unfortunately, the major account of the event is provided by the Roman historian Livy, whose ability to recount history is surpassed only by his capacity for inventing it.

Agnone's claim to direct descent from Aquilonia is based, in large measure, on the etymological evolution of the town's name from ancient to modern times. Proponents of this view suggest a sequence from *Aquilonia* to *Anglonum* (a Latin rendering used frequently in medieval documents referring to the town) to *Agnone*. This interpretation cannot simply be attributed to an excess of local campanilism and discounted out of hand. There are published opinions, some of considerable age, that regard Agnone as the site of Aquilonia. Biondo, in his work *Italia Illustrata*, published in 1510, states "et interius in depraessa valle adiacet maiellae Anglona, quod oppidum nunc in regione primarium prisci aquiloniam appellavere."[7] Orlandi, in his *Delle città d'Italia*, published in 1770, claims that Agnone was erected upon the ruins of Aquilonia.[8] The same contention is made by Sacco in his 1795 *Dizionario geografico-istorico-fisico del regno di Napoli*.[9]

In Agnone itself the idea has received considerable support. The first newspaper in the town's history, begun in 1884, was christened *L'Aquilonia*. A major arterial in the town center bears the name Via Aquilonia. One recently published local history claims outright that

Agnone is the site of the ancient city,[10] while another at least admits the possibility.[11] There is, however, considerable reason for scepticism. Ascenso Marinelli, in his nineteenth-century work on local history, contends that, although, in the third or fourth century after Christ, Agnone might have been constructed by the remote descendants of the vanquished Aquilonians, the town is not on the original site of the city.[12] Agnone lacks the evidence of monumental architecture that one would expect to find even in a city leveled by its enemies. There is also a problem posed by Livy's account in that Agnone's topography does not square with his description of the battle site. Finally, Salmon, in the most recent and thorough work on the Samnites, concludes that Montaquila, which is about 80 kilometers from Agnone, is on or near the original Aquilonia.[13]

Regardless of the ancient verities, there are modern consequences of the Samnite origins of both Agnone and the Molise. The Agnonesi regard themselves as the Samnite descendants par excellence within their region and point with pride to their presumed crucial role in Samnite and, by extension, Italian history. Both modern and older texts invoke the image of Samnite ethnicity, the notion that the inhabitants of the Molise are ethnically distinct from other Italians.[14] This distinction is believed to be manifested physiologically as well. The Samnites are said to be taller in stature and more robust in physique than the surrounding populations.

The invocation of Samnite ethnicity does not, however, occur with the same frequency nor lead to the same political and social consequences that characterize the nationalism of some of Europe's more militant ethnic groups such as the Basques, Welsh, Scots, and Bretons. In Samnium the hiatus between ancient origins and modern realities is too great and the continuity too truncated. Oscan is a dead language, so that today's speech peculiarities in the Molise are best described as a dialectal variety of Italian. Nor are non-Samnites particularly discriminated against in the Molise.

The Medieval Chronicle

The interweaving of history and local myth recurs frequently as one seeks to unravel Agnone's past. The earliest medieval example of a possible reference to the town is a case in point. In the year 833 a monastery

31

and church were constructed in Naples with the name of Santa Maria de Anglone, later called Santa Maria d'Agnone. Meanwhile, a church of uncertain antiquity but of the same name was built in the town. There are several versions of what may have happened.

By one account, a Neapolitan nobleman was bitten by a serpent near the present site of Agnone. He promised the Virgin to build a church in her honor in return for his life. He was spared and fulfilled his vow, erecting churches of the same name in both Naples and Agnone. The name Agnone, therefore, derived from the Latin term for snake, *anguis* (*angueo*). By this interpretation, the church may have antedated, and given its name to, the town.

Carlomagno rejects this interpretation and maintains that the Agnonesi, for whatever reason, built and named the church in Naples.[15] The problem is that Summonte, in his *Historia della città e regno di Napoli* (1675), attributes the naming of the Naples church to a strictly Neapolitan event. There was an enormous snake that inhabited the marshes near the city and terrorized the populace. A devout man, while journeying through the area, encountered and killed it. In gratitude he erected the church in honor of the Virgin Mary, incorporating the corrupted Latin word for snake (*angueo*) into its name.[16]

Ascenso Marinelli provides still another interpretation of Agnone's historical roots. According to him, Santa Maria di Anglono was a miraculous effigy of the Virgin Mary housed in the monastery of Santa Maria di Agnone in the town of the same name. The monastery was founded on the former site of a pagan temple of Ceres (goddess of agriculture) and staffed by Basilian fathers. Its date of origin is unknown but antedates considerably the ninth century, by which time the miraculous properties of the effigy were famous far and wide, making Agnone a favored destination for pilgrims. The founding of the church in Naples was simply an emulation and acknowledgment of the widespread fame of and devotion to the Agnone effigy of Mary.[17] Marinelli further believes, albeit from indirect evidence, that in the sixth or seventh century the Benedictine order founded the ancient monastery of San Lorenzo in Agnone on the site of a pagan temple dedicated to Hercules and Jupiter.[18] The existence of two monasteries by the seventh century, one of which was the object of pilgrimages, leads him to argue that Agnone might have been a community of considerable size and importance by that time.

On the other hand, there is negative evidence to suggest that the town remained insignificant until more recently. When, in the second half of the tenth century, the dukedom of Benevento was divided into thirty-four counties, Pietrabbondante, and not Agnone, was made the county seat of what is today the Alto Molise.[19] Similarly, when, in an early but undetermined era, a diocese was created out of the Alto Molise and a part of the Abruzzo, Trivento, and not Agnone, was made the bishopric.[20]

The earliest reliable historical documentation regarding the town dates from the beginning of the eleventh century when Agnone as a feudal fiefdom was conferred by Berardo, count of Isernia, upon his son Radoisio.[21] For the next two centuries Agnone was the property of the powerful Borrello family, counts of Pietrabbondante.[22] Successive lords of Agnone included the Carbonara,[23] Anibaldi,[24] Sabrano,[25] and Carafa[26] families.

In the fifteenth century, however, Agnone attained the rather rare distinction of being named a *città regia*, or "royal city." A document dated September 15, 1404 reads:

> Diploma of King Ladislao which reduced [the obligation] of the *università* of Agnone,[27] in perpetuity, from feudal status and service, [converting Agnone's] status to desmesne or Crown Land dominion . . . with the honors, privileges, immunity, exemptions, liberality and franchises enjoyed by the other desmesne lands of the kingdom of Sicily. It is ordered that the master *giustizieri* of the kingdom, the magistrates and the vice-regents, now and in perpetuity, recognize inviolably said *università* and its district as their own (royal) desmesne territory, annulling in the process privileges and other honors annexed to feudal service.[28]

Agnone guarded its newly won privileges jealously. When in 1417 Queen Giovanna II tried to sell the town as a fief to her counselor, Carlo Carafa, the citizens "not supporting news of such a nature concerning their reduction to the status of a baronial dominion, destroyed to its foundation the tower, that is, the fortification of their said land, in contempt of said Carlo."[29] Queen Giovanna finally reconfirmed the *università* as a part of her desmesne, pardoning the citizenry and exempting the Agnonesi from the payment of taxes for one year.[30]

In 1440 the townspeople, for reasons that are unclear, cast their lot with the force of Alfonso of Aragon that had invaded the kingdom.[31] When the Aragonese were victorious, the town reaped many benefits. In 1442 Alfonso conceded Agnone the privilege of the *bagliva*, or the right to income from fines and other sources. The taxes, or *collete*, were reduced; Agnone was to remain a part of the royal desmesne in perpetuity and could not be sold or alienated by the king's descendants. The townspeople were to pay only those taxes due directly to the royal treasury. In gratitude the Agnonesi placed a stone carving of the Aragonese coat-of-arms near the principal entrance of their town.[32]

In 1446 Alfonso again conferred privileges on Agnone and confirmed its municipal statutes. The *università* was to receive all civil and criminal fines and in return pay the salary of the king's representative in the town, the *capitano*. Agnone was conceded title to the local castle and uninhabited fiefs within its territory. These same privileges were later reconfirmed by King Ferdinand the Catholic and Emperor Charles V.[33]

Lords and Litigation

To emphasize those features of Agnone's history that underscore local autonomy is to tell a part of the story. Even though by the fifteenth century the town was a *città regia* and hence not a fief in a strictly legal sense, there continued to be many feudal estates within its confines. There were still *baroni* of Agnone. Furthermore, despite their strong wording, the royal concessions of privilege were written on paper, not infinity. Future kings would concede Agnone in usufruct (*utile padrone*) to future nobles. In time, the distinction between usufruct and possession became blurred and subject to interpretation, a fact that was to lead to frequent disputes between Agnone and its "lord."

The succession of new lords of Agnone began as early as 1453, when the king conceded the town to Paolo di Sangro in return for his military service.[34] In 1507 Prospero Colonna was named *utile padrone* of Agnone, and he confirmed the statutes of the *università*.[35] In a document of the year 1153, Luigi Gonzaga, in the capacity of *utile padrone* of Agnone, reconfirmed the statutes.[36] Shortly thereafter Agnone was listed as a part of the dowry of Isabella Gonzaga upon her marriage to Luigi Carafa, prince of Stigliano.[37] In 1638 a Luigi di Carafa is referred to as lord of Agnone.[38] In 1640 Anna Carafa, *utile padrona* of Agnone, sold her interest in the town's municipal income (*proventi*) to Bartolomeo d'Aquino for the sum of two thousand ducats.[39] In 1644, Aquino sold his debt and rights to municipal incomes to Ferdinando Caracciolo, duke of Castel di Sangro, for forty-one thousand ducats.[40] The Caracciolo family, and particularly the branch with the title *principe di Santo Buono*, were to remain Agnone's lords until the abolition of feudalism in 1806.

The nature of the relationship between Agnone and this series of outside overlords is complex. The documents reflect a curious blend of servility and aggressiveness on the part of the officials of the *università*. Whenever the overlordship of the town changed hands, local authorities dispatched an emissary to the new lord, sometimes bearing a gift of foodstuffs or artisan wares,[41] to request reconfirmation of local privilege as guaranteed by the statutes. By the mid-seventeenth century the reconfirmation entailed a money payment by the *università* to the lord. The petition might begin with such language as "your illustrious Lord's humble slaves and vassals,"[42] but there was precious little compromise of local autonomy in the main body of the text. Changes in the statutes were proposed from time to time, but always in benefit of the *università*. For a period of more than two centuries, practically every petition and amendment initiated by the *università* was approved as proposed.[43] About the strongest opposition mustered by the overlords was an occasional qualifier to the statement of confirmation that "the statutes be regulated . . . under our arbitrage."[44]

Litigation was a frequent occurrence. In 1494 Agnone was engaged in a court case with Tiberio Caracciolo, lord of Rocca dell'Abate, over a disputed boundary.[45] In 1519 the town was in litigation with Marino Caracciolo, marchese of Bucchianico, and with the *università* of Belmonte.[46] In 1572 Isabella Gonzaga, duchess of Stigliano and *utile padrona* of Agnone, sued to claim Agnone's municipal income.[47] In 1640 Agnone and Anna Carafa litigated over this same issue.[48] As early as 1627 the *università* was paying a regular retainer to an attorney in Naples to represent its interests.[49]

Legal disputes between the Agnonesi and the Prince of Santo Buono were particularly protracted and acrimonious. For more than a century, both sides appealed any verdict that was unfavorable to its position.[50] Nor was the dispute limited to peaceful tactics. In the 1750s Agnone's spokesman in its legal struggle with the prince was Filippo Longhi, who was reputed to have declared:

> The people of Agnone have never been the vassals of anyone, have never given their oath of fidelity, have never obliged themselves to accord the prince special honors nor given him noble service, as it

35

is called in feudal language, and this is because they have the right to remain free and masters of their own destiny at all costs.[51]

Because of his obstinance Longhi was almost assassinated by agents of the prince.[52] The greatest affront to the prince's authority occurred on the evening of April 25, 1786, when his representative in Agnone was murdered in the public piazza.[53]

The Feudal Society

There are two documents rich in information about the nature of Agnone society during the feudal era. The municipal charters (*statuta et capitula*)[54] date from the mid-fifteenth century (1440) and provide a glimpse of local life at the end of the Middle Ages. The "Onciario,"[55] or census, formulated in 1753, details the age, occupation, and family status of all Agnonesi and summarizes the assets and debits of every household in the town for the period just before the abolition of feudalism. Using information gleaned from both documents, while supplementing it with the fragmentary sources, it is possible to construct at least an overview of Agnone's feudal social structure.

As early as the Middle Ages Agnone was already well established as an artisan and commercial center of considerable importance. Whole sections of the charters regulate the activities of the coppersmiths,[56] ironsmiths,[57] tailors,[58] and shoemakers.[59] The clauses entitled "How the Coppersmiths Should Exercise Their Art" specify the quality of copper to be used in each object and set the price for wares sold in Agnone. They also authorized the coppersmiths to charge whatever the traffic would bear when selling their goods outside the town's precincts.[60]

Of particular interest were the ways in which the Agnonesi consciously used their statutes to both stimulate the local economy and gain access to markets in other areas for their merchants and artisans. Every Saturday, or the day of Agnone's fair "since antiquity," citizens and outsiders alike were free to sell goods of any nature without paying municipal taxes.[61] On the other days of the week, municipal taxes and duties were exacted on the sale of all goods other than foodstuffs. Outsiders (*forestieri*) were required to pay an additional tax on every sale *and* purchase, although the citizens of other towns willing to extend the same privileges to the Agnonesi were exempted from the payment of any tax on their transactions in Agnone.[62] This meant that some outsiders enjoyed an advantage over the citizens of Agnone in the latter's own marketplace. That the framers of Agnone's statutes were willing to concede such reciprocity is testimony to the town's confidence and aggressive commercial posture vis-à-vis its hinterland as early as the fifteenth century.

In horse trading there was an additional tax (*plateatico*) imposed on outsiders. The clause exempts citizens from certain other towns "since the men and persons of the territory of Agnone are free and exempt from said *plateatico* tax in those same places."[63] The place list is interesting in that it provides some idea of the far-flung nature of Agnone's trading network even in this earlier period. Included are the towns of Alfedena, Castel di Sangro, San Pietro Avellana, Pescopennataro, Sant'Angelo del Pesco, Lanciano, Rosello, Pescocostanzo, Frosolone, and Salcito, all of which remained a part of Agnone's commercial hinterland in later periods. Foggia, largest city on the Apulian plain, and more than 100 kilometers distant from Agnone by muletrack, is also listed.[64]

Agnone is situated in that part of the Molise with the greatest historical involvement in livestock raising, and the statutes contain many provisions concerning this activity. Fines were levied against the owner of errant animals.[65] The butchering of meat was carefully regulated,[66] as was the sale of wool.[67] During the Aragonese period of Neapolitan history, a major pattern of transhumance developed between the mountains of the Abruzzo-Molise and the Apulian plain. It was established by King Alfonso and modeled after the *mesta* system[68] as practiced on the Iberian peninsula.[69] The king created 3,061 kilometers of sheep and cattle walks in south Italy.[70] In the year 1474 alone, 1,700,000 sheep were wintered in Apulia.[71] The movements of the animals were monitored carefully because the flocks and herds were taxed by the royal authorities as they passed certain checkpoints. The records of the Dogana delle Pecore, or Sheep Customs, provide some idea of the extent to which the Agnonesi were involved in livestock transhumance. For example, in the year 1597, between October 25 and 30, fourteen flocks from Agnone passed the checkpoint.[72] All were under the care of several professional herders, either working on their own account or in the employ of others.

There were two institutions of paramount importance in the life of the town: the *università* and the church. The statutes and the "Onciario" bracket three centuries of local history, so it is therefore possible to gain some insight into the processes whereby the municipality and the religious establishment consolidated and enhanced wealth, power, and influence. Regarding the *università*, there is little evidence in the mid-fifteenth century statutes that it possessed a landed patrimony. Rather, the collection of taxes and levying of fines were the only two sources of municipal income. Concomitantly, there was no notion that residence in Agnone conferred upon a citizen a stake in communal property. The statutes encouraged outsiders to settle in the town. One clause even guaranteed the new resident exemption from the local head tax and municipal levies on livestock for a period of five years.[73]

Subsequently, the *università* itself acquired property. As early as 1455 the town purchased from Agostino di Normandi his one-half ownership in two uninhabited castles and estates in Agnone.[74] In 1503 Agnone purchased the fief of Cantalupo from the Carafa family for one thousand ducats.[75] Between 1484 and 1570 the town purchased all or portions of fiefs on at least eleven occasions.[76] In 1520 the *università* petitioned its lord, Prospero Colonna, for permission to defend its feudal interests against the people of the town of Rosello.[77] The *università* of Rosello had the right to cut wood and collect grasses on the fief in return for payment of a one-ducat rent due annually on August 15.[78] Depending on the context, Agnone itself could be either lord or vassal.

The emergence of a communal patrimony created through the purchase of feudal fiefs prompted the Agnonesi to modify the very notion of citizenship. In 1520 the town petitioned its lord to approve a clause that prohibited Albanians (many of whom were in south Italy as mercenaries) and malefactors from settling in Agnone. In 1524 it was proposed that any outsider desirous of residing in the town be forced to pay some sort of residence fee. The rationale was stated as follows:

> It happens that many outsiders come to live in this land and in consequence enjoy all of the fiefs and other possessions of said *università*, acquired with much fatigue and dedication of the citizens of said land, past and present, and in particular the feudal possessions of said *università* which have been bought in recent times . . . justice does not allow that said outsiders come to enjoy [these benefits] without making some honest contribution.[79]

At the same time, the *università* actively sought to increase its holdings. It was decreed that no local citizen could purchase a fief that became available within the confines of Agnone unless the *università* waived a first right of purchase.[80] Four years later, in 1528, the new local conservatism culminated in a strong measure prohibiting any outsider from settling in the town.[81]

The extent of Agnone's feudal holdings varied as the *università* acquired new fiefs, occasionally divested itself of a part of its holdings, and either won or lost court cases contesting ownership of particular estates.[82] Some idea of the magnitude of the town's feudal patrimony may be derived, however, from the fact that, when feudalism was abolished, Agnone was in possession of twelve fiefs within the confines of the *università* and one estate outside the area. The twelve local fiefs constituted 5,228 *tomoli*[83] (1,613 hectares), or about 17 percent of the total land base of the municipality.[84]

Thus, over time, the municipality of Agnone emerged as a strong corporate entity, disposed to defend the emerging town commons against the encroachments of outsiders and citizens alike. In the process, the *università* itself became tantamount to a feudal baron, owing service to the king. The original feudal obligation of providing cavalry and troops to the monarch had long since been converted to a money payment (*adoa*),[85] but the funds had to be raised to meet it. Consequently, the resources of the fiefs were allocated to the citizenry according to a system called the *candela*, a public auction to the highest bidder. "*Candela*" referred to the fact that, once the auction had been announced by the town crier, a candle was lit in the town hall. While it continued to burn, anyone could better the best standing offer. Many resources, such as the right to gather fruits and nuts, cut wood, or graze animals on particular pastures, were dispensed annually in this fashion. Other communal resources such as plowland and vineyard were allocated on a sharecropping basis. In some cases the *università* followed the lead of the church and exacted perpetual tithes against a particular field.

It is clear from the statutes that the church played a key role in medieval Agnone's affairs. The documents were themselves redacted inside of one of the town's churches and amended under the aegis of visiting Franciscan friars.[86] Several clauses outline punishments to be meted out to blasphemers[87] and those who labored on Sundays and religious holidays.[88] Similarly, people who disturbed the peace and meditation of the nuns of the Convent of Santa Chiara or the friars of the Monastery of San Francesco were to be fined heavily.[89]

The single most important clause regarding the position of the church in Agnone society is entitled "Customs and Observances in the Land of

Agnone regarding Possessions of the Church." It notes that the monasteries and churches of Agnone possessed tithes over property (*enfiteuti*) that could not be alienated from them in any fashion.[90] Lands that bore a tithe could be sold, willed, dowered, or given away by their owners; but the tithe itself was perpetual and was assumed by the new owner.[91]

The religious establishment of the town ultimately attained enormous proportions. By 1680 there were no fewer than twenty-two churches in the *cittadina* of Agnone and thirty-four churches and chapels in the *agro*.[92] Included in these totals were six monasteries and convents. The bishop of Trivento maintained a palace in Agnone, which was used as a seminary.[93] Considering that in 1648 the town was said to have had 843 households,[94] the number of religious edifices is truly staggering.

The number of secular clergyman in Agnone during the early seventeenth century also is known. In 1615 a representative of the bishop visited the town to examine the state of local Catholicism. In his report he noted that Agnone had thirty priests, twenty-eight seminarians, and six deacons.[95] This did not even include the monks and nuns in the religious orders.

Overtime, the church's patrimony grew incessantly. All of Agnone's many religious institutions acquired considerable real property as well as tithes over private and *università* holdings. By 1753, for example, the religious establishment (i.e., religious institutions and the individual clergymen combined) owned outright 11.62 percent of the town's vineyards and 62.61 percent of its plowland![96] Furthermore, the average vineyard or field held by a private citizen or by the *università* had at least one perpetual tithe against it, and many had multiple liens. Thus, of the 1,178 vineyards listed in the "Onciario," 842, or 71.48 percent, carried at least one religious encumbrance, as did 39.60 percent of Agnone's plowland.

The religious establishment played other key roles within the local economy. Each of the parish churches maintained a grain fund (*monte frumentario*) for the purpose of pious or charitable works (*opere pie*). In the not-infrequent food emergencies, church granaries were a partial guarantee against local famine. In normal times, the grain was loaned out (at interest) for sowing to those peasants who were so strapped that they were unable to set aside sufficient seed for the next year's planting.

Moneylending was another church activity. The 1753 "Onciario" lists 1,127 money loans. Of this total, 1,099, or fully 97.52 percent, of the notes were held by the various religious entities. The debt load of 21,149 ducats represented more than three times the town's municipal expenditures of 6,799 ducats in the year 1742 (or about the same period).[97] The 2,321 ducats of annual income from the combined sources of tithes and interest on notes alone had a purchasing power of 11,605 man-days.[98]

By the last century of the feudal period, the church was the single most powerful economic force in Agnone affairs. Neither the prince and local barons nor the *università* could even begin to rival it in terms of sheer economic clout. Agnone's religious establishment effectively served as the local bankers, underwriting the major portion of personal debt in the town.

The difficulty of assessing the degree to which the Agnonesi were in political and economic bondage during the feudal era should be apparent. I have discussed the centuries-long debate between Agnone and its lords over the collective legal status of the townspeople. On balance it would appear that, while the lords retained certain privileges, the townspeople enjoyed a large measure of political freedom in local affairs. Furthermore, although barons owned property in the town, the status of their Agnone estates was sometimes subject to legal hairsplitting. For instance, one document (referring to the year 1694) states that, as there were no feudal fiefs in Agnone, the feudal holdings in the town were registered in a special manner![99]

There is no indication of out-and-out serfdom in medieval Agnone in the sense that a man was bound to a plot of land and in the perpetual service of a particular lord. Rather, to the extent that bondage did exist, it took the more subtle form of *censi* and *annui* tithing that was widespread in the town. The many churches and religious institutions, the *università* itself, and many private landowners exacted perpetual tithes against harvests (as well as workshops and dwellings).

Thus, over time, a particular field or vineyard, while possibly "owned" by a peasant family, might acquire several liens in perpetuity against it. While ownership could be sold or transferred, the new owner acquired the lien obligation as well. If, then, men were not bound to the soil, the soil was itself encumbered. In fact it may well be that the result from the peasant's viewpoint was the same or worse than if he had actually been indentured. His poverty and indebtedness, an indebtedness assumed by his heirs, for all practical purposes curtailed his economic choices. At the same time he lacked the security of the arrangement in which the indentured serf received some protection and patriarchal largesse from his lord.

41

Social Classes

The common conception of feudalism is of a society characterized on the one hand by a pronounced social hierarchy with little socioeconomic mobility between the classes, or "estates," and on the other by concentration of wealth and power in the hands of a few. In a broad sense, these generalizations are applicable to Agnone.

The clergy were, in the main, drawn from the nobility and from the professional and merchant class. Accumulation of wealth, educational background, and marriage alliances all affected social standing within these circles. Taken together, the petty gentry, professionals, and merchant families constituted the elite of Agnone society.

In feudal Agnone there was generally a correlation between wealth and social status, but it was by no means absolute. On balance, in the "Onciario" the net worth of the artisan household tends to be about twice that of the peasant one. The record also shows considerable individual variation in the propensity for risk taking. There were wealthy peasants whose net worth far outstripped that of poor and even reasonably well-to-do artisans and shopkeepers. On the other hand, no peasant or artisan even approached the wealth of many of the local petty gentry.

Within the local world view, people were seen as being born into their stations of life, a fact reflected in the mentality of the record keepers. At the birth of a male infant, it was common to register his "occupation," which was invariably the same as that of his father. The 1753 "Onciario" reflects this tendency for occupational stability within family lines. In the large majority of households, all active males have the same occupation. There was, then, a closed corporate aspect to Agnone's occupational structure.

Formal education was restricted to a limited circle of families. The primary vehicles for preparing the young for adulthood were the practical roles of artisan apprentice or peasant field hand. In most instances a boy's *maestro* was his father or close kinsman. It is not surprising, then, that with a considerable degree of consistency people in Agnone today can identify a man's profession given his last name. Certain surnames cluster within certain occupations and have done so for several centuries (although the correlation is by no means absolute). This fact alone is eloquent testimony to the lack of social and occupational mobility within Agnone society.

The "Onciario" lists the occupations of all male Agnonesi and there-

42

fore provides excellent information on Agnone's economic structure during the final stage of the feudal era. In 1753 there were 1,529 males over the age of fourteen years in the town. Table 3.1 provides an occupational profile of the active male populace. Several comments are in order. Practically one out of every two male Agnonesi were listed as *bracciale* (peasant-laborer). Agriculture and artisanship remained the twin pillars of the local economy. Landownership was broad based, for even the artisan household was likely to own one or more fields and vineyards. For example, 733, or 84.94 percent of the 863 households listed in the "Onciario," has at least one vineyard in 1753. All but 20 of Agnone's households leased a portion of the commons from the *università*.[100] There continued to be considerable emphasis on livestock raising. This is seen in the numbers engaged in such animal-related activities as sheepherding, tanning, wool carding, mule skinning, neatherding, and butchering. Such artisan occupations as shoemaking, hatting, and leather working were also dependent animal by-products.

Land and livestock provided the prime investment opportunities for money and labor surpluses in feudal Agnone. A system of partible inheritance and a propensity to parcelize existing landholdings to satisfy dowry and inheritance claims have characterized the town throughout its recorded history. As a consequence, few parcels remained in a particular family line for long or retained their configuration over time. Land transactions were quite common as households with rising economic fortunes sought to invest their surplus cash while others were forced to divest themselves of landholdings to meet their obligations. Livestock partnerships were a particularly common arrangement and frequently crossed class lines. As the membership of a peasant household increased, so did the likelihood that it would become involved in labor-intensive livestock raising. The enterprising peasant household might augment its animal numbers by co-venturing with nonagriculturalists.

For its size, feudal Agnone had one of the richest and most diversified artisan traditions in all of south Italy. In part this may be attributed to the physical isolation of the Alto Molise, which made the town the trade center for an extensive hinterland of villages; but at least some of Agnone's artisan goods were traded far beyond this circle of "natural" client communities.

Clearly, in terms of sheer magnitude and fame, the primary artisan activity of Agnone was coppersmithing. Giustiniani comments in 1797 that the Agnonesi "are industrious and sell their products in surrounding

Table 3.1. *Occupational Profile of Male Agnonesi in 1753*

Peasants and manual laborers

Occupation	Number
Peasants and day laborers	747
Field hands	34
Sheepherders	32
Construction workers	21
Charcoal makers	17
Firewood sellers	14
Plowmen	14
Mule skinners	11
Neatherds	10
Total	900

Artisans

Occupation	Number
Coppersmiths[a]	138
Shoemakers	118
Gunsmiths	26
Carpenter-cabinetmakers	25
Tinkers	19
Tanners	14
Wool carders	13
Tailors	11
Bell makers	9
Hatters	9
Ironsmiths	8
Goldsmiths	7
Rope makers	7
Footwarmer makers	6
Saddlemakers	5
Silversmiths	3
Comb makers	2
Leather workers	2
Knife makers	1
Key makers	1
Engravers	1
Total	425

Professions and businessmen

Occupation	Number
Clergymen	65
Landowners	23
Independently wealthy	14
Storekeepers	11
Officials	10
Physicians	7
Lawyers	4
Magistrates	4
Pharmacists	4
Judges	2
Draftsmen	2
Overseers	1
Musicians	1
Total	148

Miscellaneous

Occupation	Number
Soldiers	15
Students	10
Watchmen	8
Butchers	7
Barbers	5
Manservants	5
Shop clerks	4
Salesmen	2
Total	56

N = 1,529

Source: "Onciario," passim.

[a] Composite total of *ramaro lavoratore* (45) and *venditore di rame* (93). The latter designation refers to the self-employed coppersmith, while the *ramaro lavoratore* was employed for wages.

towns, and distant places, as is the case with their copper wares, which are greatly esteemed."[101] Sacco, writing about the same time, notes that the town produced "various types of copper wares, which have no equal in all of our kingdom."[102] By the eighteenth century there were at least five water-driven foundries on the Verrino River providing blanks to dozens of *botteghe*, or workshops, in the town.

The goldsmiths were another artisan group with a propensity to travel widely, selling wares produced in Agnone (which included rings, earrings, necklaces, bracelets, brooches, lockets, and amulets). Gold and silver jewelry was regarded not only as an adornment but as an esteemed investment. Throughout the region, the newly betrothed customarily exchanged such jewelry before marriage.

There was yet another class of Agnone artisans who plied their trade far and wide: the men who traveled with their skills to a distant work site. The bell makers were a prime example. To this day, Agnone is famed for its bellworks, which exports its products to churches throughout the world. Until the beginning of the present century, however, transportation facilities were inadequate, and the bell makers of Agnone were commissioned to construct the bells near the edifice in which they were to be installed. Agnone's stonemasons and carpenters also traveled to other communities, where they resided for extended periods while completing a job.

Artisanship in feudal Agnone did not translate into a classical guild pattern. Coppersmiths, goldsmiths, silversmiths, and so on were not organized economically beyond the extended-family level. Indeed, it is a part of the local oral tradition that each family possessed its own techniques that were never divulged to fellow artisans. "Agnone's coppersmiths" or "Agnone's goldsmiths," therefore, existed only in a categorical sense, not as formal organizations.

Civic Accomplishment

There can be no doubt that throughout the feudal era the Agnonesi had much reason for civic pride. A number of the town's sons achieved personal fame while pursuing illustrious careers elsewhere. In 1245 the bishop Ruggieri di Borello d'Agnone was archbishop of Pontino and attended the Council of Lyon.[103] During this same period Stefano di Agnone was the royal *giustiziere* of the region of Terra di Lavoro.[104]

Orlandi provides an extensive list of Agnonesi who pursued military, administrative, and religious careers in other parts of the kingdom of Naples.[105] Ascenso Marinelli lists nine bishops and two theologians who originated in the town.[106] Fra Marco of Agnone was a missionary who was martyred in Macedonia[107] for his beliefs. Fra Arcangelo was beatified for his sanctity,[108] as was Antonio Lucci, who served as bishop in Bovino, where he defended the poor *contadini* against excesses of the lords.[109]

Other Agnonesi made their marks in the arts. Probably the most prominent was Marino Ionata, who, in the fifteenth century, authored a lengthy epic poem entitled *Il giardino*. The work was modeled after Dante's *La divina commedia* in depicting a journey through the realm of the dead. While it obviously lacked the stature of Dante's effort, it was not without literary merit and is an important document for the history of the language.[110] During the eighteenth century Stefano di Stefano achieved considerable recognition as a poet and statesman.[111]

Medicine was another field in which feudal Agnone made distinguished contributions. In 1587 the Agnonese physician Ascanio Mancinelli published a scientific treatise on rabies.[112] In the early seventeenth century Marcantonio Gualtieri of Agnone served first as the personal physician of the duke of Ossuna and later in the same capacity to the Spanish viceroys of Naples and Sicily. He also authored several medical treatises.[113] Another illustrious eighteenth-century Agnonese was the jurist Nicola Cocucci.[114]

By the end of the feudal era, Agnone itself was a center of considerable renown. In the first volume of his work *Delle città d'Italia*, published in 1770, Orlandi characterizes Agnone as a wealthy city became of its water-powered grain and fulling mills and copper foundries.[115] According to Orlandi:

> With respect to commerce the principal factors are the excellent iron products, harquebuses, and similar arms; bells; and lastly, copperware which manifest singularly fine workmanship. Wherein there continually enter into the city considerable sums of money from the diffusion of these products, as well as from the great quantity of wine which Agnone provides to many nearby places.[116]

The town was also noted for its curative waters and salubrious climate. Orlandi states that many people traveled there to convalesce from illnesses.[117]

46

Agnone was famed for its culture. Orlandi notes:

Likewise there resides [in Agnone] a large number of practitioners of many kinds, both religious and secular, who are worthy of commendation in every theological, philosophical, legal, and medical science. The city has always been esteemed for such persons, and many outsiders come there to complete a course of study.[118] For this reason Agnone is antonomastically called the city in the surrounding towns.[119]

Feudal Agnone, then, was an important urban center. It seems, in fact, that it was larger than any other town in the present-day region of the Molise. In the year 1648 Agnone had 843 *fuochi*, or households, compared with Campobasso's 826 households and the 700 households of Isernia.[120] One document places the population of Agnone in 1813— shortly after the abolition of feudalism—at 8,090 inhabitants, whereas that of Isernia was 5,089 residents.[121] In terms of size, economic complexity, and cultural accomplishments during the feudal period, Agnone outshone what are today the two most important cities in the Molise.

The Feudal Heritage

Feudalism in south Italy, as elsewhere in Western Europe, was a far-from-monolithic social order. The ever-present power struggle between the monarch, lords, church, and the *università* led to both concessions and denials of privilege that, over time, meant that social and economic arrangements in each local context acquired a degree of uniqueness. In the case of south Italy, the Aragonese monarchs were particularly prone to concede a large measure of ad hoc autonomy to municipalities as a means of countermanding the authority of the barons. There is, then, a sense in which each community had its own feudal order.[122]

There are several features of feudal Agnone society that may have contributed to the townspeople's subsequent heightened propensity for emigration in the latter half of the nineteenth century. First, the town, despite its physical isolation, was an economic and educational center of considerable importance. This meant that it received a constant flow of information concerning the outside world. Despite the rigidly hierarchial nature of social relations in Agnone and the monopolization of formal education by the few, it is likely that even the peasant or artisan Agnonese

47

possessed a world view that was less circumscribed than that of his counterpart in most other communities of the Molise.

Reinforcing some sense of cosmopolitanism was the physical movement of people into and out of the town. The fifteenth-century statutes clearly favored a free-trade mentality, both encouraging outsiders to visit Agnone's fairs and markets and encouraging the Agnonesi to engage in commerce on a regional scale. Three segments of Agnone society regularly left the town, either on a permanent or a seasonal basis. In each generation many sons of Agnone's social elite pursued military, religious, administrative, and academic careers elsewhere. Agnone's artisans doubled as traveling merchants of their own wares and in this capacity roamed far and wide. Certain artisans, such as the carpenters and bell makers, frequently traveled to work sites located at considerable distances from the town. Finally, Agnone's shepherds regularly trailed their charges to the Apulian plain. Therefore, it may be argued that it was a part of Agnone's feudal heritage to regard physical mobility as a legitimate economic strategy. Migration, in its many forms, was not a threatening prospect to the same degree as was probably the case in more closed communities lacking such experience.

The Agnonesi were also disposed to entrepreneurial activity. People of all walks of life engaged in business speculation. Regardless of his "product," each man served as his own business agent. The principal social institutions of the town, the church and the *università*, were likewise engaged in a multitude of financial dealings. Risk taking was a prominent feature of everyday life in feudal Agnone.

Feudalism in the kingdom of Naples was abolished in the aftermath of the French Enlightment, the French Revolution, and, physically, by a French invasion. Under its conservative Bourbon monarchs and lacking a numerous middle class, the kingdom as a whole was one of the areas of Europe that was least receptive to liberal thought. In Agnone, however, with its professional and merchant classes and its entrepreneurial heritage, the new philosophy had considerable appeal. Before considering the liberal era in Agnone's history, however, it is necessary to examine the broader context: late-eighteenth- and early-nineteenth-century developments in south Italy as a whole and in the Molise in particular.

4

The Liberal Challenge

While it has been possible to underscore an extraordinary degree of civic accomplishment in feudal Agnone, this must be placed in perspective by viewing it against a general backdrop of endemic poverty and political strife. Contemporary accounts of the Molise during the waning years of the feudal period depict a grim scenario. Writing in 1781, the historian Galanti, himself a native of the region, considered the Molise one of the most backward areas of the kingdom. He characterizes the situation as one of "little commerce, scarce and miserable arts, crude industries, bad roads [which are] in winter practically impassable, ignorance, crudeness, misery and oppressions." Most of the Molise was so far removed from major centers of authority that public disorder and brigandage flourished,[1] and the local authorities were little more than extortioners.[2]

Of particular concern were the miserable circumstances of the peasantry. Everyone in the peasant household had to work in order to make ends meet. The field workers consumed enormous quantities of wine just to get through their day.[3] The peasant was taxed unrelentingly and supported by his toil the whole superstructure of aristocratic and church wealth.[4] Yet despite this service he experienced severe social discrimination:

Here the peasant is poor . . . he suffers aggravations of every sort.
. . . The oppression is such that in the majority of cases it renders
the peasant depraved; he is in his poverty respectful, and by his nature given to good works, but he is resentful of the snub and of the
offense.[5]

The abbot Longano journeyed through the Molise in 1786 and confirmed Galanti's dismal portrayal of the area. Longano notes that robbery, homicide, and mendicity were all increasing sharply and that some
families were resettling in Naples to escape what was tantamount to a life
of servitude under the barons.[6] The situation of the poor people was
deteriorating rapidly owing to runaway inflation.[7] The peasants generally lacked ownership of the land and were prey to short-term lease
arrangements. Because they could be easily evicted they possessed little
leverage in their dealings with the owners. Given their fragile tenureship
they were unwilling to make substantial capital investments, which in
turn perpetuated poor yields.[8] The circle of debt in which the *contadino*
found himself could easily lead to bankruptcy, during which even his
hand tools were seized and sold to satisfy his obligations.[9]

Finally, Longano denounces the general state of corruption in the
province whereby a few wealthy people manipulated the municipalities
to their personal advantage.[10] The barons regularly bribed the royal
officials and usurped lands.[11] The church was run as a business enterprise (at times a corrupt one at that), with gross insensitivity to social
injustices.[12]

Such was the situation in the last decade of the eighteenth century, or
the waning years of the feudal era.

The Liberal Order

The collapse of the feudal system began with the Napoleonic invasion of
the Italian peninsula. In 1797 Napoleon captured northern Italy and proclaimed the Cisalpine Republic. The following year he took Rome and
installed a popular government there as well. The Bourbon king
Ferdinando of Naples sent an expeditionary force, which recaptured the
city. The success was short-lived, for the French forces regained Rome,
causing Ferdinando to seek asylum in Sicily. On January 23, 1799 Gen-

eral Championnet entered Naples and proclaimed the Parthenopean Republic in south Italy.

Unfortunately for its proponents, the new republic faltered. Napoleon extended his campaigns to Egypt, and in his absence the European monarchies launched a counterattack focused on the Italian peninsula. Ferdinando dispatched an army from Sicily under the command of Cardinal Ruffo. The republicans suffered a series of defeats, which were in part facilitated by the strong pro-Bourbon sentiment that remained throughout much of the kingdom.

Shortly thereafter, Napoleon initiated a new, successful Italian campaign. When he defeated the Austrians in the battle of Marengo, northern and central Italy were again under French control. Ferdinando was to remain as king of Naples until 1806, but only by signing a humiliating treaty that obliged him to release all of the republican prisoners.[13]

In 1806 Napoleon installed his brother Joseph Bonaparte as king of Naples. The new monarch decreed feudalism abolished. Two years later, Joseph became king of Spain, and his brother-in-law, Joachim Murat, replaced him in Italy. Murat tried to implement an enlightened administration, but Bourbon sentiment remained strong.

In 1815 Murat was forced to flee Italy, and King Ferdinando, supported by Metternich and Austrian troops, once again assumed control of the kingdom. Liberalism was far from vanquished, however, and went underground in the form of secret societies, the most powerful of which were the *carbonari*. Naples quickly became the stronghold of the movement, and in 1820 King Ferdinando, acceding to *carbonari* pressure, promised to promulgate a liberal constitution for the kingdom. He reneged on the agreement, however, and in 1821 an Austrian force captured the city of Naples, thereby putting an end to any serious challenge of Ferdinando's absolute powers.[14]

While the Bourbons remained in power from 1815 to 1860, the liberal cause was far from dormant. In 1848 the king of Naples was forced by popular demand to formulate a liberal constitution. A strong Bourbon reaction quickly set in, however, initiating a period of political repression in south Italy that was to last until Giuseppe Garibaldi's final victory, which unified Italy in 1860. Although unification of the nation represented the culmination of the liberals' efforts and realization of their dream, the triumph was somewhat tarnished when Italy became a constitutional monarchy rather than a new republic. For the remainder of the nineteenth century and the first two decades of the twentieth, however, liberalism remained a potent force in national affairs, though increasingly challenged by the emergent political left.

The Galantuomini

The above events lend themselves to a class-struggle interpretation. On the one hand, during the first half of the nineteenth century, the powerful aristocracy and traditionalist clergy remained royalist and in support of the Bourbon king. The emerging middle-class bourgeoisie, with allies in a segment of the clergy, seized upon the French invasion as an opportunity to overturn the old social order. The reaction of the *contadini* is more difficult to fathom; the peasants sided with the arisotcracy in support of the king. They remained highly suspicious of the general call for "liberty" even though they theoretically had the most to gain. The arguments that the *contadini* were either basically conservative or possibly apolitical are difficult to accept inasmuch as, time and again, the peasants organized, seized control of particular towns, and committed many atrocities against the Jacobins.

The historian Zarrilli presents a more convincing analysis. He maintains that, although the concern of the Jacobins was to topple the established social and political order in the name of greater liberty and freedom of action, few liberals championed genuine social reform for the lower classes. Thus, although the French challenge initially struck a favorable chord among *both* the middle class and the *contadini*, the French sided with the former, and the latter quickly became disillusioned.[15] Subsequent events were to confirm the peasants' suspicions, for the *liberali* sought to translate their victory into an elite social status. Designated by the newly coined term *galantuomini* ("gallant men"), they effectively replaced the *baroni* at the apex of the social pyramid.

It may also be argued that, by the late eighteenth and early nineteenth century, the middle class was a greater symbol of exploitation to the peasantry than was the arisotocracy. In the later years of the feudal period, the power of the *università* vis-à-vis the nobles had increased steadily, and control of the *università* was usually in the hands of a limited circle of local businessmen, professionals, and petty gentry. To the peasant, the local merchants, administrators, money lenders, and commodities speculators were more visibly the cause of his misery than were

52

the absentee barons. This was particularly the case given that feudal obligations such as tithes remained fixed, whereas the rampant economic inflation of the eighteenth century[16] made renewable mortgages and contracts all the more onerous.[17]

A perennial raw issue between the liberals and the peasantry was the question of land reform. The abolition of feudalism, with the prospect of the dismemberment of the feudal estates, sparked a strong strain of hope among the land-starved peasants. Their disillusionment turned to fury as the promised land reform became a usurpation by the *galantuomini*. The middle class possessed the capital to purchase lands as they became available on the open market. Many large feudal estates and religious endowments were converted into royal demesne and into town commons. The *galantuomini*, because they were in control of municipal government, were in a position to manipulate these resources or steal them outright.[18] The ultimate irony was that, as the liberal *galantuomini* sought to reinforce their claim to elite social status by becoming a landed middle class, the Bourbons came to champion the peasants' demands for redistribution of the land.[19]

The emergence of the *galantuomini* as the elite of the new social order led intially to a spate of well-intentioned reforms, and progress in agriculture was a prime target of their efforts. In 1810 Murat issued a decree in Naples establishing an agricultural society in each province,[20] and within two years one was functioning in the Molise.[21] First, it was decided that the membership should seek to rationalize farming operations and experiment with new crops. Toward these ends, two members were to plant exotic trees, and particularly South American varieties. One member (the *intendente* of the province) was to experiment with forage crops. Another man (an archpriest) was to grow new grain crops. An architect would develop new types of rural structures. The assignment of a wealthy cavalier was to experiment with woad (a dye substitute for American indigo). Two people were to seek new varieties of fruit trees. One member was to work out a system of accounting so that Molise farms could be modeled after English ones.[22]

For the *galantuomini*, the Agricultural Society and its journal, the *Giornale economico rustico del Sannio* (founded in 1819), were the source of farming knowledge. As the peasantry was illiterate, the publication was clearly for the benefit of the fledging middle-class agriculturalist. Its pages extolled the virtues of land speculation. The flavor of its articles can only be labeled as "farming by numbers," interspersed with highly technical treatises and comparisons of local yields with those in more advanced countries. At times (and to its credit) the journal advised the true novice who was having trouble to observe circumspectly the peasants at work on neighboring plots in order to learn their techniques.

The flavor of the spirit with which the liberals entered the realm of farm management is reflected in an exhortation taken from the pages of the *Giornale*:

> Rich and educated young men, if you wish to apply yourself to agri-culture, you must seek greater pleasure in the delicacies of this art; if you love to see beauty and utility in all of its many aspects, if you wish to admire the richness and luxuriousness of rural scenes, if you want to subject nature to your command, and regulate her or extract from her greater profit by means of the knowledge of the physical and natural sciences that you acquired in the course of your studies, seek to effect the most profound union possible be-tween the climate, your land, and your economic circumstances.[23]

While there is much that is laudable in these efforts to modernize one of the most primitive agricultural systems in Europe, the nature of the Agricultural Society could scarcely help but further alienate the peas-antry. One can only imagine the reaction of the *contadini* to the pro-nouncements of politicians, archpriests, and architects who were sud-denly self-styled experts on agriculture. The peasants' reliance on a conventional wisdom, gleaned from centuries of experience, scarcely squared with the new emphasis on intellectualized scientism. To rush pell-mell into the future with exotic crops and unfamiliar techniques was not the peasant style.

Another source of irritation was the liberals' myopia with respect to the pressing agrarian question of land reform. Without actually taking a stand, the society questioned whether fragmenting the former fiefs into small holdings (with the implication of peasant ownership) would not preclude proper capitalization of agricultural operations.[24] It also ex-pressed the fear that peasant cultivation of areas formerly in pasture might destroy animal husbandry in the province. Clearly, if maximum efficiency was the primary goal, a strong case could be made for medium-sized, well-capitalized operations rather than peasant tenure. This interpretation could scarcely engender peasant enthusiasm or as-suage growing suspicions of the *galantuomini*'s motives.

During the early years of liberalism, then, the land itself became a commodity; the middle class *galantuomo*, the primary speculator. For the peasantry, this did not merely represent an abstract transfer of ownership from one remote overlord to another. Rather, the new masters resided locally and were imbued with an almost blind faith in the ability of science to solve any problem. Despite their inexperience, the *galantuomini* were prone to meddle directly in the day-to-day operation of their farms. The did so with little respect for peasant opinion and wisdom. Over time, the *casino*, or rural chalet, became the symbol of the middle-class foray into agricultural management. The *casino* was a country house maintained by an owner who resided for most of the year in town. During such critical periods as the harvest, he set up housekeeping in the countryside in order to keep close tabs on operations.

Liberalism in Agnone

There is a stone monument in the busiest intersection of Agnone that bears the inscription:

To

Libero Serafini

The Nation

1899

Without hopes without Ambitions of Glory

Far from his Native Home

In Avellino the 11th of June 1799

On the gallows serenely dying

For an Oath to the Republic sworn . . .

Reference is to the political martyrdom of the town's leading proponent of the new philosophy. Serafini had a long history of opposing the feudal establishment. A notary public by profession, he was a key figure in the emergence of a Jacobin circle in late-eighteenth-century Agnone. The group contested control of the municipality with local *baroni*. At times, the confrontation was violent. Elections were rigged, and the results were overturned by the higher authorities.[25] On occasion, troops had to be dispatched to the town to monitor the voting.[26] The Jacobins denounced corruption to the provincial authorities, which led in one instance to the imprisonment of Agnone's mayor.[27] By the year 1777 the situation had deteriorated to the point that the families of the local

55

officials went about armed in fear for their safety, and the authorities in Chieti dispatched troops to police Agnone's "undisciplined" populace.[28]

The mayoral election of 1781 was particularly bitter and held in a coercive climate. Armed riflemen were posted at the polling place,[29] and Libero Serafini, himself a former mayor of the town, was forceably denied access to the hall.[30] The following year the situation was further exacerbated by the assassination of the *governatore*, or the highest ranking local representative of outside feudal authority. In 1798 a number of Agnone's young Jacobins fled the town when royal authorities cracked down on seditious behavior.[31]

The examples suffice to demonstrate that during the last fifty years of the feudal era Agnone was wracked by internal political factionalism in which the philosophical question of liberalism was already clearly at issue.

Not surprisingly, then, the French invasion of Italy triggered strong responses in Agnone. Clearly, the local professional people and at least a segment of the clergy were imbued with liberal Jacobin philosophy. On January 7, or fully two weeks before the French victory, an advance order from a French general was read publicly in the town. The populace was directed to obey the anticipated new government.

There remained, however, strong Bourbon sentiment in the area. According to one liberal chronicler, "outsiders" and "brigands" triggered a violent reaction.[32] They encountered a priest and two gentlemen in the streets of the town and opened fire on them, critically wounding one. The men, along with other Jacobins, sought asylum in the house of a notary public. The Bourbon sympathizers rained several volleys of gunfire on the refuge and finally forced entry. By that time, however, the Jacobins were well hidden in the attic. Later that night, their friends and relatives armed themselves and lifted the siege.

The next day the brigands attacked the home of the powerful Tirone family, which housed an arsenal of weapons. The Tirones and their supporters opened fire, wounding one of the assailants. Next, an attack was directed against the house of the Lucci brothers. One brigand was killed in this unsuccessful assault. At this point, the "gentlemen and most sensible" (*gentiluomini e più sensati*) townspeople armed themselves and counterattacked. The Lucci brothers, with a total of seventeen supporters, purportedly routed about four hundred brigands in one encounter.[33]

There are a number of clues in the obviously biased account that suggest that the "brigands" were not all outsiders nor all of the lower classes. Their sheer numbers suggest considerable local commitment to the Bourbon cause. At one point *dottor fisico* Vincenzo Cremonese and *dottor* don Pasquale Tamburri are identified as clandestine instigators of the brigands. Alessio di Pasqua, a former soldier in Agnone, was arrested as the prime leader and executed by the liberals.

The local Jacobins proclaimed the republic on January 13, or ten days before it was declared officially for the kingdom of Naples. Agnone was the first town in the province of Chieti to take this official step.[34] A tree of liberty was planted in the Piazza del Popolo, and Serafini was president of the municipality.[35] The Jacobins informed the French that they had arrested the Bourbons and established a civil guard.[36]

When the Parthenopean Republic collapsed shortly thereafter, Agnone was one of only three towns in the province of Chieti to remain loyal to the republican cause. As the battlefield situation worsened, the town's authorities dispatched a force of sixty men that joined other republican troops. Badly outnumbered, they were defeated and retreated to Campobasso.

Meanwhile, with the militant Jacobins absent, the Bourbons of Agnone invited a royalist force into the town, and according to the chronicler, "two miles from the city it was welcomed by many of the secular and regular clergy, with some gentlemen of the party, and a great mass of rebellious common people."[37] They entered the city amid much jubilation and cut down the tree of liberty in the Piazza del Popolo. The new mayor of the town initiated a reign of terror. Families of the Jacobins were arrested, and a commission of priests was established to mete out punishments.[38] Meanwhile, the Jacobin force from Agnone was arrested nearby as it tried to return to the town.[39] Many were sent to prison in Chieti to await trial.

Their leader, Serafini, had been captured earlier. He was tried by Cardinal Ruffo, who offered to set him free if he would declare "Long live the king!" Serafini refused, invoking his oath to the republic. As he ascended the gallows, he shouted, "Long live the republic! Long live liberty!"[40] Of the other Jacobins from Agnone, nine were sentenced to death; four were exiled for ten years; and two were perpetually banished and their property confiscated.[41] The condemned men were spared when Napoleon reasserted his domination of the peninsula.

Between 1806 and 1815 the liberals were in control of Agnone's affairs and identified strongly with the programs of the kingdom's French administrators. The town had a renowned municipal band that performed in Naples in 1809 on the occasion of the coronation of Murat and again in 1813 when Napoleon Bonaparte was feted in the city.[42] In 1813 five men from the town lost their lives fighting for Napoleon on the Russian steppes.[43]

The restoration of the Bourbon dynasty in 1815 and its persistence until 1860 clearly represented a setback for the liberals, but in many respects they continued to control local politics. In 1817, for example, Carlo Barbieri was elected mayor of Agnone. He had been an outspoken defender of the French Revolution and a dedicated Jacobin. During the events of 1799 it was Barbieri who ordered the execution of a peasant leader of the town's reactionary forces. Consequently, when the Parthenopean Republic collapsed, he fled to northern Italy, where he spent several years working incognito at odd jobs. There, he had an opportunity to observe firsthand many agricultural advances. On his return to Agnone in 1812 Barbieri established a large test plot and orchard with exotic varieties. He also initiated a free public course on agriculture.[44] That such a man could be elected mayor during the Bourbon reign is eloquent testimony to the depth of liberal sentiment in the town.

Anti-Bourbonism was reflected in other ways as well. In 1820 the king's highest ranking officer in Agnone was assassinated.[45] In 1848 when King Ferdinando was forced to accept a moderate constitution, the town's liberals were ecstatic. They vented their pent-up frustrations against the bishop, whom they identified with the Bourbon establishment. The prelate was sojourning in Agnone at the time and was subjected to considerable public humiliation.[46] For the brief period of about one year, the liberals were emboldened to sponsor frequent public discourses on the subject of freedom.[47]

That there was considerable bad blood between the town's liberal and Bourbon forces is neatly underscored by two incidents. In 1827 Giuseppe Tirone of the powerful liberal Tirone family was imprisoned for raising the tricolor flag of the republic.[48] During the proceedings he was accused of hosting meetings in the years 1816 and 1820 of the *carbonari* sect. Conversely, in 1860, after the liberal triumph in the guise of Garibaldi's victory, the mayor of Agnone ordered that the priest Biase Amicarelli be arrested as a "political reactionary" for displaying the white flag of the Bourbon monarchy.[49]

The Social Balance

In principle, liberalism emphasized individuality, free enterprise, and achieved rather than ascribed social standing. In practice, it frequently led to unbridled competition in which some of the competitors, and notably the *galantuomini*, were clearly advantaged. Both those who, in the feudal era, enjoyed privileges (the barons and church) and those who experienced privation (the peasants and manual laborers) suffered at the hands of the liberals. The heralded "triumph of the middle class" was at everyone else's expense.

Nowhere was this more apparent than in Agnone, the liberal bastion of the Molise. Relatively speaking, the town had a large number of professionals, businessmen, and master artisans, many of whom sought to underscore their new social status by monopolizing the local economy and particularly its land base. With respect to the latter, there were essentially four possible sources from which the aspiring *galantuomo* could aggrandize his holdings: the baronial estates, the church's patrimony, the town commons, and private small holdings.

Baronial estates. Despite land-reform legislation mandating the abolition of feudalism, it is clear that many of the baronial estates of south Italy escaped immediate dismemberment. The barons' losses were more in the area of political power than economic clout. The harried aristocrat desirous of protecting his estate had a number of ploys at his command. He could engage in lengthy obfuscating legal maneuvers. If his holdings surpassed the new legal limits size of estates, he could vest ownership of different tracts in individual members of his immediate family.

Viewed from the perspective of Agnone, in 1816 (ten years after the abolition of feudalism) the heirs of the baron Gigliani still owned 4,011 *tomoli* of land, or fully 15 percent of the total land base of the municipality. In addition, they possessed a mill, a warehouse, four artisan workshops, and ten dwellings.[50]

Church patrimony. If the baronial estates remained largely intact, the same may not be said for the church's influence and patrimony. Liberals regarded the church's patrimony as a blatant symbol of social injustice and a ready source from which to finance the new order.

The assault on ecclesiastical power and wealth did not begin, however, exclusively with the liberal reforms of the early nineteenth century. It is estimated that in the eighteenth century, at the time of the coronation of the Bourbon king Carlo III, fully two-thirds of the productive lands of the kingdom of Naples were owned by the church and exempt from taxes.[51] In 1740 he prohibited the construction of new monasteries and churches. The following year Carlo ratified a concordate under which the previously exempt church lands were to be taxed at one-half the rate of ordinary private property. Any new acquisitions were to be subject to full taxation.[52] In 1786 a law was promulgated that placed the economic affairs of the religious orders under governmental supervision and audit.[53]

The intrusions on ecclesiastical privilege culminated in the decrees of 1807 and 1809 whereby the French ruler in Naples suppressed all but a few of the religious orders in the kingdom, mandating that they divest themselves of their properties.[54]

During the period of French liberal rule, the church suffered reversals in every area of its operations, and despite considerable support of the deposed Bourbon king among the clergy, many of the anticlerical liberal reforms survived his restoration to the throne. In 1815 Ferdinando decreed that accounts of the teaching orders of nuns would be subjected to government audit and regular taxation. The convents were to retain only those properties for which they could produce incontrovertible documentation of ownership.[55] In 1816 it was decreed that parish accounts be reviewed annually by the local authorities.[56] In 1818 the number of dioceses in the kingdom was reduced at royal demand.[57]

During the remaining years of the Bourbon reign, the church was to make somewhat of a comeback, but under the watchful eye of the civil authorities. Once church hegemony in the kingdom's political and economic life was broken, neither liberals nor Bourbons were particularly anxious to see it restored.

It is clear that the antichurch measures of the early nineteenth century were effective. In 1809 the bishop of Trivento noted that his bishopric was impoverished owing to recent civil legislation. The laws prevented town councils from appropriating municipal funds to pay the customary tithes to the diocese. Civil marriage had also been instituted, thereby depriving the church of another of its former sources of revenue.[58] In 1812 the clergy of Agnone, as a body, petitioned the local administrations unsuccessfully for payment of certain tithes that had been in arrears since 1805 and 1808, respectively.[59]

Parish finances were also in desperate straits. In 1811 the *mense*, or parish funds, of Agnone's seven parishes collected a total of only 182 ducats, 30 *grane*, an amount insufficient to cover their expenses.[60] By the end of the decade the physical plant of San Marco had all but collapsed. Its organ had been transferred to the ex-monastery of San Francesco. The altars, choir loft, and art objects were removed to other churches in Agnone and throughout the diocese. San Marco's bell had been commandeered by the government (probably for its scrap-metal value).[61]

In 1835 the church of San Nicola was in a lamentable state of disrepair. The parish priest petitioned the *intendente* for assistance because the parish's patrimony was so reduced that it produced less than four ducats annually.[62] Documents from the 1830s make frequent reference to the fact that the *opere pie*, or charitable funds, of Agnone's parishes were so strapped that even individual requests for aid had to be directed to the town council rather than the churches.[63] Furthermore, the parishes relinquished most of their fiscal autonomy to civil authorities. Parish accounts were subject to regular audit and revision by the town council, and the local officials sold at annual auction the wheat and must of all of Agnone's churches.[64]

The religious orders were the particular targets of the liberal government. In 1807 all monasteries and convents not used for teaching purposes were closed. In 1809 there was an unsuccessful attempt to convert Agnone's Celestine monastery into a diocesan seminary. Shortly thereafter, the physical plant collapsed into ruins.[65] The Capuchins were able to maintain a "family" in the town by virtue of a special exemption issued in 1812,[66] but they were placed under strict governmental control. The friars even had to petition the authorities for permission to leave the area.[67] The town council controlled the monastery's finances and allocated an annual stipend of thirty-three ducats for its maintenance.[68]

Because the Clarists were a teaching order of nuns, the Convent of Santa Chiara was permitted to function, yet it was in difficulty. An undated document from the early nineteenth century claims that

> the income is quite small for the maintenance of the nuns. Because of the absence of 375 ducats in rents [due from] various borrowers . . . on capital of nearly 7,000 amortized by the Royal Court and [the loss of income] from other notes and property titles that is uncontrollable, the nuns support themselves in proper propriety from the weekly tuitions that are paid by their many students.[69]

Between 1824 and 1830 the convent's accounts were deficit in every year save 1828. During the period the overall negative balance was 638 ducats, 45½ *grane*.[70] Even the modest income from tuitions began to erode. In 1825 the convent had thirteen private students, whereas by 1839 there were only five.[71]

In terms of its landed patrimony, Agnone's religious establishment suffered severe losses, and particularly in the early years of the liberal era. A comparison of church holdings in the 1753 "Onciario" with those listed in an 1815 cadastre shows a marked decline in land ownership. The 1753 figures were approximately nine time greater. Furthermore, by 1815 the ownership base of the religious patrimony had narrowed. Two of Agnone's seven parish churches had no lands. The number of landed chapels was down from twenty-two (in 1753) to seven. The clergy as a whole no longer possessed a common landed patrimony. The charitable endowments were not mentioned in the cadastre, and the landed *monte frumentarii* (*opere pie*) of individual parishes were down from seven to four in number. In the case of all but the Capuchin monastery and the Convent of Santa Chiara, monastic buildings had become the property of the commune, as had such productive holdings as the flour mill owned formerly by the Monastery of San Francesco[72] and the copper foundry of San Marco.[73]

Almost without exception, the purchasers of church lands were the *galantuomini*. For example, in 1812 the businessman Giuseppe Tirone offered to purchase a vineyard from "the suppressed parish of San Pietro."[74] He later acquired a vineyard from the Monastery of San Francesco.[75] In 1817 he rented, for a period of six years, the lands pertaining to the former Celestine monastery.[76] In 1816 the *possidente* (landowner) Camillo Cocucci acquired thirteen parcels belonging to the Convent of Santa Chiara, while Nicola Cocucci bought thirty-eight parcels, two houses, and a house site. An analysis of the remaining purchasers shows that they were either already substantial landowners or in possession of considerable urban property.

Town commons. Zarrilli contends that throughout much of the Molise the *galantuomini* seized control of local government and then used their positions to usurp portions of the town commons illegally.[77] There is evidence that this was the case in Agnone. In 1885 a government agent investigated the status of the town commons. After his first findings, a crusading newspaper noted: "It is several days since the desmesnal investigations began. They are proceeding well, and it is with pleasure that we applaud how the *contadini*, by admitting and declaring the small area that they usurped, have given a brilliant example to the gross usurpers."[78] Two years later, the agent published a report that claimed that many of the lands then held in private ownership by wealthy families had been usurped in the early part of the century and hence actually belonged to the municipality.[79]

It is clear, however, that such usurpations happened over a considerable period of time. The 1815 cadastre lists 1,866.41 hectares of land in municipal ownership.[80] This is a somewhat greater figure than the 1,613 hectares of land held by the *università* in fiefs at the end of the feudal era.[81]

Private small holdings. The primary source of land for the *galantuomini*, then, was the marketplace. During the early nineteenth century there was pronounced parcelization of landholdings in the town. The cadastre that was formulated in Agnone about 1815 lists 7,838 individual plots, excluding house and other building sites. In the 1753 "Onciario" there were 1,178 vineyards that averaged 0.6588 hectares in size. Sixty-three years later, the number of recorded vineyards had almost doubled to 2,297, and their average size had declined by almost one-third to 0.4626 hectares.

Fortunato blames such parcelization in south Italy on the land reform accompanying the abolishment of feudalism. To be sure, the peasants were assigned parcels, but each family qualified for only a maximum of 0.83 to 1.5 hectares depending on fertility. Consequently, the new proprietor had insufficient property to survive in agriculture. Thinly capitalized, he was unable to take adequate care of even this small parcel. According to Fortunato, the majority of such holdings were "reclaimed by the municipality for nonpayment of liens, or sold for little money to a local proprietor, or finally ceded to a usurer for contracted indebtedness."[82]

Increased parcelization of landholdings, then, did not mean a broadened base of landownership. During the thirty-one–year period from 1814 to 1845, the absolute numbers of landowning households in Agnone was almost halved. In terms of ratios, in 1814 there was one landowner for every 7.94 inhabitants, whereas by 1845 there was one landowner for every 16.98 inhabitants.[83]

The cadastre begun in 1815 provides information regarding the transfer of land titles over several generations, and it is evident that the *galantuomini* were aggressively engaged in land acquisitions. For example, the cadastre lists the following holdings for the businessman (*negoziante*) Donato Amicarelli: one parcel of olives (1 *misura*), five parcels of vineyard (16 *tomoli*), thirty-eight parcels of plowland (139 *tomoli*, 13 *misure*), one parcel of unproductive land (1 *tomolo*), for a total of 156 *tomoli*, 14 *misure* (or 48.32 hectares). 48.32 hectares of land represented a sizeable agricultural estate in Agnone terms. In addition, he possessed an artisan workshop, two warehouses, and six dwellings. Amicarelli's large number of small parcels suggests that he was acquiring peasant holdings as they came on the market. In the year 1816 alone he purchased or foreclosed on nine additional parcels of grainland, which totaled 33 *tomoli*, 12 *misure* in size and which belonged to six different owners.

The new climate of land speculation and aggressive free enterprise undermined the security of the peasant *colono* (renter) in several ways. Not only was he routinely outbid by the *galantuomini* for the available parcels; the lack of agricultural experience of the *galantuomini* in itself subsequently led to forfeitures. The sharecropping renter, who in feudal time enjoyed some certainty of continued access to a field by virtue of his client relation to a powerful and economically stable patron (baron or church), was now faced with the prospect that the thinly capitalized, inexperienced *galantuomo* owner might suffer bankruptcy.

Between 1838 and 1860 the official journal of the province lists dozens of such sales in Agnone alone. An example was the case of Pasquale Galasso (*proprietario*), son of Marco Galasso (*negoziante*). Marco, in 1815, owned four houses, a warehouse, a wine cellar, and eighteen parcels of land totaling 73 *tomoli*, 12 *misure*. By 1838 his son Pasquale owned five houses, a warehouse, a wine cellar, a copper foundry, a fulling mill, a grain mill, and forty-one parcels totaling 148 *tomoli*, 7 *misure*. Yet Pasquale's patrimony was undergoing forced sale at public auction at the insistence of his creditors.[84]

If, then, the new owners possessed the initial capital or credit to acquire the land, they could not as a rule afford steady and substantial losses. They viewed agriculture as a business investment, and one that was to be carefully cost-accounted. The owner-manager could be ruthless in attributing poor yields to his peasant employee's ineptness or dishonesty. The *galantuomo* proprietor was also prone to invest in nonagricultural enterprises where serious business reversals might lead to a loss of his landholdings as well. The new owner might void the existing contract with the peasant who actually cultivated the land.

In sum, during the first decades of the liberal era, Agnone's *galantuomini* acquired church lands through distress sales and, to a lesser degree, usurped tracts of the commons. They also speculated aggressively in the land market, thereby acquiring many parcels formerly owned by the peasantry. In these fashions, they quickly monopolized the town's land base. Given the value system of south Italian society, in which land ownership correlates with social prestige, such acquisitions were motivated by more than simple economics. Rather, they represented a process whereby the *galantuomini* consolidated and validated their claim to elite social status.

Power and Influence of the Galantuomini

A further source of pressure on the poor derived from the political control of the town by the *galantuomini*. An electoral list for the year 1821 provides a measure of the extent of the liberals' control over municipal affairs.[85] It states that literacy, reputation among the populace, and an ability to lead were desirable qualities in candidates, while financial liquidity and a certain amount of capital were requisites for officeholding. There were 181 eligible people identified as being of the following professions:

44	landowners	6	bellmakers
16	lawyers	6	carpenters
12	shoemakers	4	merchants
12	peasants	4	land surveyors
11	coppersmiths	4	gunsmiths
9	physicians	6	other professionals
5	notary publics	25	other artisans
7	goldsmiths	10	other manual laborers

The list is clearly weighted against the peasants and manual laborers, who, while constituting more than one-half of the populace, had only twenty-two (or 12.15%) of the eligible candidates. The seventy-one artisans, representing 39.23 percent of those qualified, more nearly approximated the proportion of artisans in the total population. The remaining groups had access to political office that was all out of proportion to their numbers.

The discrimination is even more pronounced than the list of eligibility would imply. The same document lists former municipal offices (if any) held by those eligible. Here, it is possible to appreciate the extent to which the *galantuomini* monopolized political power. Of the fifty-seven men who had held posts, there twenty-three *proprietarii* and thirteen lawyers. Other professionals and merchants numbered eleven. Only five artisans and three peasants and manual laborers had previously held an office.

Even this limited participation of the working classes in the political process could provoke resentment. When, in 1821, Giacinto Gambarale, a tanner and butcher, became *cassiere*, or treasurer, of Agnone, the *intendente* received a letter of protest. Gambarale was denounced as being of "obscure family origins." It was noted that in Agnone the post of treasurer had always been entrusted to "able subjects, honest and humane, and not to persons born amidst manure." Gambarale's appointment was therefore a disgrace for a town made "illustrious by *galantuomini*, professors of law, medicine and surgery, and other professionals . . . merchants and landowners."[86]

Control of local government allowed the *galantuomini* to influence public policy in their favor. In 1816 there was a grain scandal. It seems that several members of the *decurionato* (town council) profiteered through emergency grain sales to the public granary.[87] In 1817 the attempts to create a public grazing area out of a former fief held by the *università* were opposed by a landowner who was accustomed to renting his lands for that purpose. This same man held the post of treasurer of Agnone.[88]

Even more ominous for the lower classes were the partly successful efforts of the newly propertied, politically powerful *galantuomini* to shift the tax burden off of the land and onto the consumer. During the first half of the nineteenth century, there were many formal requests in Agnone, mostly from *galantuomini*, to have existing tithes owed to the *università* on parcels of land either reduced or canceled.[89] In 1811 the populace was assessed a special head tax that amounted to 161 ducats.[90] In 1814 Agnone showed a considerable deficit in its budget. The authorities had managed to collect only a quarter of the amount owed in taxes because the wealthiest citizens, acting in concert, were successfully avoiding their obligations.[91] The local officials received orders from the *intendente* to raise the money through new extraordinary levies.

The deliberations of the town council are revealing. The first suggestion was to tax livestock, meat, and fish. To their credit, the councilmen rejected this on the grounds that it would most harm the "miserable class" that depended on livestock raising. It was decided that taxes would be levied against salt (all consumed more or less the same amount) and dwellings (since almost every Agnonese owned his own home). In the words of the council, "in this fashion the burden would fall equally upon everyone without fear of fraud."[92] While more equitable that the earlier proposed livestock tax, the decision failed to adjust for wealth differences. It reflected the belief of the *galantuomini* that every citizen ought to bear the same tax liability. The peasant's hut was to be taxed in the same fashion as the gentleman's mansion.

There were constant efforts to place taxes on basic necessities, hence exacerbating the already precarious circumstances of the poor. In 1820 the town council reduced assessments on merchants and increased them on meat, bread, and pasturage.[93] An 1827 document shows that the tax base for the town was being calculated on the basis of the estimated grain consumption of the populace.[94] In the early 1830s the mayor of Agnone was denounced for his arbitrary decision to impose an additional head tax on livestock.[95] In 1833 the mayor placed new taxes on fish, fruit, and other foodstuffs. Wine was absolved only after stringent public protest.[96] Clearly, the liberals' policy was to tax people rather than property.

The New Demographics

The economic and political triumphs of the *galantuomini* increased considerably the burden on the peasantry and working class. Yet another development further exacerbated the situation, namely, a population explosion. Throughout much of the feudal era it seems that Agnone's population remained fairly stable. In 1648 there were 843 households in the town; the 1753 "Onciario" reports only 863 households.

The "Onciario" lists a total population of only 4,823. Yet an 1811 document places the number of households in Agnone at 1,227, containing a total of 7,725 people.[97] A government census résumé for the year 1813 records 8,090 residents;[98] by 1830 there were 8,593.[99] In an eighty-year period, the population had almost doubled.

The specific causes of this dramatic increase are difficult to pinpoint. There is, however, little evidence that in-migration was a factor. For example, in 1813 twenty-three people emigrated from Agnone, whereas only six settled in the town.[100] In 1830 thirty people emigrated, and there were no new residents.[101] In 1845 there were seventeen emigrants and no in-migrants.[102] So it would seem that Agnone gave more migrants than it received. This impression is reinforced by the fact that of the 2,319 who died in the town between 1885 and 1892, only 34, or 0.01 percent were born elsewhere.[103]

The critical factor in Agnone's population increase must therefore have been an excess of births over deaths. The town was not unique in this regard. Handlin notes that such eighteenth- and nineteenth-century growth tripled Europe's population over a 150-year period. Inasmuch as this antedated the widespread use of modern medicine, hygienic practices, and dietary improvements, there is, as yet, no entirely satisfactory explanation.[104] Crosby suggests that it may in part have been due to the growing acceptance of New World cultigens that complemented the traditional Old World ones.[105] Certainly by this time, maize, beans, squash, tomatoes, and potatoes were all being cultivated in Agnone. An 1811 document notes that "potatoes are used by the poor people for food."[106]

According to official résumés, in 1813 there were 106 more births than deaths in Agnone.[107] Within the five-year period 1820–1824, just two of Agnone's seven parishes increased the population by 399 people.[108] Projecting this as a five-year growth of 9.5 percent, in slightly more than thirty-five years the population would have doubled. There were, of course, other factors that prevented such a growth rate from becoming established. Aside from the question of emigration, epidemics were capable of halting and even reversing population increase temporarily. In 1830 there were 310 births and 380 deaths.[109] In 1837 Agnone, along with much of the kingdom, was ravaged by cholera. During an eighty-seven–day period 306 people succumbed to the disease.[110] In 1845 there were 302 births in the town and 367 deaths.[111]

It seems clear that as Agnone's population increased there was an attempt to intensify cultivation. The area of vineyards in the town expanded from 2,514 *tomoli*, 16 *misure* of land in 1753[112] to 3,025 *tomoli* in 1816,[113] a gain on the order of 20 percent. Over the same period, grainlands purportedly quadrupled from 2,274 *tomoli*, 20 *misure* in 1753 to 11,034 *tomoli* in 1816.

The 1816 figure for grainland deserves analysis. Because it served in part as the basis for taxation, it is unlikely that producers would declare more land than was actually in production, so it may be regarded either as accurate or as an understatement. At the same time, it represents 41.12 percent of Agnone's total land base (versus 21.05% of the municipality in grain production as of 1970).[114] From internal evidence in the document it is clear, however, that 5,766 *tomoli*, or more than half of the declared grainland, carried the dual classification of *montuoso e boscoso*, mountainous and forested. Grain production was therefore being extended into more marginal areas of the municipality.

This intensification, then, was only at the expense of other aspects of the local economy: animal husbandry and silviculture. In 1810 the town had 14,016 sheep and goats;[115] by 1834 their number had declined to 11,572 head.[116] The remaining forests were also under illegal assault as the desperate peasantry increasingly engaged in the surreptitious felling of trees on the commons.[117] In 1850 the town authorities complained that over the years the peasants had plowed and cultivated many former areas of pasturage and woodland and that the resulting plots were of only minimal agricultural utility.[118]

Any increases in Agnone's agricultural yield through intensified cultivation were more than offset by population pressure. In 1838, although Agnone produced 20,000 *tomoli*[119] of grain, it consumed 24,000 *tomoli* and exported 12,000 *tomoli*, which meant that the town had to import 16,000 *tomoli* to cover its needs. Despite the 6,400-*tomoli* harvest of maize, the Agnonesi consumed 12,000 *tomoli* and had to import 5,600 *tomoli* to cover the deficit. The shortfall in barley was 3,200 *tomoli*. Only in potatoes (12,000 *tomoli*) was the town self-sufficient.[120]

There is evidence that as grain production intensified, the quality of the yield declined. In 1821 worried local authorities resolved to build a lime kiln on communal ground to provide fertilizer because the previous year's grain had been so poor as to be unsuitable for seeding.[121]

Infant mortality rates and life expectancy frequencies provide graphic evidence that the pernicious effects of population pressure and declining standard of living were not felt equally in Agnone's social classes. Given Agnone's rigorous climate and the poor insulation and heating systems in the dwellings, it is not surprising that the documents on infant deaths frequently list pneumonia and other respiratory ailments as the cause. An examination of the parish census for San Emidio, begun in 1841 and closed in 1863, provides some idea of the frequency of such deaths in the town.[122] Of the 2,134 births listed, 647 of the infants died before their second birthday. Thus, 1 of every 3.3 infants did not survive.

The San Emidio parish census lists 155 births among the profession-

Table 4.1. *Life Expectancy in Early Nineteenth-Century Agnone*

	Peasants and manual laborers (N = 556)	Artisans (N = 138)	Professionals and merchants (N = 88)
Age at death (in years)			
Mean	48.78	43.55	60.11
Median	50.07	44.50	65.60
Mode	40.00	50.00	80.00
Total *N* = 782			

als and merchants and 41 deaths, or a ratio of 1 fatality for each 3.78 births.[123] The artisans produced 893 children and experienced 231 infant deaths, or an even more favorable 1 death for each 3.87 births. The *contadini*, however, produced 908 children and suffered 326 infant deaths, or a mortality rate of 1 death for each 2.79 births. It is clear, then, that infant mortality in nineteenth-century Agnone correlated with standard of living. The high rate suffered by the *contadini* was one more sign of their poverty and misery. The impersonal nature of the above statistical profile pales before the tragedy of the Stefano family, for example. Between 1846 and 1860, this peasant and his married son fathered twelve infants, all of whom died within two years of birth.

Life expectancy for adults was similarly conditioned by living circumstances. An analysis of 782 death certificates from the years 1820–1829 is interesting in this regard.[124] The sample includes all people ten years of age and older who died in Agnone during the decade and whose occupation is given.[125] Table 4.1 divides the sample into three groups: the peasants and manual laborers, the artisans, and the professionals and merchants. As the table shows, the life expectancy of the professionals was considerably higher than that of the other classes. This may be attributed to such factors as superior diet, better medical care and freedom from hard physical toil. Of the professionals in the sample, 59.62 percent were sixty years of age or older at death versus 33.33 percent of the peasants and 32.94 percent of the artisans.

Of particular interest is a comparison of the infant mortality rates and life expectancy of the peasants and the artisans. Whereas among the peasants a death occurred for each 2.79 births versus 1 for every 3.87 births among the artisans, once the critical childhood years were traversed, the peasants enjoyed a somewhat higher life expectancy. Thus the mean age at death for peasant males in the sample was 49.19; for peasant women, 48.42 years. Artisan males survived on the average 46.71; years; the artisan women, 38.49 years. Difficult working conditions in the artisan *botteghe* probably made the difference. For example, 22.35 percent of the male artisans in the sample died between the ages of 14 and 29 (the apprentice years), whereas only 15.53 percent of the male *contadino* deaths were of the same age group.

The Disaffected

Population pressure, inadequate agricultural yields, lack of capital, foreclosures, usury, price increases through commodities speculation, consumer taxes, and natural disasters all conspired to harshen the life circumstances of Agnone's lower classes.

During lean periods the poor, and particularly the peasants, were extremely vulnerable. In 1814 the parish priests of Agnone requested assistance from the government for "the thousand indigents in our commune who are gravely ill from a pernicious fever that derives from Puglia and from the extreme poverty."[126] In 1815 the harvest was poor. Bread prices more than doubled, and interest rates soared to 40 percent. Agnone's poor were reduced to eating boiled grass and became so weakened that many died of fever.[127] In 1816 troops had to be sent to the town to restore public order after an abortive attempt of the millers to alter the traditional weights and measures in their favor.[128]

In 1817 Agnone suffered severe crop loss during a summer hailstorm. The poor were again faced with the prospect of famine, and they had lost their seed grain for the next year. A killer epidemic exacerbated their suffering. During the year there were 1,078 deaths in Agnone, or about one-eighth of the population.[129] The town council responded by petitioning the provincial authorities for permission to divert local road maintenance monies into a relief fund.[130] Shortly thereafter they also subsidized creation of a municipal *monte frumentario*, or grain reserve.[131] The idea was to provide the poor with seed grain at one-sixteenth of a *tomolo* annual interest on each *tomolo* borrowed in an attempt to break the ruinous cycle of usury in which many of Agnone's peasant cultivators found themselves.

According to one early-nineteenth-century (circa 1817) account,

Agnone's peasants could no longer afford to eat wheat bread and had to substitute cornmeal in its stead. Their wine consumption was reserved for festive occasions and for the hardest work periods of the year. Salt pork was their only meat, and few had more than a single change of clothing. It further notes that "at one time all of the peasants cooked their vegetable *minestra* in a small copper vessel . . . but at present the majority are not privy to such an aid and substitute for the copper vessel a clay pot."[132] This is a particularly graphic indicator of rural poverty in a town that housed one of south Italy's most flourishing copper industries.

Sanitary conditions were deplorable. The *contadino* "always shares his room with the chickens, and his bed is over the pig sty and donkey stall; for this reason throughout the night he breathes an unsanitary air." Furthermore, few peasant dwellings were equipped with proper chimneys, so their inhabitants were constantly inhaling smoke.[133]

Alcoholism was a prevalent problem with the artisans. In commenting on wine consumption, the chronicler notes that

> the abuse of this beverage is most frequent among the artisan class, who from lunch until nightfall consume wine constantly. Because of such a criminal practice some work remains unfinished, there are quarrels in families, and a series of misfortunes results.[134]

Excessive drinking among the artisans was likely related to the extremely bad working conditions in the *botteghe*. Apprentices were regularly mistreated. Hours in the workshops were long, frequently from before sunup until after sundown and for a minimum of six days a week. Some artisans, such as the tailors and shoemakers, worked Sunday afternoons as well. The *botteghe* themselves were dingy and poorly ventilated. In many of the trades the workers were exposed to extreme heat, dust, and smoke from the forges.

The examples serve to underscore the precarious circumstances of the poor and underprivileged. One graphic indicator of their inability to compete in the postfeudal society is the figures for mendicity. In Agnone between 1814 and 1845 the number of *mendici*, or beggars, increased tenfold. The ratio changed from 1 beggar for every 129.34 inhabitants in 1814 to 1 for every 15.39 Agnonesi in 1845.[135]

The situation in Agnone mirrored the deplorable circumstances of the region as a whole. A report by Cantalupo, authored in 1834, notes that two-thirds of the peasants in the Molise were landless.[136] Sanitary conditions were appalling; criminality was on the increase; beggars were proliferating;[137] and many workers were migrating to other areas.[138] Del Re, writing in 1836, confirms this dismal evaluation. He notes that because of rural poverty, twenty-four thousand workers left annually for seasonal jobs of up to seven months duration in the Capitanata and Terra di Lavoro.[139]

Nicola de Luca, describing the situation in 1844, notes that intensified cultivation of the former fiefs had exhausted the soil and thereby cut the yields while at the same time reducing the overall livestock numbers in the province.[140] Progressive sterility of the soil, exorbitant taxes, and usury had forced many peasants into bankruptcy. Since the abolition of feudalism the majority of peasant holdings had passed into the hands of the *galantuomini*.[141] Referring to the *contadino*, de Luca writes,

> Everything sold, he is covered with rags, he nourishes himself with acorns roasted on a fire, with roots and grasses, and in the dreariness of winter in swarms he presents himself in the public piazzas extending his honorable hand in order not to die of hunger.[142] . . . He who actually cultivates the soil in the Molise does not own even his hoe.[143]

There is a sense, then, in which the victory of the *galantuomini* was both too swift and too complete. By disrupting ancient social and economic arrangements and pursuing a single-purposed policy of self-aggrandizement, the liberals contributed mightily to a budding economic crisis that ultimately affected them as well. Without peasant consumers, the artisans lacked much of their clientele. With both peasants and artisans unable to pay, professionals were forced to provide their services for practically nothing or remain inactive. Nor were the landowners immune, for bankrupt peasants were unable to pay their rents. In many instances, the value of land had been halved since the abolition of feudalism. By 1844 only the civil servants were relatively well off because they had fixed salaries and because the depressed economy had reduced local prices somewhat.[144]

This general economic climate produced high interest rates (frequently 25%),[145] because of every ten loans made, five would certainly result in default.[146] The Molise was caught in a vicious economic circle. Interest rates remained exorbitantly high as a hedge against probable loss, which in turn made it impossible to capitalize the recovery that would reduce the risk for everyone concerned. Despite the original optimism of the liberals, by mid-century the province was in a state of economic paralysis.

Athens of Samnium

The dismal chronicle of abuses is only a part of the story, for in many respects it can be said that liberal energies carried Agnone to the very principle of its historical achievements. By the middle of the nineteenth century, the town was famed as a cultural center, identified throughout the region as *l'Atene del Sannio*, or the "Athens of Samnium." This reputation rested primarily on the pedagogical accomplishments of a segment of the citizenry.

I noted in the last chapter that, by the waning years of feudalism, the town was famed for its teachers. Given the liberals' commitment to education and scientific experimentation, it is not surprising that during the liberal era Agnone's academic role was both broadened and strengthened. Before the abolition of feudalism, education in the kingdom had been monopolized by clerics; during the initial years of the liberal reform, strong efforts were made to limit their role as educators. The liberals were engaged in a frontal assault on church privilege and property and hence feared an ecclesiastical backlash. The confrontation also turned on major philosophical differences that made the liberals suspicious of theological pedagogy.

Yet, the kingdom clearly lacked sufficient numbers of secular teachers to replace the priest-scholars. For example, in 1811 Agnone had only two secular primary school teachers of boys, "who are active according to the number of students who seek them out," and no girls' teacher "for lack of a qualified woman."[147] Before suppression of the religious orders, the Monastery of San Francesco alone had provided two school teachers specialized in science, theology, and philosophy. Several other friars had instructed Agnone's youth in reading and writing.[148] Consequently, in 1817 there were abortive attempts in the town to reopen the monasteries of San Francesco and San Berardino as educational institutions.[149]

Over time, it became apparent that liberal fears of the clergy as a monolithic opposition force were simplistic. Academically oriented

74

churchmen found much in the new philosophy to their liking. In places like Agnone, clerics were recruited from all social classes and reflected the attitudes of their progenitors. Thus, within the town, elitist priests drawn from the aristocracy formed a coalition of convenience with peasant priests in support of the Bourbon cause. On the other hand, many of Agnone's clergymen were members of the same professional, merchant, and successful artisan families that constituted the backbone of liberal support. It was the latter who would ultimately emerge as the driving force in the town's nineteenth-century academic and cultural momentum.

By the decade of the 1830s there was considerable activity discernible on the educational front in Agnone. Several local people of both secular and religious backgrounds made application for licensing as teachers. In 1833 there were five private schools in the town, each with one teacher.[150] By 1835 Agnone had no fewer than eight private institutions, as well as two primary schools for boys and a primary school for girls.[151]

By the mid-1830s, then, Agnone was emerging as a principal educational center of the Molise. In 1830 the town had 2.61 percent of the population of the province; in 1845, 2.82 percent.[152] Yet in 1835 the sixty-two boys attending primary schools in Agnone presented 4.28 percent of the province's male primary school population; the twenty-eight female pupils were 5.92 precent of the provincial total. In private instruction, the figures were even more impressive. The census lists the numbers of students for only five of the eight private schools and the Convent of Santa Chiara. The forty-five pupils represent 7.64 percent of the private student population for the entire Molise.[153]

During the 1840s educational institutions in Agnone proliferated. In 1842 three Savastano brothers—a priest, a lawyer, and a physician—opened a school. The priest taught Latin and Italian letters, the lawyer taught jurisprudence, and the physician specialized in philosophy and mathematics. Students came from surrounding communities to attend these classes. The three brothers were politically liberal and were forced to close their school during the reactionary period that followed the events of 1848.[154] At that same time, a pre-law school, founded in 1844, was closed on political grounds.[155]

In 1848 one of Agnone's most scholarly sons, the priest Francesco Antonio Marinelli, returned from Naples (where he had been a successful educator) to found a private school in the town. Marinelli was joined by another renowned Agnonese priest-scholar, Ippolito Amicarelli.[156] The Istituto Lucci offered three classes and immediately attracted a substantial number of pupils. The first year there were more than fifty students from towns other than Agnone.[157] Another source places the total student body at one hundred.[158] The following year the numbers increased.[159] The institution closed at the end of its second year in the face of political opposition. The teachers were all accused of corrupting the youth with their liberal ideas. Two faculty members, Ippolito Amicarelli and Ascenso Marinelli, were forced to flee.[160]

In 1851 both men returned to Agnone, where each initiated private schools.[161] During 1852 and 1853 the four teachers of the original school of 1848–1849 again collaborated in founding a larger institution. The new Istituto Lucci was an immediate success. No fewer than 150 students from Agnone and surrounding towns attended classes.[162]

Gamberale provides a vivid description of the academic climate in Agnone during 1852–1853:

> He who in those two years would have happened upon Agnone for the first time might have believed that he was in one of those German towns, made famous for their culture and for their happy student banter. Agnone seemed to have become one big boarding school.[163]

These developments were not without their economic impact. Gamberale notes that "Stores of every kind improved their trade, and for that reason new businesses emerged and the old ones were transformed and improved."[164]

At the same time, schooling was clearly class specific and reserved for the children of the *galantuomini*. When Gamberale speaks of the respect shown the founders of the school, he notes, "Everyone esteemed them and demonstrated their feelings, everyone, *even the artisans*, spoke of them with reverence" (emphasis supplied).[165] The students themselves constituted a social elite. The whole town followed their progress, and "the names of the better ones were repeated by everyone."[166]

Despite the fact that the new school attracted students from many surrounding communities, it was the creation of a few families of Agnone. Extended kinship ties interlocked the faculty and student body. The dominant pattern was for the priest-uncle to serve as mentor-exemplar for the scholarly nephew. The education of the latter frequently culminated in the profession of religious vows, thereby perpetuating the longstanding close identification in Agnone of certain elite families with the religious establishment.

Thus, when the priest Francesco Antonio Marinelli founded his school, he enlisted the services of his two nephews Ascenso Marinelli and Giuseppe Nicola D'Agnillo both recently ordained. Luigi Gamberale, who was ultimately to become the most illustrious graduate of the school, was the nephew of Vincenzo Gamberale (a priest who had a private school in Agnone before 1848).[167] Luigi's first schooling came under the tutelage of Giovanni Gamberale, who was also his uncle and a priest.[168] Luigi Gamberale decided to enter the Istituto Lucci in part because his first cousin was affianced to Amicarelli's brother.[169] When the school was first closed in 1849, Ascenso Marinelli and Amicarelli sought refuge in Naples and resided there with Baldassare La Banca. La Banca, Marinelli's kinsman, was preparing for the priesthood. He had studied with Francesco Antonio Marinelli in Naples before the latter's return to Agnone in 1848.[170] When La Banca was jailed in Naples for his involvement in the protests of 1848, it was Vincenzo Gamberale, Luigi's uncle, who was instrumental in securing his release.

The examples could be multiplied.[171] Clearly, in mid-nineteenth-century Agnone, political liberalism, religious vocation, and educational mission were the shared traits of a rather restricted network of intimates whose relationships were frequently reinforced by extended family ties.

An Intellectual Portrait

The local pedagogical successes of Agnone's nineteenth-century educators were only a small part of the intellectual contribution of this extraordinary group of Agnonesi. The school founded in the town in 1848 was essentially the work of young men. The eldest of these, Francesco Antonio Marinelli (1817–1892) was just thirty-one years of age at the time. Between 1848 and 1860 Marinelli and his close associates Ippolito Amicarelli (1823–1889), Giuseppe Nicola D'Agnillo (1827–1916), and Ascenso Marinelli, were to devote their efforts to the creation of a sound educational establishment in Agnone. With the liberal triumph of 1860, these men, all of whom were in the prime years of life, were able to parlay their budding reputations and strong liberal credentials into successful academic careers elsewhere. They, as well as the somewhat younger Baldassare La Banca (1829–1913) and Luigi Gamberale

(1840–1929) displayed a burst of intellectual energy that at times attracted national and even international attention. In terms of their individual careers, their noteworthy accomplishments were as follows:

Francesco Antonio Marinelli. In 1861 Marinelli was president of the Lycee of Aquila. In 1863 he served in the same capacity in Chieti. From 1867 through 1881 he was a superintendent of schools in such diverse places as Chieti, Teramo, Benevento, Potenza, Macerata, Livorno, Pisa, and Campobasso.[172] He founded two important schools in the city of Campobasso.[173] Marinelli was remembered more for his pedagogical contributions than for his writings. His publications were brief and few in number.[174]

Ippolito Amicarelli. Between 1861 and 1865 Amicarelli served as a deputy to the first Italian Parliament. He held posts as professor and later as president of the important Liceo Vittorio Emmanuele of Naples. Amicarelli penned several poems, one unpublished play, and works concerning the nature of the Italian language.[175]

Giuseppe Nicola D'Agnillo. Between 1861 and 1867 D'Agnillo taught at the lycees of Chieti and Pavia before returning to Agnone shortly before 1868. In that year two plays authored by D'Agnillo, *Griselda* and *Duchessa di Bracciano*, were performed in Naples and received favorable critical acclaim.[176] Unable to cope with success, he withdrew to Agnone, where he became a recluse.

Ascenso Marinelli. In 1865 Marinelli became a professor in a gymnasium of Reggio d'Emilia. On two separate occasions he taught in Sicily.[177] His publications include a work on language and a book of moral platitudes.

Baldassare La Banca. In 1861 La Banca became a professor of philosophy in the Lycee of Chieti, where he remained for three years. He subsequently taught in lycees of Bari, Milan, and Naples. In 1878 he taught in the Liceo Vittorio Emmanuele of Naples, where Amicarelli was president.[178] In 1879, on the strength of his publications, La Banca acquired a professorship at the University of Padova and later taught at the University of Pisa. In 1886 La Banca was given the first chair of the history of Christianity at the University of Rome. As this was a step in the abolition of the department of theology, the appointment placed him at the center of a major controversy.[179] La Banca was an extraordinarily prolific writer. His many books and articles include philosophical treatises and essays on religion and literature as well as political and pedagogical polemics.[180]

Luigi Gamberale. Gamberale likewise became a prominent educator. For many years he was the president of an important boarding school in Lucera.[181] Him many publications included pedagogical works and collected essays. A devotee of English and German authors, he also produced a critically acclaimed three-volume translation of Walt Whitman's *Leaves of Grass* and a volume of translated English and German verse.

How does one evaluate these men and their contribution? Collectively, they laid the bases for Agnone's pretentious claim of being the "Athens of Sannio." But then, according to Gamberale, they would have been the first to reject the sobriquet as venal.[182] Viewed individually, the life's work of each was either flawed or deficient. The two Marinellis and Amicarelli were not prolific writers; La Banca and Gamberale were incisive critics and pedestrian eclectics rather than truly original thinkers. D'Agnillo's career was tragically aborted. The upshot is that they have not demonstrated staying power. Today none receives (or merits) more than a footnote in the history of Italian letters.

On the other hand, viewed collectively and from the perspective of the town, the impact of their accomplishments was truly impressive. Their efforts, influence, and example represented the culmination of nineteenth-century liberal philosophy in Agnone. They, more than any other single factor, converted Agnone into a liberal showplace.

Liberalism's Triumph and Its Cost

In conclusion, the challenge of liberalism triggered significant realignments of the society, economy, and polity of the kingdom of Naples. These included the abolition of feudalism with attendant curtailment of the power and wealth of the *baroni* and the church, and the emergence of the *galantuomini* as the dominant force in the social equation. Ill-prepared for the new laissez-faire competitive climate, the peasant's lot actually worsened during the liberal era. The resulting confrontation between the successful middle classes and everyone else was generic throughout south Italy but particularly pronounced wherever the liberals either gained the uppper hand, or at least successfully challenged the hegemony of the traditional elite. Agnone was such a place. From the outset, the town was the torchbearer of liberalism in the Molise, and it was the region's only community to remain faithful to the cause throughout the stormy nineteenth century.

By midcentury, there were clear signs of impending problems. With its physical isolation and the rather archaic nature of the local economy, Agnone was ill-suited for the competition in the arena of a unified and modernizing Italy. Furthermore, the accomplishments discussed in this chapter were essentially the product of a single social class, the *galantuomini*. The events of 1860 and its aftermath clearly demonstrate the depth of political alienation felt by Agnone's peasants, manual laborers, and artisans. By the early 1870s there was a trickle of transatlantic emigration from the town. The trickle became a torrent that was ultimately to undermine Agnone's viability as a significant urban center.

5

The Emigrants

For the more than a century since Garibaldi unified the nation, emigration (and the related question of internal migration) has been an overriding social concern in Italy. Both its causes and its consequences have been debated incessantly throughout the period. The sheer magnitude of the movement could scarcely be ignored inasmuch as between 1871 and 1971 approximately twenty-six million people emigrated, and slightly more than half returned to Italy.[1] Emigration was opposed by the nineteenth-century parliamentarian fearful of the drain on the nation's human resources and concerned that the agricultural system would collapse for lack of a pliable class of tillers.[2] It was prohibited by a vainglorious leader, as Mussolini sought to swell the population for his ill-starred drive for national glory. Yet it was encouraged by some governmental agencies like the Cassa per il Mezzogiorno as a critical factor in the economic development of the Italian South. Condemned and extolled, emigration has become a tangible symbol of the most profound questions confronted by post-Garibaldian Italy: modernization of the nation, amelioration of class and regional distinctions within it, and Italy's role in the world economy.

Causes of Emigration: Theory and Polemics

Before resuming the task of the present work, namely, a microanalysis of the situation in one south Italian hill town, it is well for me to review briefly the main issues in the literature on south Italian emigration. Over time, the question of why south Italy provided such a pronounced emigratory trend has moved from "self-evident" economic push–pull reasoning to more subtle social-structural and cultural interpretations. That is, the argument that the migrants left a blatantly impoverished south Italy for a variety of destinations all of which proferred at least some semblance of improved economic circumstances is no longer regarded as a sufficient explanation.

Foerster, in his classic work *The Italian Emigration of Our Times*, was an early and eloquent exponent of the economic push–pull model. He detailed at length the physical conditions such as overpopulation, inadequate rainfall, deforestation with subsequent land erosion, prevalence of malaria and natural disasters such as earthquakes. The peasant's lot was further worsened by an abusive system of taxation and by land tenureship arrangements that resulted in an indifferent class of latifundists side by side with tenants of tiny, inadequate landholdings on the one hand and a class of underemployed, landless agricultural work force on the other. Foerster concludes that "so grave has been the economic maladjustment which has come to rule in South Italy that one need not long ask why it should prompt emigration."[3]

More recently, MacDonald, in a series of seminal articles, notes that shared poverty did not translate into a propensity to emigrate in all parts of south Italy. Rather, he argues, in places like Apulia where, after feudalism was abolished, the *baroni* were successful in repurchasing their estates, pronounced class distinctions remained between the landowners and the landless rural proletariat. The latter became prime candidates for strikes and radical political action. Their shared interests galvanized them into a cohesive political force disposed more to class confrontation with the landowners than resort to emigration as an avenue of personal mobility.

Conversely, he argues, in areas of the South where land redistribution, by whatever means, led to broader based ownership of small holdings, the proprietors—be they peasants, artisans, or small businessmen—were individualistic competitors less prone to act in concert. At the same time, they lacked the foil of the *grosse proprietaire* against whom to vent their rage. Thus, as the economy of south Italy deteriorated and the alternative of overseas emigration became available, the small-scale proprietors opted to leave, either as a means of permanent escape or ultimately to return in order to purchase additional land with accumulated savings, thereby improving their status within the south Italian context. This local investment of emigrant capital in itself tended to reinforce a broad-based and more equitable distribution of property in the sending communities without, however, alleviating their collective poverty vis-à-vis the outside world. Thus, the bases for continued emigration remained.

Key to MacDonald's argument are the twin assumptions that the basic unit of south Italian society is the nuclear family and that fierce loyalty to it precludes the formation of more broadly based mutual-assistance associations such as farmers' cooperatives.[4] This view was further developed by Banfield, who coined the term *amoral familism* to describe a world in which each nuclear family maximized its own interests to the detriment of all others.[5] Banfield regards this lack of associative spirit as one of the prime causes of endemic poverty in the Italian South. His work has influenced a number of students of Italian immigration in host societies.[6]

Still more recently, this interpretation of emigration causality based on endemic poverty and social-structural deficiencies has undergone partial revision. Lopreato concurs with much of MacDonald's and Banfield's reasoning but insists that additional attention must be given to cultural factors. According to Lopreato,

> emigration from southern Italy is not primarily a question of seeking one's fortune. To a very large extent it has become a question of escaping what a peasant from Basilicata has recently referred to as "the inferno of the peasant's life," a culture of tragedy and persecution. This the peasant no longer tolerates.[7]

Both Barton and Briggs cite late-nineteenth- and early-twentieth-century evidence to question the stereotype of the peasant emigrants as a homogeneous class of downtrodden, ill-educated people fleeing from circumstances beyond their individual and collective control. Rather, both note that the ranks of the emigrants were more heterogeneous than had been thought.[8] Briggs emphasizes that, although the quantity and quality of south Italian schooling was poor by any standard, in the late nineteenth century there is ample evidence of a growing concern for formal education among the lower classes.[9] Similarly, the argument that the lower classes lacked any sort of associative capacity is simply over-drawn. Rather, the period witnessed florescence of worker mutual benefit societies throughout south Italy.[10]

Since the work of Barton and Briggs, Bell has examined the emigration issue in one north Italian and three south Italian communities. He conducted quantitative tests of some of Foerster's earlier assumptions such as the correlations between climatic and economic trends and emigration and found them to be positive. He came to the interesting conclusion, however, that the emigrants were more prone to leave during good times than bad, as a modicum of financial success permitted them to capitalize a move abroad.[11]

Bell, more than any other student of the subject to date, emphasizes the impact of emigration on the home communities and the importance of the individual emigrant's capacity to make well-reasoned choices when faced with the emigration alternative. Correctly, he notes that most Italians opted not to leave. The question, then, was:

> Stay in the village, move to the nearest city, seek work in Milan or Turin, emigrate to Germany or France, cross the Atlantic to Argentina or the United States, go alone, travel with spouse and children, help finance a brother's passage—these were choices, strategies of survival or calculations of gain.[12]

Barton, Briggs, and Bell make an admirable attempt to modify the image of the peasant emigrant from that of pawn and victim of Old World injustice reacting passively to forces pushing him out of his natal community and attracted by the pull of a life in a New World. Previous analyses of immigrant adaptation to host societies were, when they employed such a view of emigrants, hard pressed to explain their propensity once abroad to organize into voluntary associations and emphasize educational achievement in pursuit of their ethnic group interests. Given the implications of the stereotype, once it was accepted, the only explanation seemed to be that such behavior was simply a response to New World conditions rather than an extension of Old World propensities.[13]

Barton and Briggs are more proponents of an "Old World cultural baggage" school of thought in which immigrants arrive with more than their dirty laundry; rather, they import behavioral models as well. By demonstrating that peasant immigrants were more the architects of their own destiny than was previously acknowledged, Barton and Briggs provide a useful and stimulating redress of a simplistic stereotype.[14]

The arguments regarding the causes of south Italian immigration may thus be summed up as follows:

1. Every observer, whether a nineteenth-century social commentator or a twentieth-century social scientist, concurs that abject rural poverty is characteristic of south Italy. This constitutes a necessary and, for some, a sufficient cause of emigration.

2. For contemporary observers and a few social scientists, the related question of overpopulation is critical. There is less consensus on this point. Lopreato downplays its importance;[15] Bell views it as paramount;[16] and Barton and Briggs ignore it altogether.

3. Social-structural factors including the emphasis on the nuclear family, the lack of voluntary associations, and the presence or lack of pronounced class distinctions correlated with narrowly or broadly based patterns of land ownership are critical to the analyses of some observers such as MacDonald and Banfield.

4. Finally, there is a more eclectic approach, best represented by Barton, Briggs, and Bell, that accepts much of the above but insists on including cultural considerations as well as the potential emigrant's capacity to make rational decisions after assessing the alternatives, including that of not leaving at all.

These, then, are the principal arguments that have been advanced to account for the massive emigration of south Italians. In eclectic fashion, they inform much of my subsequent analysis of emigration from Agnone. At the same time, I seek to refine some of the points where they fail to square with the Agnone data. Although one cannot generalize from a single community to all of south Italy, it is unlikely that Agnone was unique.

The Political and Economic Preconditions

Garibaldi's victory and the unification of the Italian nation were greeted with suspicion by the lower classes of south Italy. To the extent that the events represented a liberal triumph, they exacerbated the already profound alienation of the peasantry and manual laborers. The liberal faith in the ability of science, education, and unbridled free enterprise to cure the ills of the Mezzogiorno had been cruelly disabused in practice. During the period following the abolition of feudalism, the lot of the peasant and manual laborer had actually worsened.

Despite certain parliamentary inquiries and well-intentioned attempts at reform, the new national government made little headway in resolving the endemic social and economic problems of south Italy. Franchetti, writing in 1875 of his travels in the Molise, provides a vivid description of the desperate straits of the lower classes. He notes that the typical peasant was landless and received a bare minimum for his labors. In most sharecropping arrangements, half or more of the grain harvest went to the landowner as well as the major portion of the grape crop.[17]

The peasant regarded anyone dressed in city clothing as a *galantuomo* and treated him with extreme deference:

> For the peasant the *galantuomo* is omnipotent. If he doesn't have him for a patron, then he has him for a creditor. He needs him for his communications with the governing authority, which doesn't understand the peasant's language and whose language the peasant often fails to understand. He needs him to fill out tax declarations when they are to be paid, to file his petitions, to defend his rights, to obtain from the authorities licit favors and at times illicit ones. . . . In sum, in any situation or circumstance that he finds himself, the peasant is always dependent upon the *galantuomo*.[18]

Consequently, the *contadini* remained antagonistic to the new order and retained Bourbon sentiments,[19] occasionally taking up arms and struggling with force born of desperation to replace upon the throne a king who promised to make the *galantuomini* respect the law. "They have the books, we the guns" was the word that spread from town to town.[20]

Between 1860 and 1875 the peasantry therefore constituted an explosive political element in south Italy. Disenfranchised and disillusioned by the lack of land reform,[21] the peasants lent their support to brigands. The political overtones of the brigandage, which has been likened to a thinly disguised civil war, were clear. On occasion, bands attacked town halls to destroy records, control of which provided the means whereby the *galantuomini* maintained hegemony in local affairs.[22] The magnitude of the brigandage was quite impressive; in the Molise one band alone killed 258 people in a ten-year period.[23] The bands operated independently, however, and without a clearly conceived ideology and plan of action.[24] In time, they lost popular support and disappeared from the scene. Zarrilli notes that, by 1875, "in effect the landed bourgeosie of the Molise no longer had anything to fear from a peasantry exhausted by the long revolt of brigandage, tired, and by then resigned to their misery. While our peasants no longer became brigands, there began the tragedy of emigration."[25]

In Agnone to this date, among the lower classes there is an expression, "Let's make the thirtieth of April," that serves as a euphemism for popular revolt. The specific historical disturbance is no longer remembered, but the symbolism remains. Reference is to the events of April 30, 1860, and they may be reconstructed from the courtroom testimony that followed.[26]

On the day in question, several *contadini* were told by a local baker that no more bread was available in the town. This triggered a demand that the bakers be arrested for illegal speculation. It was believed that many *galantuomini* had cornered the private grain supply and manipulated municipal stockpiles to create a shortage.

A large crowd assembled that included a few artisans and many peasants and manual laborers, armed with farm implements. With shouts of "Long live the king" (referring to the Bourbon monarch Francesco II), they decided to attack the houses of the "proprietors." The local police were frightened into a state of inertia by the size of the multitude, which was estimated at two thousand people. The demonstrators forced entry into the residence of the municipal registrar, Francesco Antonio Tamburri. Tamburri's frightened son signed a promissory note in the amount of four hundred ducats.

Next, they attacked the residence of the former mayor Giuseppe Mª Sabelli. They accused him of having dissipated and misappropriated the several thousand ducats' surplus that he had received from the former administration. The crowd sacked the house, stealing valuable objects and smashing everything else.

The dwelling of the Pietro de Horatiis family suffered the same fate. The priest Angelomaria de Horatiis was wounded with a dagger. Pietro de Horatiis was the caretaker of the Monte dei Pegni, or the municipal pawnshop. The pawned objects were taken. While the purpose of this organization was to provide low-interest loans to the lower classes,[27] in point of fact, in the Molise these institutions tended to be badly managed and easily manipulated by unscrupulous people who were themselves, like Pietro de Horatiis, *galantuomini*.[28]

The crowd turned its attention to the Convent of Santa Chiara, but before the door could be forced, the nuns signed a promissory note in the amount of one-hundred ducats. By then it was late at night, and there had been much drinking. Some people retired to their homes, while others continued to assault the dwellings of forty other *galantuomini*, most of whom were forced to sign promissory notes as well.

Meanwhile, the mayor had armed a few trusted men and was gradually restoring order. He stationed guards to protect the dwellings of many officials, including that of one of his kinsmen, a local judge. In an altercation that ensued at the judge's house, one of the rioters was shot to death. A few days later the *intendente* of the Molise and the chief officer of the provincial police arrived with troops to restore order.

The class affiliations of the rioters may not be doubted. In the proceedings most of the defendants declared themselves illiterate and too poor to retain a lawyer. The targets of the rioters are also revealing. The local administration, the Monte dei Pegni, and the convent were all visible symbols of oppression to the lower classes of Agnone.

This popular revolt was particularly unnerving to the *galantuomini*. Unlike previous disturbances, which contained strong elements of political factionalism in which all segments of local society were represented in some measure on both sides of the dispute, the revolt of the thirtieth of April was clearly a class phenomenon. Both during and after the events, the *galantuomini* closed ranks. Most of the testimony was elicited from *galantuomo* witnesses and was unanimously condemnatory. Indeed the very title of the proceedings is revealing. The case file is labeled "Process relative to the devastation and looting enacted against one class of persons. . . ." Subsequently, seventy-six people were arrested, including a number of women.

On September 7, 1860 a triumphant Garibaldi entered the city of Naples. He prepared a plebescite in late October in which the electorate of the kingdom, by overwhelming majority (1,302,064 yeas to 10,312 nays), accepted annexation into the nation of Italy. The election did not, however, measure the extent of Bourbon support in the kingdom. There continued to be considerable resistance to the new developments.

In Agnone, between the seventh and fourteenth of October, there was armed insurrection.[29] It seems that "certain elements" sowed discontent among the *contadini* and lower classes as well as the false rumor that a legion of troops was in Isernia and poised to restore the Bourbon monarchy. The *contadini*, in return for their support, had supposedly been promised carte blanche for six months to redress old scores. On October 7, a large group of charcoal makers and peasants assaulted the police barracks of Agnone. The policemen deserted their posts. The crowd burned the tricolor flag, replaced it with the white Bourbon standard, and marched through the town shouting, "Long live the king. Long live Francesco." The rebels held Agnone for eight days. They dispatched an emissary to nearby Schiavi d'Abruzzo to order that populace to revolt as well or be invaded by a force from Agnone. The agent threatened to execute "the *galantuomini* and *liberali*" of Schiavi.[30]

In subsequent years Agnone had its share of brigandage. To a degree, this cut across class lines as well-to-do sympathizers of the old order and the conservative element in the clergy lent clandestine support to the outlaws. In 1861 three prominent persons from the town were accused of serving as go-betweens for bands of brigands hiding in Agnone's forests.[31] The duke of nearby Pescolanciano was also implicated as a sympathizer of the brigands.

In June of 1862 four brigands, who were identified as *contadini*, kidnapped and held for a one-hundred—ducat ransom a young man who was traveling through Agnone's forests.[32] That same year, three butchers from Agnone learned that brigands had stolen many cows and went to their hideout to try to buy the meat. On their return, they encountered a government patrol and were arrested for collaboration.[33] Again in 1862 the charcoal makers of a particular forest were accused of living with and protecting its *briganti*. When a forest warden was killed, it was alleged that the charcoal makers had used the brigands to rid themselves of a long-standing enemy.[34]

A contested election held in 1863 also produced considerable discord. It seems that the supporters of a particular conservative candidate for the office of commander of the local militia mobilized the vote of the *contadini* and provided them with premarked ballots as they approached the urn. The election was voided by the local officials on the grounds that the *contadini* had been coerced, cajoled, and bribed into voting as they did. The officials noted that the *contadini* were "habitually reluctant to intervene in public elections" and that they probably did so only under duress.[35]

As supporters of the former Bourbon monarchy and residents of the strongest bastion of liberalism in the Molise, then, the peasants and manual laborers of Agnone were regularly manipulated and profoundly alienated. On these grounds alone they were preconditioned for emigration. At the same time, it was the peasantry that paid the greatest price for Agnone's difficult terrain and arduous climate. Landslides are a common occurrence in the town and are capable of sweeping away several farms and dwellings at a single stroke.[36] Crop failure was a constant threat. In 1879 a severe and lengthy winter caused near-famine conditions in the town;[37] in 1884 the harvest was sparse,[38] as it was again in 1886, when a violent hailstorm raked the area.[39]

Natural disasters were, of course, not restricted to the late nineteenth century and in themselves scarcely explain why the Agnonesi began emigrating in that period. Of more probable relevance was the question of critical space. That is, as Bell has pointed out,[40] rates of emigration are positively correlated with population size given available natural resources. In Chapter 4 I noted that between the mid-seventeenth century and 1830 Agnone's population almost doubled, thereby exacerbating the decline in the standard of living for the lower classes. This pattern of rampant population growth continued unabated over the next forty years.

Estimates of Agnone's population during the latter half of the nineteenth century run as high as fourteen thousand inhabitants,[41] a figure that is probably inflated and attributable to excessive chauvinism. The official Italian census of 1871 places the resident population of Agnone at 11,073.[42] Of these, 11,019 were listed as "stable" residents and 54 as "transient." Also, 596 people with legal residence in Agnone were "absent." So the total legal population of the town in the year 1871 was 11,615.[43] Thus, in a little over a century, Agnone,'s population nearly tripled.

If, from a per capita standpoint, the critical space for each Agnonese had narrowed considerably by the 1870s, a series of economic developments within the New Italy added to the burden. Protectionist policies designed to cushion the fledgling national market led instead to a disastrous drop in agricultural exports and a sharp decline in the agricultural price index.[44] Added to this was the fact that the new government demonstrated a voracious appetite for taxes to finance necessary nation building.[45]

In 1884 the local newspaper *L'Aquilonia* reviewed the causes of emigration of peasants from Agnone and concluded that the two major factors were excessive taxes on consumers' goods and usurious interest rates that at times surpassed 20 percent in the town.[46] As the local tax base was now predicated on the high population figures for the town before the departure of the first transatlantic emigrants, further emigration was now increasing the burden because fewer taxpayers remained to share the load.[47]

To these problems may be added the fact that inflation was rampant during the latter part of the nineteenth century and the early years of the twentieth. In the words of one Agnone newspaper: "The items of prime necessity have increased a third, doubled or even tripled compared to a few years ago. The poor father of a family, be he a worker, artisan, or modest employee, does not know how he can get by."[48]

The peasant was a shadowy figure in the pages of Agnone's newspapers. When he is mentioned at all, it is usually either as a social problem or as the victim of natural disaster. From such articles it is possible to catch a brief glimpse of a world characterized by considerable violence and tragedy. Robbery,[49] homicide,[50] assaults,[51] and infanticides[52] were not unusual for rural Agnone. On occasion, peasants were arrested for stealing the crops of the *galantuomini*,[53] and a particularly frequent crime was the illegal cutting of timber on the town commons.[54] In 1863, for example, the authorities actually prosecuted 624 cases of illegal felling of trees, many of which involved several defendants.[55]

Consequently, when by the 1870s, owing to improvements in sea travel, a lowering of fares, and the expansive nature of the economies of both the United States and the Rio de la Plata region of southern South America, transatlantic emigration became a viable alternative, the lower classes of Agnone were, out of a sense of desperation, prime candidates. Politically alienated by decades of unfulfilled promises of land reform, mired in endemic poverty, dependent on a rapacious class of *galantuomini* for what was, by any yardstick, a meager existence, the peasantry was further squeezed by relentless population increase throughout the first seven decades of the nineteenth century. For Agnone's *contadino*, then, the act of emigration, even though to an uncertain destination and destiny, could scarcely be regarded as extravagant risk taking. By concentrating its efforts, a peasant family, sometimes seeking aid from its extended kin network, pooled its resources to provide one or two of its young adult male members with passage. The whole process was quickly facilitated by agents and agencies, some operating for private gain and others commissioned by the Argentine government,[56] who recruited emigrants with the promise of loans and other forms of assistance. For Agnone's poor, emigration held at least the prospect of escape from misery.

I have chosen the term *misery* deliberately with the knowledge that considerable debate has centered on depiction of the south Italian peasant's life as the world of *"la miseria."*[57] While I agree with Lopreato and Saltzman's contention that the imagery of *"la miseria"* results in part from research designs that emphasize poverty, conflict, and suspicion,[58] I also believe that a historical perspective is required. A generation of social scientists has documented the relative social and economic deprivation of the south Italian peasant by conducting post–World War II field studies in the region. If the image of the world of *la miseria* emerged from such investigations, how much more appropriate would it have been in 1870? In Agnone today the peasant continues to manifest such a generally low standard of living compared with the other social classes that a detailed description of his existence and self-image would support, at least in part, a depiction of *la miseria.* Yet today's peasant benefits from subsidized medical care, a rural school system, old age pensions, and other government programs. He can acquire a low-interest and partially subsidized loan from the Cassa per il Mezzogiorno to improve his dwelling and modernize his agricultural operation. Given the depopulation of the last century, he can now acquire access to virtually all the land he can work. Also, it is a rare household that has not benefited from the feedback of emigrant savings.

The Magnitude of Migration

In 1871 the Molise had one of the lowest rates of emigration of any region in Italy. For that year there were only 134 emigrants, of whom 90 went to the Americas. This gave the area only .06 emigrants per 100 inhabitants.[59] The following year, however, emigration increased markedly, to 809 emigrants, or 0.23 per 100 inhabitants.[60] Destinations listed were: 609 to Buenos Aires, 91 to Montevideo, 85 to Brazil, and 24 to European nations. Of the total, 492 listed their occupations as *contadino*; 228 were without occupation; and information was lacking for 63. The remaining 26 persons included 15 artisans, 7 industrialists, 3 landowners, and 1 priest.[61]

Emigration to the Americas subsequently declined. Josa notes that, officially, in 1876 there were only 5 transoceanic emigrants from the Molise. By 1878 this figure had increased to 311. In 1883 there were not fewer than 4,305 Molisani emigrants.[62] Between 1886 and 1900 there was an annual average of 7,551 emigrants from the province.[63]

These figures are not further refined according to the emigrants' towns of origin, and they document only "official" emigration. That is, the totals are compiled from the applications of those who emigrated along the legal channels established by the government for the purpose. There is evidence, however, that clandestine departures were also common. Those with police records[64] and minors unable to secure parental approval[65] were prime candidates. At one time, it could be claimed that, of four known murderers in Agnone, three had succeeded in escaping justice by emigrating.[66]

It is impossible to determine the precise magnitude of transoceanic emigration from Agnone during these years. The obituary of Raffaele Iannicelli contends that he was Agnone's first South American emigrant. Iannicelli first migrated to Rome, where he became an apprentice tailor. In 1858 he emigrated to Argentina.[67] According to another source, the first Agnonese to emigrate to South America left in 1866.[68] By 1870 departures from the town to Argentina were frequent.[69] Ascenso Marinelli notes that by 1872 he was sometimes employed by local families to translate letters written in Spanish received from relatives in Argentina.[70] The emigrants in question were illiterate and hence employed the services of professional Argentine *escribaños*, or scribes.

Josa states that Agnone was the first town of the Molise to respond to the opportunity of transatlantic emigration.[71] Furthermore, in his analysis of the early years of emigration from the province, he finds that the Agnonesi constituted the largest single contingent among the earliest Molisani emigrants.[72] The newspaper *Biferno* noted in 1884 that "Agnone would be the largest city in the Molise if 5,000 Agnonesi had not emigrated for the Americas."[73] The same year the newspaper *L'Aquilonia* estimated that one-third of the town's population was in the New World.[74]

By this period it could be said that emigration in Agnone was a mass movement and that there was growing local concern over its consequences. The January 1, 1885 issue of *L'Aquilonia* noted that seventy-five Agnonesi had just departed for America, and thirty-eight were planning to leave shortly.[75] The following month, twenty-nine Agnonesi embarked in Genoa for South American destinations.[76] In April the newspaper noted:

> Emigration. It is always with us. Our cocitizens do not want to have anything to do with Italy. And until some stable means is provided to improve the [conditions of the] working classes, emigration will increase and in frightening proportions. In less than four days, from our subdistrict more than eighty have departed!![77]

By all indications, the first wave of emigration from Agnone was directed exclusively at Argentina. Under the direction of President Roca, the 1870s was a period of pacification of the Indians of the pampas.[78] New areas were opened to European colonists. The landed oligarchy, or *estancieros*, saw considerable economic advantage in sharecropping a portion of their vast estates. European peasants, in the main Italian, [79] were given short-term leases to a few hundred acres of virgin but potentially arable land. The conditions were frequently stringent,[80] and the tenant faced easy eviction after having exhausted his energies in breaking the root systems of the native grasses; but for the Italian *contadino* they proved more attractive than the same arrangements on a tiny parcel of Old World hillside.[81]

By the mid-1880s there were signs that the Agnonesi were selecting a broader range of destinations. The April 17, 1884 issue of *L'Aquilonia* published a letter from a man residing in Montevideo. He noted that, because of Uruguay's stormy political history, few people from the Alto Molise had established residence there. He urged those contemplating emigrating to consider the country inasmuch conditions were much improved.[82] In the same issue, there is an article that describes economic conditions in the United States in an unfavorable light. The very appearance of such an article suggests, however, that a North American destination was becoming a viable consideration for Agnone's emigrants. An 1886 article states: "In the last days of March many of our citizens departed for the United States, from whence they recently returned."[83]

By this time, chain migration was a major factor in perpetuating the movement of Agnonesi to the New World. *L'Aquilonia* reported in 1886:

> At 8 A.M. on September 25th we found ourselves on the *Largo della Vittoria*. It presented a sad and tormenting spectacle. By now it is clear that, before we know it, the entire town will end up in the Americas, but it is always painful and discomforting, for those who

remain, to witness the departures of cocitizens to distant shores; to see them return and then depart again, taking with them still more relatives. . . . Yet another 25 emigrants gave their goodbyes to their friends, hugged their tearful wives and inconsolable relatives . . . and these scenes are repeated every 15 or 20 days, and they are increasingly more frequent.[84]

Statistics concerning the emigrants' savings provide another indicator of the magnitude of emigration from Agnone. The major savings repository for the emigrants was the Cassa Postale di Risparmio, the Italian postal service. For the year 1887, throughout the twenty-five communities of the district (*circondario*) of Isernia, there were 3,371 savings accounts with a total of 607,711.51 lire. Agnone's 1,016 passbooks and 317,769.36 lire represented almost one-third of the accounts and more than one-half of the total savings for the district. The town of Isernia, though almost as large as Agnone, had only 191 accounts and 22,525.20 lire.[85]

By the 1890s the Agnonesi were well aware of conditions in several New World countries. Letters from relatives in the Americas, the accounts of returnees, and articles in the local press were all sources of such information. Nor was the news always favorable or presented in adorned fashion. The June 10, 1894 issue of the *Eco del Sannio* noted:

> For now we say that the situation in Argentina continues to be most entangled and irresolvable, that the civil war in Brazil continues . . . that the situation in Uruguay is relatively stable and that affairs in the United States are progressively more uncertain due to the lack of work and the increasing agitation by the many jobless—or strikers.[86]

In 1896 the newspaper cited the need for the Italian government to intervene to protect the emigrants abroad. The newspaper noted recent anti-Italian acts in Brazil and the lynching of Italians in New Orleans in 1891.[87]

Yet despite such gloomy prognoses, few, apparently, were dissuaded; Agnone was infected, in the words of one pundit, with "emigromania." By 1895 it was estimated that, between the artisans and merchants scattered in other towns and provinces of Italy and the emigrants in the Americas, fully two-fifths of the Agnonesi were residing elsewhere.[88]

The following year, 576 emigrants left for the New World.[89] Given that the 1901[90] census placed the total town population at 9,827 inhabitants,[91] estimate that in 1896 alone nearly 6 percent of the townspeople emigrated! Of that year's emigrants, 413 left for Argentina, 127 for the United States, and 36 for Brazil.

In 1897 a letter was sent to the newspaper *Il nuovo risveglio* discouraging anyone from emigrating to Argentina as unemployment there was rampant.[92] A few months later, the newspaper described massive layoffs in Buenos Aires and reported that eight hundred south Italians had lost their savings when a Genoese banking agent went bankrupt.[93] In 1898 the *Eco del Sannio* warned that, though peasants might find menial jobs in Argentina, Agnone's more specialized and educated workers would encounter grave difficulty.[94] In 1901 the paper stated that, in Argentina,

> foreign labor (and particularly Italian) is too abundant whether in Buenos Aires or in the interior. . . . This is so much the case that many workers and peasants cannot find work, even at a reduced wage, and a large part of them should return to Europe.
>
> In this state of affairs the Commissariato [for Emigration] advises our workers and peasants not to emigrate in risky fashion to that republic. Rather, they should procure explicit assurances from relatives and friends that they will quickly find work once they reach their destination.[95]

In the same issue, the readership is warned against the recruiters from a certain Brazilian Amazonian sugar-processing company in which poor living conditions were producing a frightful mortality rate among the workers.[96]

With such adverse publicity about conditions in South America, it is not surprising that increasing numbers of Agnonesi elected a North American destination. Of the 1,024 people listed as absent from the town in the 1901 census, 429 were in Argentina, 339 in the United States, 155 in the "Americas," 10 in Brazil, 4 in Uruguay, 2 in Mexico, 2 in Chile, 1 in Australia, 1 in Canada, and 1 in Switzerland.[97]

In 1902 the national Commissariato dell'Emigrazione commissioned a committee in Agnone to protect the interests of emigrants from the Alto Molise and a part of the province of Chieti. The new *comitato* met monthly to discuss "that which morally and economically concerns emigration."[98] Its main function was to provide potential emigrants with information on passport application, conditions in the country of destination, and travel arrangements. It was also to process complaints from emigrants who had been illegally exploited by officials or shipping agents.[99]

By 1902 the Agnone press was warning potential emigrants not to leave for the United States without first securing a U.S. entry permit because those arriving in New York without one were being sent back to Italy.[100] The next year an article explained how one could circumvent this by emigrating to the United States via Canada.[101] That same year the *Eco del Sannio* warned the Agnonesi not to attempt to emigrate to the Transvaal without proper documentation, as they would be denied entry.[102] The newspaper also reported that Italian immigrants were receiving very bad treatment in France.[103] On the brighter side, in 1903 associations for the protection of Italian immigrants were formed in both Buenos Aires[104] and New York.[105]

By 1903–1904 the focus of emigration had shifted even more strongly from South to North America. There were 576 emigrants from Agnone during this two-year period,[106] of whom 501, or 87 percent, listed New York as their destination.[107] At the same time, a 1903 article noted that, as a result of bad conditions in Argentina, many people had returned home, while "various others have left Buenos Aires to go to New York."[108]

Such secondary migration was not at all uncommon. For example, Camillo Lauriente emigrated to Argentina, returned to Agnone, married, and reemigrated to Canada, where he worked on the railroad. He settled for many years in Trail, British Columbia, where he became a successful storekeeper. He later retired to Spokane, Washington.[109] Salvatore Marcovecchio first emigrated to the United States but then continued on to Buenos Aires, where by 1913 he was well established.[110]

By the first decade of the twentieth century, Agnone was declining in importance as a significant staging area of emigration from the Molise. Whereas in 1896 the town provided 576 emigrants, which amounted to 4.36 percent of the provincial total of 13,224,[111] that number was halved to 576[112] emigrants for the two-year period of 1903–1904,[113] and it represented only 2.74 percent of the Molise's sum of 21,013.[114] This was at a time when the province had the highest emigration rate in all of Italy, or 337 emigrants for every 10,000 inhabitants.[115]

The reduced role of Agnone in the total emigration from the province should not, however, be interpreted as a diminished propensity of the Agnonesi to emigrate. Not only were other areas of the Molise awakening to the opportunities of emigration and therefore swelling the ranks of the transoceanic migrants, but Agnone's long-standing involvement in emigration had, by 1900, seriously reduced its pool of potential candidates.

There were signs that emigration at the relatively reduced rate of 1903–1904 was a more manageble proposition for Agnone. The newspaper *Eco del Sannio* noted that, whereas the 1902 figure of 384 emigrants was enormous, the situation was far from critical because a high number of returnees from the Americas and a favorable balance of 120 more births than deaths meant the town's population had remained stable for the year.[116]

Unfortunately for this study, after 1903 Agnone's newpapers only infrequently listed the names and destinations of the emigrants, and the passport book for 1905–1908 is missing from the municipal archives. There is reason to believe there was a considerable drop in the emigration rate for at least a part of this period, for a 1909 article in the *Eco del Sannio* notes that emigration was picking up again after a pause caused by the 1907 decline in the U.S. economy.[117]

At the same time, the United States was tightening its immigration regulations. In 1909 it imposed literacy tests for the newcomers.[118] The following year a Connecticut chapter of the Daughters of the American Revolution published an immigant guide expressly for people from the Molise.[119] Despite this gesture of goodwill, there were signs of disenchantment. In 1912 newspapers throughout the Molise declared the probable innocence of two men from the province being tried in the United States for murder,[120] and one Agnone newspaper editorialized against the candidacy of President Wilson because of his anti-immigration stance.[121] The following year there was further tightening of U.S. immigration rules, particularly with respect to literacy, prompting another Agnone newspaper to call for creation in the town of an emigrants' school.[122] Argentina, too, was becoming less attractive for the potential emigrant. The period immediately before World War I was one of considerable anti-foreigner xenophobia in the South American nation.[123] Conversely, in 1914 an Agnone emigrant wrote a letter to the *Eco del Sannio* extolling the advantages of Trail, British Columbia, inviting other Agnonesi to come there.[124]

On balance, then, during the decade preceding World War I, the

Table 5.1. *Agnone Emigration, 1909–1913, by Destination*

Year	Argentina	United States	Canada	Brazil	Europe	Totals
1909	59	325	1	0	1	386
1910	88	228	2	0	2	320
1911	20	158	6	3	0	187
1912	77	239	7	1	1	325
1913	54	303	16	2	0	375
Totals	298	1,253	32	6	4	1,593

Source: "Libri dei passaporti," Archivio Comunale di Agnone, 1909, 1913.

Agnonesi were aware of potential problems, and particularly anti-foreigner sentiment, in the two nations that had formerly received the large majority of the town's emigration. By this time, however, there were substantial colonies of Agnonesi in both the United States and Argentina. The potential emigrant need not fear immigration-in-the-abstract because he could presumably count on kinsmen and friends while situating himself in the host country. It is interesting to note that in the period 1909–1913 the rate of emigration from Agnone is comparable to that of a decade earlier (see Table 5.1). With the exception of 1911, more than three hundred people left the town annually, and fully 78.66 percent selected a U.S. destination.

Africa deserves a parenthesis in the history of the town's emigration. During the late nineteenth century, Italy initiated a drive for African colonies that was to last through the Mussolini years. In 1887 Giovanni Tirone, a military officer and a member of a prominent Agnone family, was killed at Dogali, Eritrea (the Italian equivalent of the battle of the Alamo).[125] In 1896 the *Eco del Sannio* reported that sixteen Agnonesi were on military duty in Africa.[126] In 1912 it was claimed that twenty-four Agnonesi had been serving in the current Tripoli war and that five young men were leaving for it shortly.[127] The Italian government sought to attract colonists for its newly won African territory. In 1913 a thirty-eight-year-old peasant applied for passports for his wife and six children, listing Tripoli as his destination, although he later withdrew his application.[128]

The Emigrants' Profile

Who were the emigrants? There is little doubt that Agnone's first trans-atlantic travelers were in the main peasants and manual laborers. An 1884 report says:

> Because of the poor grape harvest, a large number of peasants will leave for the Americas. And they are right. Here one works without hope of even earning a living; there one works, and even more than here, but the work in the final analysis is compensated, and the *despotism of our wealthy* [citizens] is entirely forgotten.[129] (emphasis theirs)

It is also clear that the mass departure of the peasantry, both in Agnone and its hinterland, directly affected the life circumstances of others, and particularly the artisans:

> They, it is necessary to say, were too numerous in Agnone, and therefore the production of artisan industry surpassed considerably the needs of the populace. Indeed this was so much the case that even in the remote past Agnone's artisans emigrated to surrounding towns, some permanently. . . . But with the facilitation of the means of communications, with the destruction of small industries by large ones, and with the emigration of the *contadini*, the artisans too have had to leave beautiful Italy, squeezed by necessity.[130]

The parish census for San Pietro, formulated in 1882 and kept current through 1885, provides some idea of the social class distribution of emigrants at that time.[131] Of the 224 males fourteen years of age and older listed in the census, 107 were peasants and charcoal makers, 91 were artisans, 12 were *galantuomini* (professors, engineers, landowners, priests, and businessmen), 4 were in service activities (2 sacristans, 1 organist, and 1 policeman), and for 2 people occupation is unspecified. There were 8 men in the category *spezzino*, or storekeeper.

Of the 107 peasants and manual laborers, 31 (or 1 in every 3.45) were residing in the Americas. Of the 91 artisans, 15 (or one in every 6.06) was likewise an emigrant. None of the 12 *galantuomini* or the 4 service providers had emigrated. Of the 8 *spezzini*, 3 were in the Americas.[132]

An analysis of the 1901 town census provides considerable evidence concerning the nature of emigration from Agnone at the turn of the present century.[133] Of the 2,875 males over fourteen years of age, 1,737

100

were peasants and manual laborers; 831 were artisans; 184 were professionals and merchants; 20 were in service activities (policemen, coachmen, doormen); and 103 were listed as *negoziante*, or businessmen. Of the 2,875 adult males, 646, or 1 in every 4.45, was residing in the Americas. Of peasants and manual laborers, 416 (or 1 in every 4.17) had a New World residence, as did 176 (or 1 in every 4.72) artisans. There were only 4 of the 184 members of Agnone's social elite residing abroad (or 1 in every 46), and none of the 20 persons in service activities was absent from the town. Of the 103 *negozianti*, 50, or almost half, were in the Americas, but many of these men were clearly of humble origins, for other members of their nuclear family were entered as *contadino*.

It is likely that during the early years the majority of emigrants were young, unmarried males. At least this is the superficial impression that one gets from a reading of the few published obituaries of those who ultimately succeeded in the New World.[134] By the mid-1880s, however, there was more variety in the makeup of the emigrants. In the words of one observer:

> Every morning they leave in throngs, and every morning with heavy heart one witnesses a desolating scene. Every morning in the *Largo della Vittoria* between those who leave and those who come to see them off there is an interminable glut of people.
>
> There are infinite handshakes and lingering goodbye kisses. When, finally, the crowded carriages move off slowly, like a third-class procession, there is only one sound that rises to the stars, a prolonged, acute, tormented cry that seeks out the inner recesses of the heart.
>
> Poor souls!
>
> They leave in fives, tens, twenties, and at times as entire families; men, women, old and young.[135]

The "Libri dei passaporti" provide a rich source of information about the sex, age, and family status of the emigrants from Agnone. I have already noted that in the two-year period 1903–1904, 576 people left the town. These included ten nuclear families comprising a total of forty-one persons. There were forty cases of married women and offspring (109 individuals) traveling together to join their spouses in the New World. There were six instances of two kinsmen traveling together (a man and his nephew, a man and his daughter, a widowed mother and daughter, a brother and sister, and two cases of two brothers). The remaining 410 emigrants traveled on their own (although usually in the company of other Agnonesi). In 1903–1904, emigration remained a predominantly male enterprise, but not nearly to the extent as in former years. In all, there were 165 female (or 28.65 percent of the total) emigrants during the two-year period of whom 51 were children (ages unspecified) traveling either with their mother or as members of nuclear families. There were 74 married women, 34 spinsters, and 6 widows.

More than two-thirds of the emigrants, or 409 persons, were males. Of this total, 40 were children (age usually unspecified) traveling with one or both parents. Fully 228, or 55.75 percent of all males and 39.58 percent of the total number of emigrants, were married men.

From the figures, it is clear that by 1903 the most likely emigrant was a male who was neither single nor necessarily young. The mean age of the married male emigrants was 32 years, and the median age was 30.38 years, although the modal age was 23 years. The last figure suggests that a particularly prime candidate for emigration was the newlywed husband.

Almost four times as many married men (228) as married women (60) departed Agnone during the period. This is one strong measure of the extent to which separation was a critical feature of the emigration process. By the 1901 census period, fully 1 out of every 5.73 of the town's married male heads of household was absent and working in the Americas.[136]

It might be argued that in psychological terms, both for the emigrant and his family, the departure of a married man was particularly trying. The adventuresome single young man certainly experienced loneliness and was missed, but the absence of a husband-father-provider placed an extraordinary burden on all concerned. The wives who were left behind came to be known as the *vedove bianche*, or white widows.

On the other hand, it may be that, in the patrilineally extended family household of Agnone, the sense of separation for members of the emigrant's nuclear family was ameliorated by their collective living arrangements. Also, I have argued elsewhere that the per capita income of households in Agnone was augmented as size of membership increased.[137] One might therefore expect that on both psychological and economic grounds the extended family household was better able to tolerate and finance emigration of one or more of its members.

It is therefore particularly interesting that the majority of husbands listed in the 1901 census as absent in the New World were heads of nuclear family households. This would seem to reinforce the interpretation of MacDonald and others who argue that the atomistic nuclear family unit was a prime seedbed of candidates for emigration. It would also call into question Bell's assertion that a modicum of prosperity, rather than abject poverty, favored emigration. Clearly, by the turn of the century, emigration of the main productive member was viewed as a viable economic strategy in those households in the least prosperous phase of their developmental cycle.

While the emigrant likely found solace and support in the New World from established kinsmen and friends, there is also evidence of another mechanism for coping with loneliness. In the 1903–1904 records, in eleven cases an emigrant was sponsored by his or her father, in nine by an uncle.[138] Of the total, eleven were males and nine were females, and their mean age was thirteen years. The eldest was eighteen, and the youngest, ten. It would seem, then, as the emigrant became established in the New World, but before he was able to bring out his entire family or himself return to Italy, he might send for one of his children, a niece, or a nephew.

In this fashion the transfer of a family from the Old World to the New was as likely to be drawn-out process as an event. That is, by the time the nuclear family unit was reunited, years might go by during which members resided on both sides of the Atlantic. A family established in the New World might ultimately send back to Agnone for an elderly member who would otherwise be abandoned. During the 1903–1904 years there were eight examples of a child sponsoring a parent. In all but one case the parent was over fifty, and in four instances he or she was widowed.

Conversely, return visits, particularly by the successful, emerged as a common pattern. At times, entire families from the New World visited their Agnone relatives.[139] More commonly, however, just one or two members were able to make the journey. Such visits tended to be lengthy. In 1900 the *Eco del Sannio* reported: "Good journey! is our wish for our friend Michele Sammartino, who today leaves for Argentina after seven months spent . . . among family, relatives, and friends. The pain of separating is mitigated by the sweet thought that in Buenos Aires he is awaited with keen desire by his son Pepino."[140]

Another discernible practice was for established New World families to send one or more of their children back to Agnone to be educated. In the 1901 census, of the ninety-three students with residence in Agnone's boarding schools, nine were born in the New World (including four in Brazil, two in Buenos Aires, two in "America," and one in New York). This could mean a separation of considerable duration. In 1905 the wife of Francescopaolo Marinelli returned from Argentina to Italy because her young son, whom she had not seen in six years, was critically ill in Agnone.[141]

Even in death, the emigrant was likely to remain of local concern. By the early 1900s it was common for the churches in Agnone to celebrate funerals for people who died in the New World.[142]

The Human Costs

The story of the travails of nineteenth-century transatlantic emigrants, with the imagery of human cargos and huddled masses, is well known.[143] The emigrant ran a gauntlet of potential exploiters on both sides of the Atlantic. It might take several years before he or she became reasonably established in the New World; many were literally destroyed in the process. In the words of one Agnone newspaper, "They find another firmament, other mountains, other people, another civilization. They adjust to the most difficult tasks. Few are they who make a fortune; many are those who are quickly seized by strong disillusionment; many encounter death in those distant lands."[144] An Agnonese emigrant wrote in a letter to the editor of the *Eco del Sannio*;

> The small percentage of emigrants who return to their birthplaces with four liras in their pocket cause the rest of the cocitizens to lose their heads and not think of the hundreds of their companions who are hard up, exploited by infamous speculators, disheartened by adverse fortune . . . or who, weakened by vices, pain, and nostalgia for the homeland that they will never see again, await death.[145]

Another emigrant chose to vent his sorrow in verse:

The Emigrant
Here, in this land
where melancholy assaults inner peace
where people pass by without noticing you
and where every corner emanates a sigh

where breathing is just existing
where for those born in the distant lands
talking becomes an obsession
due to the difficulty of expressing oneself
where the woman suffers the misfortune
of falling prey to constant toil
where life becomes a deception
and every prediction an error.
Here, in this land
where time becomes an eternity
and a moment of happiness a rarity
I remember my gentle homeland
and suffer nostalgia and regret.[146]

Separation, nostalgia, loneliness are the recurring words in the emigrant's lament, and at times there were examples of truly poignant human tragedy. Two articles from the newspaper *L'Aquilonia* illustrate the point:

Signore Achille Borsella, Agnonese, 37 years of age, emigrated to Buenos Aires in 1872. His family has never heard from him again despite many efforts. They therefore came to us so that, through the medium of *L'Aquilonia*, we could advise all the cocitizens who are resident in the Argentine Republic [of the problem].[147]

The *contadina* Celesta Carlomagno, forty years of age, while she was working in a grainfield . . . was struck by a lightning bolt that instantaneously rendered her a corpse. For the past 12 years the poor woman had her husband in the Americas from whom she has never received any news, and here she leaves behind a young son in abandon and misery.[148]

Separation, then, was the inescapable cost of emigration, and one of its consequences was an increase in adultery.[149] Given the overriding concern in south Italian society with female virtue, this was indeed a socially disruptive development. At times it could lead to violence and tragedy, when a jealous husband returned from America to confront his wife's lover.[150]

Infanticide was another by-product. One Agnone newspaper article notes:

At the beginning of December a certain C. A., 35 years of age, wife of M. N., emigrated five years earlier to America, gave birth to a baby, fruit of an illicit relation with one R. G. . . . With the purpose of hiding the disgraceful fact and therefore salvaging her honor, C strangled the infant, consigning it to someone else to be interred secretly.[151]

There existed in Agnone a long-standing mechanism for dealing with illegitimate births. The commune had a tradition of paying for the care of abandoned infants by consigning them to wet nurses.[152] At times, the babies were simply left on doorsteps, but there was also a formal drop point known as *la ruota*, or "the wheel." This was a lazy susan mechanism installed in the exterior wall of one of Agnone's chapels. A person could maintain anonymity while abandoning a baby because the operation could not be observed by anyone on the inside.

During the first half of the nineteenth century, the vital records include an occasional illegitimate birth. For example, for the ten-year period from 1820 to 1829, there were 3,410 births in the town. In 23 cases, or 0.67 percent of the total, the identity of the father was unknown.[153] Conversely, between 1880 and 1889, of 4,435 recorded births, there were a total of 240 children listed as *abbandonati*, 5.41 percent of the total.[154] Whereas in the earlier period about 1 in every 148 infants was illegitimate, by the late nineteenth century 1 in every 18 births recorded in Agnone entailed an abandoned baby.[155]

By the 1890s the questions of infanticide and infant abandonment had become a burning civic issue. In 1897 the *Eco del Sannio* editorialized against continuance of the *ruota*. It noted that poor women had converted wet nursing into a business. For a woman to have milk for the abandoned child, she already had her own infant at her breast. In some cases women accepted more than one abandoned infant, meaning that three babies were dependent on her milk supply. Her natural tendency was to favor her own offspring; hence the infant mortality rate among children consigned to wet nurses was staggering. The newspaper branded this as a form of delayed infanticide, and one that went unpunished.[156]

In 1900 the town council abolished the *ruota*, and the newspaper reported:

The *ruota per gli esposti*, instituted in Agnone in remote times for those unfortunates who, as fruit of vice, or at times because of the poverty of their parents, came to be abandoned, has now been suppressed for humanitarian reasons and in the public interest.

The number of foundlings has here experienced a frightening increase, and it is lamentable [to note] that the major contingent derives from distant and neighboring towns. It was to be hoped that improved moral and economic conditions among the the populace would have diminshed the number of poor victims of passion, but the hopes were delusive; and possibly the main cause, if not the only cause of such evil, is to be found in the persistent emigration. . . .

It is not fair that the commune and the province spend ten thousand liras annually, of which almost half goes for foundlings from other towns.[157]

The Emigration Mentality

Despite the many hazards and drawbacks, by the end of the nineteenth century, emigration was a state of mind with a momentum all its own. Masciotta writes concerning the Molise as a whole:

Emigration today has become a sport, a custom, a mania, a fever. Everyone emigrates: the proletariat, small- and medium-scale landowners, artisans, peasants, professionals without clients, priests, the unemployed, everybody. . . .

America has become for our young generation a voluntary necessity of life. One believes himself to be morally incomplete if he does not go there for at least a little while.[158]

Furthermore, having once experienced a new life in a foreign land, the returnee faced a difficult, and frequently unsuccessful, readjustment:

The few years spent in America as a laborer make him a demanding man, a man who has need of beer, of liqueurs, of steak, and in the evening even of a little bit of theater or horse racing. Returned amongst us with many new needs, few of which he can satisfy here, he feels nostalgia for foggy Pennsylvania or Canada, and he no longer works with desire because he finds the work to be almost uncompensated. And thus, having spent the savings scraped together abroad in the town taverns, he once again procures a passport for a second or third voyage.[159]

Emigration, then, was a tremendously complex social question. In the main, its driving force was youthful imagination fueled by the success stories of a few. For many a person, unbridled enthusiasm and energy seemed more than a match for any adversity, and so they departed in droves, and their departures touched upon practically every aspect of life in communities like Agnone. Families were deprived of members, fields of their tillers, workshops of their artisans, patrons of their clients, priests of their parishoners, towns of their taxpayers. Consequently, the merits and demerits of emigration were debated incessantly. Gamberale, in a public discourse delivered in Agnone in 1902, phrased the question eloquently:

Some say that emigration is the cause [of the town's decline]. Possibly so, at least in part. But consider that emigration, clearly the cause of many ills, is itself an effect. It began . . . in malaise . . . in hardship. . . . Therefore, don't condemn our emigration; don't question whether it was and is a blessing or a handicap. It was a necessity, and a necessity is not and cannot be said to be a voluntary evil.[160]

6

The New World Agnonesi

It is far too general to state that the townspeople emigrated to North or South America or even to the United States, Canada, Argentina, and Brazil. Although there were cases of individual globe-trotting emigrants from Agnone who presumably spent much of their lives abroad without the company of other Agnonesi,[1] many of the emigrants clustered in a few communities where, in some cases, there emerged a true, self-aware colony. What commonly occurred was *chain migration*, a phenomenon that, as Tilly notes,

> moves sets of related individuals or households from one place to another via a set of social arrangements in which people at the destination provide aid, information, and encouragement to new migrants. Such arrangements tend to produce a considerable proportion of experimental moves and a large backflow to the place of origin. At the destination, they also tend to produce durable clusters of people linked by common origin.[2]

This two-way flow of personnel, capital, and ideas certainly characterized emigration from Agnone and provided the basis for an ongoing dialectic between the town and its emigrant diaspora. The specifics are the subject of this chapter, although I must begin with the caveat that it is impossible to quantify the proportion of the emigrants that engaged in chain migration. Apostasy with respect to continuing loyalty to birth-place removed an emigrant from awareness and hence from this analysis. Also the phenomenon of chain migration is itself better described in degrees rather than in terms of simple presence or absence.

I have noted that the first emigrants from Agnone went to Argentina. Many were peasants and manual laborers before leaving Agnone and entered the ranks of the Italian sharecroppers of the pampas, but this is not the entire story. In later accounts published in Agnone of the tribulations of the early emigrants, there is mention of a group of townspeople who became wandering peddlers on the pampas. These men are described as undergoing great hardship and solitude as they traveled the plain in wagons loaded with trade goods.[3] They were thus continuing the Agnonese tradition of engaging in ambulatory commerce. It is also likely that they were, in the main, ex-artisans rather than ex-peasants. The newspaper *L'Aquilonia* noted that the artisan emigrants "who do not find the means to exercise their own art for the hoped for gains, can find other work that is in greater demand; something that the peasant cannot do."[4]

By the end of the 1870s some of the emigrants were settled in urban areas, notably Buenos Aires. In 1879 two Agnonesi resident in the city organized a festival to celebrate the feast of the Madonna del Carmine.[5] The following year there was a revolution in Argentina, and an ex-soldier from Agnone formed a military unit in Buenos Aires composed of unemployed Italian immigrants and called the Legione Agnonese.[6] By 1883 the festival of the Madonna del Carmine was a major event for the city's Italian colony.[7] That same year a voluntary association called La Giovane Italia was founded in Buenos Aires. Of the thirty-three founding members, seventeen were Agnonesi.[8]

In 1884 a group of Alto Molisani (in the main, Agnonesi) formed a voluntary association, Il Circolo Sannitico, in Buenos Aires.[9] The organization persisted into the first decade of the twentieth century and was to play a major philanthropic role with respect to Agnone. In Argentina it operated as a social club, held an annual ball,[10] and ultimately founded its own orchestra.[11] It also functioned as a burial society.[12]

At the same time, it is clear that the Agnonesi participated in activities of the broader Italian community.[13] Baily analyzed a sample of forty-six Agnonesi resident in Buenos Aires between 1881 and 1910 and found that no fewer than forty-two were members of the Colonia Italiana, one of the largest and most important immigrant mutual-aid societies in the city.[14]

The Buenos Aires colony tended to confirm the generalization that Argentina attracted Agnone artisans. In Baily's sample twenty-three, or 50 percent of the total, were engaged in an artisan trade, including six goldsmiths and seven tailors.[15] Of equal interest was the fact that the Agnonesi in Buenos Aires manifested a strong tendency to cluster residentially. Baily found that "forty-two of the forty-six (91%) lived or owned a store within an 11 by 20 block area in the center of the city."[16]

Other communities of Argentina with considerable numbers of Agnonesi included Ballesteros, Bellavista, Mendoza, Tucumán, and Belleville. In 1896, when the larger Italian colony of Belleville organized a celebration, the president, treasurer, and secretary of the committee were all Agnonesi.[17] In 1897 Felice Andrea Carlomagno, a successful grainbuyer from Agnone, was named Italian consul for the town.[18]

If some of the earliest emigrants worked as itinerant peddlers on the pampas, by the end of the century others were enjoying fabulous business success in South America. In Buenos Aires there were three Agnonesi who owned their own shipping and banking agencies. Ruggiero di Paola owned a money exchange and lottery ticket outlet with three hundred employees.[19] Luigi Santarelli, a former goldsmith, owned a funerary wreath factory that employed sixty people.[20] Francesco Campercioli owned a pasta factory that began in 1885 with three employees and had twenty by 1910.[21] The Sabelli family had a large store in Mendoza,[22] as did the Amicarelli family in Ballesteros[23] and the Cervone family in São Paolo, Brazil.[24] In Tucumán the Iannicelli brothers were successful jewelers.[25] Tommaso Marinelli was enjoying great success in the same line in Brazil. He first opened a jewelry shop in Rio de Janeiro and later moved the business to Manaus, where he made a large fortune.[26]

There were certain enterprises owned by Agnonesi that were particularly impressive. Nicola Serricchio was one of three partners in a hat factory in São Paolo founded in 1900 and by 1907 producing 370,000 hats annually.[27] By 1911 production was up to 1,550 hats daily.[28] In Mendoza province of Argentina, Giustino Piccione, his son Gaetano, and his son-in-law Raffaele Sammartino created an enormous winery. By 1912 the enterprise, under the label "Marca Piccione," was winning international acclaim.[29] That year it founded a small town, Rodeo de la Cruz, which had 126 homesites.[30] By 1913 the enterprise was capitalized at a value of 3½ million pesos. It produced 50,000 hectoliters of wine annually and employed 384 workers.[31]

Another enormous entrepreneurial undertaking was the agricultural produce–purchasing agency of the Carlomagno brothers headquartered in Belleville, Argentina, but with branch offices in San Marcos, Chanares, Oliva, and Buenos Aires.[32] Founded in 1875,[33] by 1899 it was exporting large quantities of grain and hay to Brazil and South Africa.[34] In 1909 the Carlomagnos were negotiating grain deals directly with the British and Brazilian governments. That year alone they exported 250,000 quintals of wheat and 1 million bales of hay.[35]

In evaluating the successes of the South American emigrants, it might be claimed that "the Agnonesi, who in their town had a chance to study, since there exist many institutes of instruction, have known how to better themselves, and to hold high the prestige of their country in the industries, sciences, arts, and commerce of America. They are not the dwellers of the seedy quarters of the city."[36]

To the degree that Agnone's elite emigrated at all, then, they were prone to elect a South American destination. In part this seems to have been dictated by the language and opportunity structure of the receiving areas. A professional person from Agnone was more apt to be able to pursue his career effectively in a Latin country where learning the language was relatively simple than in the Anglo world of North America.

By the mid-1880s several Agnonesi were contributing to the cultural life of the Rio de la Plata nations. In 1884 Antonio Paolantonio, the former civic orchestra leader in Agnone, was touted as one of the finest musicians in Buenos Aires.[37] It was he who played at the balls of the Circolo Sannitico. Roberto Savastano became a pioneer journalist in Montevideo. In 1885 he founded the newspaper *La colonia italiana*, which lasted for five years.[38] He subsequently published *L'operaio italiano*, *Il Garibaldi*, and *La mosca* (the last in Spanish).[39] An 1897 issue of an Agnone newspaper acclaimed the Agnonese Girolamo Carosella as one of the most famous sculptors in Buenos Aires.[40] In 1903 an Argentine-born descendant of Agnonesi visited Italy to continue studying piano after graduating from the conservatory of Buenos Aires.[41] In 1911 the work of an Agnonese playwright, *Los Apaches*, was performed in the Argentine capital.[42] In 1912 a young woman from Agnone won second prize in the musical competition of the conservatory of the province of Cordoba.[43]

The emigrants continued the town's strong educational tradition in the South American nations. In Montevideo the journalist Savastano's wife founded a girls' school for the Società Italiana, Lega Lombarda.[44] In

1888 an Agnonese was named to a teaching post in the Istituto della Società Colonia Italiana;[45] in 1906 Antonio Apollonio was named professor of Italian in the Colegio Nacional de Uruguay (in Argentina);[46] and in 1908 a professor from Agnone was teaching piano in a Buenos Aires school and directing its orchestra.[47] In 1913 Nicola Iannelli was named by the Bolivian government as professor of anatomy, veterinary science, and plant pathology in the school of agronomy of Cochabamba.[48] Agnone's press regularly published the scholastic achievements of the town's New World descendants. These included the exam results of grammar school children[49] and university accomplishments of maturer students alike.[50] In 1900 the newspaper *Il cittadino agnonese* reported that eight of the town's descendants were registered at the University of Buenos Aires.[51]

Other emigrants excelled in the professions. These included a director of public works for the city of Buenos Aires,[52] a head accountant for a railroad,[53] a public accountant,[54] a public administrator in Paraná,[55] a physician,[56] a veterinarian,[57] and the inspector of municipal clocks of the city of Caracas, Venezuela.[58]

Information on the Agnonesi in North America is sketchier than that for the South American colonies. This may well have been a function of the general tendency of the town's newspapers largely to ignore the peasants and workers. In a speech given in Agnone by Paolo Borsella, a jeweler resident in New York City,[59] on the occasion of the departure of Dr. Giuseppe de Horatiis for the city of Detroit (where he planned to establish a medical practice), the uniqueness of the event was underscored:

> The Agnone colony in North America is mainly composed of workers who, engaged in difficult tasks and a continual struggle to exist in the midst of heavy and sad vicissitudes, recall the sadness with which they left their country in order to return there someday in different circumstances. . . . Years ago North America was regarded here as the land which only a peasant could enter. No professional risked himself in those faraway regions.[60]

Consequently, during the same years that Agnone newspapers made frequent mention of the accomplishments in the arts and professions of individual Agnonesi in the Rio de la Plata nations and Brazil, there are few comparable news items from North America. Two physicians, Daniele of Youngstown, Ohio and de Horatiis of Detroit, the artist Carosella in the latter city, and two other artists (F. A. Di Paolo[61] and

Girolamo Carosella[62]) in Toronto were the exceptions. The major business success of a North American resident Agnonese documented in the Agnone newspapers was that of Michele Massanisso, who founded a cigar factory in Providence, Rhode Island.[63]

The raw-boned nature of the North American experience was reflected in the coal-mining economy of Youngstown, Ohio; the steel mills of Pueblo, Colorado; and the frontier life of Trail, British Columbia. It is also inferred in the letter sent in 1889 fron Philadelphia to the newspaper *Il risveglio sannitico* by a man who had spent seven years wandering about the United States and who was presently boarding at the restaurant owned by the Agnonese Francesco Lollo. The writer unleashes a double-edged observation that is as much a critique of Agnone society as it is a comment on life in the United States: "In this land there are no daddy's boys who don't work because they disdain work and who live as parasites. . . . In America work is the apotheosis, no idleness as is the case in all Catholic countries which create festivals to render man dependent and servile."[64]

The Diaspora

While each New World concentration of Agnonesi presented its own peculiar characteristics and group life, viewed collectively they constituted a veritable diaspora for the town. This diaspora did not emerge inadvertently and merely as a function of the sheer numbers emigrating. Nor in referring to diasporic ties do I mean the continued contacts between individual emigrants and their Old World kinsmen and friends. Rather, what is of particular interest is the fact that Agnone as a community, and particularly the elite, consciously attempted to retain the loyalties and orchestrate the activities of the emigrants. Indeed, initial success and ultimate failure in this regard were the major factors in both the town's late-nineteenth-century fluorescence and its subsequent twentieth-century decline.

The primary vehicle of communication between Agnone and its diaspora was the town's press. Its first newspaper, *L'Aquilonia*, began publication in 1884, or almost two decades after the earliest transatlantic emigrants left the town. From the outset it depended heavily on an American clientele. During its second month of existence, the newspaper noted with satisfaction that it had just received 40 subscriptions from Buenos

Aires and anticipated receiving 60 more shortly.[65] By the end of the first year, it had 121 subscribers in the New World.[66]

By 1886 the newspaper was in financial trouble, and it appealed (unsuccessfully) to its subscribers in America to buy it a printing press.[67] The following year it put out a special call for new American subscribers, noting that "in large measure *L'Aquilonia* survives and will continue to survive through the support from America."[68] Shortly thereafter, it folded, but in 1888 it was started up again in response to several hundred requests from abroad.[69]

That same year a rival newspaper, *Il risveglio sannitico*, began publication as well. The competition for the support of the emigrants was fierce. When, in 1889, a Buenos Aires Italian-language paper sided with *L'Aquilonia*, the editor of the *Risveglio sannitico* angrily replied that his paper would continue even if it had to get by without American subscriptions.[70] That same year *L'Aquilonia* ceased publication, as did the *Risveglio sannitico* one year later, in 1890. Agnone was then without a local press until the *Eco del Sannio* was founded in 1894. In succeeding years other short-lived newspapers made their appearance. Inevitably, the prime audience was the New World emigrants, without whose support the journalistic effort was deemed unfeasible. For example, the first issue of *Il nuovo risveglio*, begun in 1895, contained an open letter "to our citizens residing across the ocean":

> This newspaper . . . is not a matter of indifference to you, because one of the motives which inspired its publication was the thought of keeping you who are such a part of our preferred Agnone, knowledgeable about all that is thought and done for the good of our town. . . .
>
> And you who are in the distant regions of the Americas where you went in search of work and fortune, keep always alive the thought of our Agnone. . . .
>
> When tired from the labors of the day you return to your houses . . . when your thoughts turn to the land of your birth, grateful will you be to read a newspaper from which you can learn . . . *those which are the most urgent needs of our town.*[71] (emphasis mine)

In seeking to orchestrate the loyalties of the emigrants in benefit of the town, Agnone's newspapers, despite their other differences, spoke with one voice. Nor was the message ambiguous. *L'Aquilonia* in 1889

115

suggested that the New World Agnonesi found a philanthropic society for the town.[72]

At the same time, the newspapers facilitated continued ties between the emigrants and their relatives in Agnone. *Il nuovo risveglio* published a *piccola posta* section of messages. Written in shorthand, and at times in code, they provide insight into the dynamics of separation. Selections from one issue include:

1. R. Ap. C. D'A. Enr. G.—Long silence hurts me. Distressing news. I greet you with great affection. All of your family well.
2. Andres d'Onofrio—Azul [Argentina]—received remittance Lire 100. Your mother Lire 30. Await letter. Greetings. Fontana.
3. R. Di Paola—Rep. Arg.—Received your letter with Lire 50. Many thanks. Greetings to all. F. Camperchioli.
4. C. e P. Carlomagno—Repub. Argent.—For a long time no news of you. I am waiting. Greetings. Custode.[73]

For the illiterate and semiliterate sectors of Agnone society, this must have been a particularly valued service. The message could be delivered orally at the newspaper office and might capture the attention of a literate emigrant in the New World, who might then pass it on to its intended recipient.

Emigration Agents

During the last decade of the nineteenth century, the Argentine colony represented the largest and oldest segment of Agnone's diaspora. In January 1887 the newspaper *L'Aquilonia* announced that Ruggiero Apollonio (a relative of the paper's editor) was leaving shortly for Buenos Aires to found a bank and business "and study there the means to repatriate, in whatever fashion, at least a portion of our numerous emigrants."[74] It further stated that "his main purpose is not that of amassing wealth, of which, after all, he is not in need, but rather to contribute as much as possible to the moral and economic status of the Agnone colony."[75] By May, he still had not departed for the New World. The paternalistic overtones of the venture were clearly apparent in a new article on the impending journey, exhorting the Agnonesi in Argentina to meet Apollonio's boat:

I am writing you with happy news; within a few days Ruggiero Apollonio, friend of the workers who labor for the prosperity of their family and their country, will arrive in your midst. Your friend, as you know, and as you may imagine, does not emigrate in search of lucre and vulgar speculations . . . he comes to you to know and study the virtues of the place where such a large part of Agnone resides, and to attempt, if it is possible, to create there a focus . . . a center of relations between you and us, between the emigrants and their home towns. Your emigration, if it is desired that it should always and generally produce good results, has need of a directing principle; one that is serious and constant, that guides it, harmonizes its aspirations, and that constrains dissipated energies into a single force. In sum, that makes of the emigrants almost a family in which, one for all and all for one, you work to obtain desired prosperity without losing sight of your native town, which expects much from its distant sons.[76]

In July there was an announcement from Argentina of Apollonio's impending arrival, which suggests that his reception on the other side of the Atlantic was not shaping up quite as well as anticipated:

Shortly there will arrive in our midst the honorable lawyer Ruggiero Apollonio of Agnone, a cultured and distinguished person, who does not come to Buenos Aires to defend lost causes, nor to lose the causes already won, but rather to open a large import house of products from South Italy.[77]

By the following year Apollonio had a firm that was funneling remittances back to Agnone. He also had his own representatives in Agnone itself.[78]

Meanwhile, in that same year, another Agnonese, Francescopaolo Marinelli, established a bank in Buenos Aires.[79] Marinelli emigrated from Agnone to Argentina when he was fifteen years old. He first worked as a postal agent in Lomas de Zamora before opening a small store in Buenos Aires and a larger one in partnership in the town of Tuy. He went back to Italy in 1884. In 1888 he returned to Buenos Aires, where he founded an import house specializing in south Italian wines and viands. According to later accounts, Marinelli was so successful that he sent for two of his brothers to help him.[80] For the Agnonesi, the agency became a veritable social center and a clearinghouse of news regarding friends and relatives from all over Argentina. It also provided information regarding employment opportunities in the Argentine nation.[81]

The stage was therefore set for the emergence of the kind of factionalism that is common throughout Agnone's history. In 1896 the newspapers reported that the two agents were contesting the leadership of the Buenos Aires colony. Significantly, and understandably, the Agnone press refused to take sides.[82] Both agencies sought to expand their services. Marinelli established his own representative in Agnone, whereas Apollonio's local agent, Michele Amicarelli, moved to Naples to assist emigrants both in their departures and arrivals from that port city.[83] By the following year the competition between the agencies, as reflected in their ads in the Agnone press, was fierce. Apollonio advertised that his agency provided "unique services." Marinelli claimed that his concern "didn't engage in speculations in the money exchange with *untouchable* and *sacrosanct* savings, as *in truth* some others do and would like to do" (emphasis his).[84] Both men were conscious of the business consequences of maintaining a good image in the town and consequently were frequently willing to serve as fund raisers for Agnone's civic projects.

For example, in 1889 Apollonio sent fifty liras and pledged two hundred more to help the town purchase land for an urban beautification project.[85] The following year he raised five hundred liras among the emigrants to help rebuild a bridge in rural Agnone that was in bad condition.[86] In 1900 Marinelli raised three thousand liras for construction of a monument to Libero Serafini.[87] In 1906 he organized a festival in Argentina that raised six thousand liras for the Giardino d'Infanzia, or orphanage, in Agnone.[88]

Meanwhile, there were other efforts by Agnonesi to establish New World banking and shipping agencies. In 1901 Erasmo Amicarelli of the Naples-based Amicarelli agency (and Apollonio's representative in Europe) traveled to New York to establish ties with American banks and with the Agnonesi of North America. He advertised his trip and offered to carry news and gifts on behalf of any Agnonese with relatives in New York City.[89] His efforts to establish a North American base proved abortive.

During the last decade of the nineteenth century and the first of the twentieth, several other Agnonese emigration agencies emerged. Carlo Vecchiarelli, a jeweler in Buenos Aires, opened a maritime agency and money exchange.[90] Feliciantonio di Paola and Camillo Carlomagno established a subagency for emigration in Agnone that represented several shipping lines.[91] Filippo d'Agnillo was the Agnone representative of several German shipping lines that regularly serviced Boston, New York, Montevideo, and Buenos Aires.[92] Antonio Vecchiarelli was one of two partners in the Banca Europa of Philadelphia, which, in addition to banking services, acted as an employment bureau.[93] The local Agnone shoe store operator C. Mastronardi represented the Milan-based Società "Anglo-Italiana," which arranged transportation and provided maritime insurance.[94] Elia di Pietro was the Agnone agent of the shipping firm of Felice Mastronardi Fratello (both Agnonesi) of Buenos Aires.[95]

Of all these agencies it was the original Marinelli firm that prospered most. In 1900 Enrico, brother and partner of Francescopaolo, returned to Agnone from Argentina[96] to establish an emigration and exportation agency in the town.[97] By working closely together, the two agencies were able to expedite for their clients legal and banking matters on both sides of the Atlantic.[98]

For his part, Francescopaolo Marinelli became a leading socialite in Buenos Aires. He served on the board of directors of many of the city's Italian and non-Italian social clubs alike.[99] In 1907 he was elected president of the Association of Shipping Agents of Buenos Aires.[100] In 1911 he set sail for Agnone after more than a twenty-year absence from the town. When he landed in Genoa, overcome with emotion, he suffered a stroke and died. An entire issue of the *Eco del Sannio* was devoted to the life and works of the man who had become one of Agnone's leading benefactors.[101]

The statistics on the accomplishments of the agency were indeed impressive. Between 1890 and 1900 it remitted 38,732 money orders to Italy, and between 1901 and 1910 it sent 149,742 others. Between 1901 and 1905 the remittances totaled 5,879,062.51 liras. The agency offered its own savings accounts with deposits approximating seven hundred to eight hundred thousand liras annually. From its inception through 1910 it had sold 23,281 boat tickets from Argentina to Italy and sent 19,928 tickets to Italy for people traveling out to Argentina. The capital worth of the firm stood at four million liras at Marinelli's death.[102]

Enrico Marinelli returned to Argentina with two of his sons in an attempt to consolidate his family's position in the shipping business.[103] The loss of Francescopaolo was critical, however, for in its first year of operation after his death, the agency remitted only 1,257,622.20 liras to Italy.[104] Meanwhile, they were receiving competition from a new agency founded by the Mastronardi brothers of Agnone.

The evidence, then, while sketchy, suggests that the role of the emigration agent entailed far more than simply that of facilitator of economic transactions. The Marinelli agency in Buenos Aires, for example, was a gathering place for many Agnonesi of the city and consequently a source of information about developments in Agnone. It was also a purveyor of imported south Italian foodstuffs. Hence, it dealt in nostalgia and camaraderie as much as in bank drafts. It seems probable that the agency functioned as a safe haven for the newly arrived immigrant as well as a source of housing and employment information.[105] The agents, as well as other successful Agnonese businessmen, were frequently cast in the role of personal benefactors of the town and were called upon to organize the colony to channel the beneficence of other Agnonesi toward their natal community.

Pesos and Dollars

The emigrant press and a locally based network of shipping agents both served as vehicles to strengthen the ties between Agnone and its diaspora. The newspapers informed the emigrants of local needs and projects and regularly lectured them about the quality of loyalty; the agents served as convenient and willing representatives abroad of Agnone's local interests. In 1900 it could be said of the Agnonesi of Buenos Aires: "Agnone, strong and beautiful city of the Sannio, has here in America a flourishing *colony . . . that has given admirable proof of love of birthplace and solidarity*"[106] (emphasis theirs). The ties between emigrants and their birthplace assumed many forms and supposed an enormous feedback to the town of money from the New World.

The late nineteenth and early twentieth centuries witnessed considerable economic development in Agnone, and much of it was underwritten from abroad. As early as 1885 *L'Aquilonia* noted: "What mitigates somewhat our dismay at the by-now-incessant emigration to the Americas [is the fact that] it signifies economic improvement, and families which feel the need for new and more extensive dwellings."[107] By 1899 the number of new dwellings was so large and the magnitude of correspondence arriving from the New World so great that it was necessary to affix street numbers to all houses in the *cittadina* to facilitate mail delivery.[108]

There was, then, a construction boom at the end of the nineteenth century fed by the demand for residential improvements. The returnee emigrant's penchant to upgrade his natal residence or construct a new one has been noted in other areas of south Italy as well.[109] Home improvement offers the twin advantages of immediate betterment of one's standard of living and evident ratification of one's success abroad through conspicuous consumption. In Agnone it is clear that such forces were at work inasmuch as the building boom was not in response to a housing shortage. At the same time that new construction proceeded apace in the town, many emigrants resident in the New World were offering to sell houses in Agnone.[110] It was during this period that the distinction between a populated and bustling "new Agnone" and an abandoned and quiet "old Agnone" began to emerge.[111]

Similar developments were discernible in the commercial sector of local life. From time to time the newspapers announced the openings of new businesses such as a hotel, jewelry stores, restaurants, and bakeries.[112] Some were initiated by local entrepreneurs who were simply responding to the accelerating tempo of business activity; others were fashioned directly out of emigrant savings, such as the "American Bar" established by Pasquale Carosella on his return to Agnone.[113]

There were also attempts to found new small-scale modern industries in the town. In 1909 a local man acquired technology from Manchester, England to manufacture men's and women's socks.[114] Another founded a firm specializing in mosaic work.[115] Two new mills were established in the town.[116] As the *Eco del Sannio* noted in 1906, "It is truly encouraging that the Agnonesi are beginning to employ their own capital in industrial speculations."[117]

By the end of the nineteenth century, Agnone possessed two banks, the Banca Sannitica and the Banco Operaia Cooperativa. It is difficult to determine the extent to which the banks were initially dependent on emigrant remittances for their success. The lists of stockholders of each suggest that the original capitalization derived almost exclusively from residents in Agnone. Also, it is clear that the official Cassa Postale di Risparmio of the Italian postal service garnered the lion's share of emigrant savings sent back to Italy. Despite this fact, in 1901 the Banca Operaia could claim considerable growth during the first fourteen years of its existence. In 1887 savings accounts totaled only 2,793.31 liras, whereas at the conclusion of 1900 they amounted to 146,764.33 liras.[118] Over the same period the number of shareholders in the bank had increased from 218 to 290; the value of their investment, from 12,653 liras to 20,275 liras.[119] The following year the Banca Sannitica reported that after only two years in existence it had 183 shareholders with a combined investment of 54,025 liras and that it closed the year 1901 with 517,143.43 liras in deposits.[120]

Within a decade, emigrant savings were critical sources of funds for the two banks. The Banca Operaia reported 1,598,304.08 liras on deposit at the end of 1910. During that year the bank had processed 1,474,269.41 liras alone in remittances from the emigrants (not all of which remained on deposit, of course). The bank directors, in their annual report, stated: "No one can deny the great advantage that our bank has brought to Agnone's commerce with the emission of remittances on the Credito Italiano, Banca Commerciale, the agency of Cavaliere F. Marinelli in Buenos Aires, the American Express Company, the Nuovo Banco Italiano of Buenos Aires, and others."[121] They hailed this source of funds as unsurpassed in importance by any other.

Meanwhile, during the same year, the Banca Sannitica reported 1,801,757.82 liras on deposit in savings accounts. Its annual report noted that 204,142.46 liras were received from abroad, primarily from the agency of Francescopaolo Marinelli of Buenos Aires. This represented an increase over the previous year of 86,604.80 liras in emigrant remittances.[122]

During the years of their existence, Agnone's two banks played a major role in the town's economy, which in turn would have been impossible were it not for the many millions of liras they received from abroad. In one of its annual reports, the Banca Operaia underscored a major difference between such major financial institutions as the Banco di Napoli and small local ones like the two in Agnone. The former discharged a purely economic function and sought to maximize gains; the latter served a civic function. While the local institutions sought to make a profit for their shareholders, they were primarily interested in benefitting their community.[123]

Clearly, Agnone's two banks discharged this role well. In at least three ways they contributed to the well-being of the town. First, they provided low-interest loans to borrowers at a time when most local enterprises were facing an uncertain economic future. It may be argued that

122

this source of capitalization forestalled (though did not prevent) the ultimate demise of Agnone's artisan industries. Second, the banks provided
funding for civic projects that would have had considerable difficulty in
securing financing from more demanding and critical financial sources.
As a prime example, when a local railroad was capitalized, the Banca
Sannitica purchased 7,500 liras worth of shares, and the Banca Operaia,
2,500 liras.[124] Later, when the railroad was in financial crisis, the
Banca Sannitica purchased 150,000 liras of additional shares, and the
Banca Operaia, 50,000 liras.[125] Third, the banks contributed regularly
and generously to local charities. They also supported public works. For
example, in 1910 the Banca Sannitica gave 500 liras to the town for construction of a badly needed bridge over the Verrino River.[126] In 1913 it
furnished 7,000 liras to finance a study of Agnone's water and sewer
systems.[127]

In many respects the railroad project both symbolized Agnone's late-
nineteenth-century plight and galvanized its civic energies. At issue was
nothing less than inclusion in Italy's transportation infrastructure and,
hence, participation in the emerging modern world. The Agnonesi were
keenly preoccupied with this question. In the context of the new Italy,
manufactured products from the north were now assured ready access to
southern markets. Not only were Agnone's artisans competing with
northern assembly line efficiency; they were handicapped by local high
transportation costs. In the late nineteenth century, Agnone, with all of
its regional administrative importance, was still an isolated mountain
town linked to the outside world only by a series of tortuous mule trails.
Commenting on the state of affairs, one newspaper noted:

> The copper industry in Agnone would be flourishing if our brave
> producers could, with quick and economic means of transport,
> present their goods in the markets of population centers. Rather,
> [they are] constrained to put them up for sale at a vile price and
> with grave self-damage in order to meet the competition.[128]

Specifically, by the 1870s an Isernia-Sulmona rail link was under
consideration, but Agnone was in danger of being bypassed. Unfortunately for the town, it was located at considerable distance from the most
direct trajectory, and the intervening mountainous terrain presented a
costly obstacle. Nevertheless, in 1884 Agnone sent a delegation to the
hearings on the routing to argue for inclusion.[129] That same year the
provincial government voted to back the request that the railroad be

123

placed as near to the town as possible.[130] The following summer, however, it was the decision of the Ministry of Public Works to exclude
Agnone.

The rail link was completed some twelve years later, and the town of
Carovilli was its closest point to Agnone. The Agnonesi reacted with
considerable bitterness. The turn of events was a strong blow to their
civic pride and self-image. Just before the inaugural ceremony, one
Agnone newspaper noted that it was humilating to be an appendage of an
insignificant town like Carovilli,[131] while another commented: "At the
foot of a mountain in a small plain completely surrounded by an age-old
forest . . . the traveler will find a train station, and high over the main
portal written in large letters will be CAROVILLI—AGNONE.
Alas!"[132]

Bruised civic pride was not the only adverse consequence for the
Agnonesi. As the *capoluogo*, or chief town, of a subdistrict, or
mandamento, Agnone was the administrative center for Caccavone,
Castelverrino, Belmonte, and Pietrabbondante. In 1875, however,
Pietrabbondante initiated an attempt to secede from the subdistrict in order to join that of Carovilli. The main reason was the distance and the
extremely poor state of the Agnone-Pietrabbondante road.[133]

This was viewed with alarm in Agnone because it would have a serious
economic impact. The administrative offices of the *capoluogo* were subsidized in part by payments from the communities constituting the
subdistrict. Also, if the inhabitants of Pietrabbondante no longer had to
come to Agnone on official business, local stores would lose a part of
their clientele. Agnone opposed the move. In 1901 Pietrabbondante
was, at its own request, annexed, nonetheless, by Carovilli.[134] Proxim-
ity to the new rail link had been the telling argument, thereby
underscoring the political as well as economic seriousness of Agnone's
earlier defeat on the railroad issue.

The Agnonesi did not accept their fate passively. Rather, the railroad
issue mobilized public support and provided the basis for what was probably the town's greatest civic accomplishment: creation of a locally
owned and operated railroad. Immediately after announcement of the
trajectory of the Isernia-Sulmona line, there was sentiment in the town
for creating a branch rail link.[135] At first the effort centered on getting
the government to fund a Carovilli-Agnone-Vasto branch line.[136] In
1907, when a landslide destroyed a part of the Isernia-Sulmona road
bed, the Agnonesi renewed their demand that the railroad be rerouted

closer to their town.[137] When attempts to get government financial support failed, the Agnonesi embarked on the monumental task of underwriting a branch line themselves. Local newspapers, banks, and political factions suspended their differences to provide unanimous backing of the project.

A key to the success of the endeavor, however, was support from the emigrant diaspora. When the shares were first offered for sale in 1908, the *Eco del Sannio* remarked, "We desire that, as they have always done, our brothers of the Argentine Republic, Brazil, and the United States, demonstrate once again their solidarity with the motherland."[138] By January of 1909 the newspaper could announce with pleasure the first sales in the New World: Nicola Serricchio of Sao Paolo had purchased shares in the amount of 5,000 liras, and Dr. Michele Daniele of Youngstown, Ohio bought 1,000 liras worth.[139] At one point, there was growing concern over the silence from Argentina, but by summer the committee announced that 66,800 liras of shares had been subscribed in that nation. The *Eco del Sannio* reported with satisfaction:

> Agnone has its own sons dispersed throughout the world, where they honor her name in the arts, the sciences, the military, industry, and in the most varied of human activities. Yet this pleasant niche of the Appenines is always the foremost image in their dreams. At the opportune moment, none denies [Agnone] the benefit of his skill and his personal effort; none refuses to withdraw from more favorable investment a small part of his savings to employ it in less profitable yet more noble fashion—the redemption of his own town.[140]

By 1909 the Agnonesi had created a private corporation and secured financial commitments from the town councils of Agnone, Belmonte, Castelverrino, and Pietrabbondante.[141] In 1910 the plan was approved by the government, and there was public jubilation.[142] Construction required more than five years, and the railroad was inaugurated in 1915,[143] on the very day that Italy entered World War I. It remained in service until destroyed during the Second World War.

Saints and Madonnas

The religious devotion of the Agnonesi provided another source of New World funds for the community. This statement must, however, be

125

qualified. I have noted the decline in the fortunes of the church during the first half of the nineteenth century. During the remainder, church-state relations deteriorated further. After the unification of the nation, the new Italian government created the Cassa Ecclesiastica dello Stato as an agency for the administration of all church wealth within its territory. In 1866 the convents and monasteries were abolished by government decree. With the exception of parish churches and seminaries, church edifices became the property of local and provincial government, to be used for public purposes such as schools and hospitals. In 1870 the Italian government conquered the remaining territory of the Vatican State, thereby destroying the temporal power of the papacy. The resulting rift between church and state was to last until the concordat of 1929 negotiated with the Mussolini government.

In communities like Agnone the church-state confrontation lent considerable secular legitimacy to anticlericalism, which quickly translated into a dearth of religious vocations. In 1814 the town had hosted the largest number of clerics in the Molise. Of the total population of 8,278 people, 60 were priests, 8 were friars, and 25 were nuns.[144] This meant that the town had 1 religious for every 89 residents. By the turn of the twentieth century, Agnone's religious population had been more than halved. In 1901 there were 29 priests, 7 nuns, and 3 seminarians out of a total population of 9,827,[145] or a ratio of 1 vocation for each 252 inhabitants. In reporting the ordinations in 1889 of two local youths, an Agnone newspaper commented on the state of affairs: " 'The seed has been lost!' Such is the popular expression for saying that in Agnone for many years down to the present, there hasn't been [even] a dog that embraced the priesthood."[146]

Such sentiments notwithstanding, Agnone's many churches and chapels were replete with effigies of saints and manifestations of the Blessed Virgin Mary. Personal commitment to a particular one was a long-standing feature of local religious practice. The worshipper, in effect, acquired a spiritual protector or protectress. Given the perilous and uncertain nature of their undertaking, it is not surprising that the emigrants were particularly fervent in such devotion. In the words of one emigrant, "Let the pious Madonna della Libera, intercessor of my home, concede to me the consolation and the happiness to return to live in the sweet land where I was born!"[147]

In 1885 the priest Felice Sammartino returned to Agnone after a fifteen-year sojourn in the New World and purchased a golden crown worth three thousand liras for the effigy of the Madonna della Cintura in the Church of San Nicola.[148] In 1888 *L'Aquilonia* exhorted the Agnonesi in the Americas to send funds to replace the vestments of the effigy of Agnone's patron saint San Cristanziano, as they had recently done for the effigy of San Rocco.[149] The same year the Agnonesi in the Americas contributed a part of the expenses of the *festa* of San Rocco in the parish of San Amico,[150] and seventy-five donors in Buenos Aires collected 151.50 pesos for a new pedestal for the effigy of the Madonna della Mercede.[151]

As standard procedure, whenever there was a need to collect funds, a committee was formed in Agnone, which named its overseas representatives. The latter were expected to contact the other Agnonesi and Alto Molisani residing in their respective areas. In Buenos Aires the local representative was frequently Francescopaolo Marinelli.

In 1895 there was a special bicentennial celebration honoring the Madonna dell'Addolorata held in Agnone. Donations totaling 600.00 liras were received from 186 people resident in Buenos Aires.[152] The following year 68 people in Argentina subscribed 553.65 liras for the *festa* of the Madonna della Cintura.[153]

In 1897 the Congrega di Carmine made lavish arrangements to celebrate the six hundredth anniversary of their patroness, Maria Santissima del Carmelo. As the sodality of the peasants and workers, the *congrega* had a large membership, much of which was in the Americas.[154] The celebration, lasting several days, consisted of religious ceremonies, public discourses, athletic events, processions, dances, firework displays, and banquets. Several thousand visitors came to Agnone for the festivities.[155]

The organizing committee later published a full report describing the events and listing all of the donors and the amount of each donation.[156] There were, in all, 1,349 donors who subscribed a total of 5,384.35 liras; 734, or 54 percent of the donors, were resident in the Americas. The emigrants contributed 3,489.35 liras, or 65 percent of the total. The average donation from New World residents was 4.75 liras, whereas that of the 615 Old World residents (602 from Agnone and 13 from Bagnoli del Trigno) was 3.08 liras. The committee appointed fourteen individual fund raisers (*cooperatore*) in Buenos Aires alone. The distribution of the New World contributors is shown in Table 6.1.

By the end of the nineteenth century, the churches and religious sodalities of Agnone were organizing to tap New World funding for their

Table 6.1. *New World Contributions to the Maria Santissima del Carmelo Anniversary Celebration, by Location*

	Number of donors	Liras donated
Argentina		
Buenos Aires	487	2,170.35
Mendoza	38	375.00
Bella Vista	34	65.00
Paraná	25	40.00
Cordoba	22	107.00
Tucumán	22	125.00
Villa Mercedes	15	36.00
United States		
Philadelphia	81	325.00
Youngstown	7	31.00
Colorado	1	15.00

respective annual *feste*. In 1898 the Congrega di Carmine was again sending out solicitation forms to its representatives in Argentina.[157] That same year sixty-five people in Pueblo, Colorado sent 366 liras for the *festa* of the Madonna dei Miracoli in the parish of San Antonio;[158] twenty-seven people in Argentina sent 105 liras, and fifty-nine donors in the United Sates sent 166 liras for the *festa* of the Madonna della Mercede;[159] and fifty-four people in Pueblo, Colorado gave 260 liras for the *festa* of San Rocco.[160]

During the following few years, efforts were intensified to raise money both for *feste* and for special church projects. In 1899, 144 people in New York; 15 in Youngstown, Ohio; and 1 in Mendoza, Argentina donated 732.25 liras to the church of the Santissima Trinità for purchase of a new bell.[161] In 1901 the *Eco del Sannio* reported that an artist was gilding the church of San Biase and that two donors in Argentina and four in New York has thus far made contributions. The paper added, "We exhort our other devoted cocitizens resident in America to send their offering for such a worthy work."[162] In 1903 the Agnonesi of Pueblo sent more than 100,000 liras to the church of San Antonio for the purchase of a statue of the Madonna dei Miracoli.[163] The following year there was a new drive to purchase a silver crown for the effigy.[164] At the same time, there was a fund-raising effort to restore an altar in the church of San Nicola.[165]

By the first decade of the twentieth century, the amounts of money sent and the numbers of *feste* supported were both increasing markedly. In 1905 alone, 134 people in Youngstown contributed to the *feste* of the Madonna della Libera;[166] 55 people in Springfield, Massachusetts donated 216 liras for the *festa* of Santa M^a degli Angioli in Fontesambuco;[167] 15 persons in Hubbard, Ohio donated 60 liras for the *festa* of the Madonna della Mercede;[168] 46 people in Youngstown and 8 persons in Canada donated 255 liras for the *festa* of Rosario;[169] 65 donors in Denver, Colorado,[170] 87 from Pueblo, 61 from Youngstown, 35 from Hubbard, 74 from Fernie, British Columbia, and 23 from Rodeo de la Cruz, Argentina donated a total of 1,074 liras for the *festa* of San Rocco;[171] and 39 people in Chicago, 12 in Youngstown, and 2 in Argentina made donations for the *festa* of Carmine.[172]

One other measure of the rapid increase in donations is seen in the fact that, in 1904, 36 residents of Springfield donated 136 liras for the *festa* of Santa Maria degli Angioli;[173] the following year 55 Springfield residents donated a total of 216 liras for the same event;[174] and in 1909, 205 people in the Massachusetts community donated 504 liras.[175]

Several comments are in order. First, the pattern of religious donatons reflects further refinement in the organization of chain migration from Agnone. To a large extent it may be said that the colony of Pueblo was the enterprise of the parishoners of San Antonio; the colony of Springfield, the overseas extension of the hamlet of Fontesambuco; and the colony of Youngstown, the work of the hamlet of Villacanale.

Second, from the pattern of such donations, it is possible to ascertain that during the first decade of the twentieth century, Agnone's North American colonies were proliferating. In 1907, 14 donors from Philadelphia contributed to one *festa*.[176] That same year, contributions for the *festa* of the Madonna della Libera came from 89 donors in Montreal, Canada.[177] In 1910, donors for the *festa* of San Rocco included 73 people from South Chicago and 32 from Canton, Ohio.[178] And in 1913 donations for various *feste* were received from 60 people in Jersey City, New Jersey; 44 in Niagara Falls, New York; 21 from Salida, Colorado; 47 from Tooele, Utah; 18 from Pocatello, Idaho; and 19 from Trail, British Columbia.[179]

Third, it is clear that by this time the New World colonies were underwriting the major portion of Agnone's ceremonial life. In 1907, 426.00 liras of the 579.55 liras expended for the *festa* of the Madonna dei Miracoli, or almost three-fourths of the total, came from abroad.[180] This did not simply mean shifting the burden of financing existing festivals at their traditional levels onto the emigrants; rather, the New World input itself stimulated rapid elaboration and proliferation of Agnone's ceremonial life. Festivals that were formerly low key and restricted to a single parish became ostentatious and community-wide. In 1903, for example, the Confraternità of Maria Santissima Addolorata, first founded in 1691 but inactive for many years, was reconstituted with an annual *festa*.[181]

Masciotta, in commenting on this phenomenon, expresses doubt that the donors were moved by religious devotion. Rather, he attributes their "generosity" to a desire for personal recognition: "Vanity and nothing else inspires them, knowing that on the festive occasion their name will be 'shouted' in church by the priest, with the indication of the amount sent and its precise purpose, that is, for music, for the fireworks, for the procession of the saint's statue and so forth."[182]

The organizers pitted the various New World colonies against each other as a point of honor, as Agnone's parishes, parish priests, and religious sodalities all tried to outdo one another. In 1905 the organizers of one *festa* claimed:

> The Festa della Libera, which for just a few years had been celebrated with outward pomp, has now acquired a special importance, such that it has almost surpassed the other truly important *festa*, that of Carmine. This is due to the strong support of the emigrants in America and to the activities of a willing and able committee.[183]

In 1912 this *festa* alone cost 2,324.35 liras, of which 1,495.50 liras were collected in the New World (primarily in Argentina).[184] Only 339.85 liras were subscribed in Agnone proper. Each member of the organizing committee had to pay 16.80 liras to cover a deficit. The next year no one in Agnone would serve, so the entire committee was appointed in the Americas.[185]

At the same time, there was a growing awareness that costly ceremonialism was getting out of hand, and some dissenting voices were heard. In 1906 the *Eco del Sannio* noted:

> The officials of our several *feste* could in fact channel a part of the money that comes from the Americas into any work of public utility, instead of wasting it to entertain people. We wish to persuade

our distinguished cocitizens who are in the Americas of the practicality of such a use. The saints are not honored only with rockets, but with any work that produces well-being.[186]

Public Works and Charities

The ostentatiousness of the religious *feste* was self-evident, and their expense chagrined the more practically minded; it is not really accurate, however, to suggest that all or even most of the charity from abroad was earmarked for devotional purposes. Agnone's diaspora actually initiated some public projects for the town and lent substantial support when asked to contribute to others.

The emigrants were particularly amenable to supporting projects that stimulated campanilistic public pride. In 1895 the Circolo Sannitico of Buenos Aires donated a gilded banner to the town to commemorate the four hundredth anniversary of the discovery of America.[187] It was to be used in Agnone's public ceremonials and serve as a visible link between the town and its Argentine colony. The following year 381.50 liras were raised from 101 donors in Argentina to purchase flags for all of Agnone's elementary schools.[188]

Both collectively and individually the emigrants provided charitable donations for the afflicted and underprivileged. In 1884 the Circolo Sannitico collected funds to relieve the victims of cholera in south Italy.[189] The next year thirty-two people in Buenos Aires sent a medal and diploma to Dr. Tirone of Agnone in recognition of his bravery and devotion during the epidemic.[190] In 1895 the Circolo Sannitico collected 403 liras from seventy-eight donors for distribution to the poor of Agnone.[191] In 1910 it was reported that "Signore Adolfo Apollonio this year, as in the past, has sent from Buenos Aires to his uncle Cav. A. Savastano the sum of 100 liras to be distributed personally to the truly poor of the commune, in memory of his father Ruggiero Apollonio."[192] Two brothers in Argentina sent 30 liras to the newspaper *Eco del Sannio* for the purchase of school supplies for the three poorest students in each of Agnone's five rural schools.[193] In 1900, when Giovanni Ionata was reelected mayor of Agnone, a committee was formed in Corrales, Argentina, which sent him congratulations, a plaque commemorating his victory, and funds to be distributed to Agnone's poor.[194]

There were two major charitable undertakings that were to preoccupy

131

the Agnonesi throughout the late nineteenth and early twentieth centuries: the attempts to found the Asilo d'Infanzia for impoverished and orphaned children and a hospital for the Alto Molise. Both projects struck a responsive chord among the emigrants.

From the outset, it was recognized that, for the fund-raising effort for the orphanage to be a success, an appeal would have to be made to the New World Agnonesi. In 1885 *L'Aquilonia* announced: "We predict that outsiders and citizens alike, and especially persons in America, will come forth with generous donations."[195] During the year 12,000 liras were raised, although there is no record of what proportion came from the New World. In 1887 fourteen donors in Buenos Aires sent 162.25 liras to the orphanage fund,[196] and in 1880 an additional 85.00 liras were collected in that city.[197]

In the spring of 1904 a committee was appointed in Agnone to raise funds for the proposed new institution. A similar committee was named in North America and another in Buenos Aires.[198] The initial response from the Americas was not good. For the next several months only isolated and rather modest amounts came in from the emigrants. It was not until October of 1905 that thirty-two donors from Youngstown sent donations.[199] At about the same time Giuseppe Marinelli, a jeweler of Buenos Aires, personally gave 440.00 liras and raised among his clients a total of 1,072.50 liras. It was decided to display his photograph in the new building.[200]

In March of 1906 the *Eco del Sannio* noted: "With regards to our honorable citizens in America, who are always the first to encourage the good institutions of our town, with the exception of a few well intentioned persons, they have not yet shown signs of life, whereas their aid would complete this work that will honor Agnone."[201] In October, a new appeal went out to the New World Agnonesi.[202] The following month Francescopaolo Marinelli of Buenos aires organized a benefit ball held on board a ship anchored in the city's port. The effort raised six thousand liras, and by the end of 1906 Agnone's Argentine colonies had raised a total of ten thousand liras.[203]

In successive years New World donors continued to respond to the needs of the orphanage. In 1907 Giuseppe Marinelli of Buenos Aires sent one hundred liras to sponsor a party for the children.[204] In 1908 Tommaso Marinelli of Brazil sent five hundred liras.[205] In 1911 eight persons in Argentina gave fifty-two hundred liras to the project,[206] and the following year two persons sent an additional eight hundred liras.[207]

The other major civic undertaking of the period was the attempt to found a hospital in the town. Unlike the successful Asilo d'Infanzia, this effort failed, but the process also illustrates the interaction between Agnone and its diaspora. In 1878 the town council considered a proposal to establish a hospital in the vacant convent of San Berardino.[208] By the middle of the next decade, the effort was beginning to coalesce in the New World. In 1885 many Alto Molisani residents in Buenos Aires met to form a fund-raising committee for it.[209] Within a few months, a large number of people had agreed to pledge two-hundred liras each over a forty-month period. They requested that the town council make the convent available for the site.[210] In 1889 the Argentine committee had fifteen-hundred liras on deposit.[211]

The following year one of Agnone's wealthiest citizens, Feliceandrea Sabelli, died and left two hundred thousand liras for the hospital, raising false hopes.[212] The will was contested by his other heirs, initiating protracted litigation.[213] The hospital project was shelved for the time being.

Meanwhile, there was another development as Pasquale Mario, an extraordinary person, entered the scene. Mario was born in Agnone in 1844 into an impoverished family. A street urchin, he survived by traveling about to nearby towns to sell string, buttons, needles, and thread.[214] He impressed the powerful Falconi family of Capracotta, which offered him a chance to study mechanics. Later he went to Switzerland, where, after several years, he became the owner of a major watch factory in Neuchâtel.[215] He ranged far afield, selling his products, even organizing annual safaris to the African interior to trade his watches for native goods, which he then sold in Europe. He owned his own yacht, which he used to travel extensively throughout the Mediterranean.[216]

During his most active years, Mario demonstrated little interest in Agnone and made the pages of the local press only infrequently. In 1884 *L'Aquilonia* carried a brief announcement that, as president of the Società Italiana of Neuchâtel, Mario was sending cholera relief funds to Naples and its surroundings.[217] In 1897 the *Eco del Sannio* announced that Mario had returned to Agnone for a visit after a thirteen-year absence.[218] Thus began an intense and relatively brief love affair between Mario and the town. He purchased a home in Agnone, which he used almost every summer.[219] He became a benefactor of the Asilo d'Infanzia. In 1903 the *Eco del Sannio* observed: "Our distinguished cocitizen

Cavaliere Pasquale Mario, who brings such honor to our town, and who carries out his uncommon activities in distant regions, returns from Egypt and the Sudan, where he contracted a bad case of pneumonia. For several days he is with us to breathe his native air."[220] On his many trips, Mario began to collect stuffed examples of African fauna, which he then donated to Agnone's technical school for student study.[221]

Meanwhile, the halting effort to fund a hospital in Agnone was continuing in Buenos Aires. In 1904, fifty-five donors raised 227.25 liras for the project.[222] In November of 1906 Mario stunned the town by announcing that, if the council would concede the use of the ex-convent of the Capuchins, he would personally finance the project.[223] The council accepted but then did a hasty about-face. While in Switzerland Mario had become a fervent Protestant, and the local Catholic clergy were aghast at the prospect of a consecrated Catholic facility falling into his hands.[224] A short time later an incensed Mario placed 171,931 liras on deposit as a show of good faith and left for Africa on business.[225]

The following October he withdrew his offer, denouncing the council's actions.[226] The shocked council restored its original offer of the convent, but Mario was too angered to respond. Four years later he gave an emotional and bitter address to the Agnonesi in which he lamented that

> he had lived in Naples, surviving on bread and fruit alone, and for 50 years he had worked 18 hours a day and saved every cent he earned, always having in his soul the ideal of donating to the poor of his town a place to alleviate their sufferings, a place where they could restore their health, or die in peace.[227]

In later years Mario declined to visit his natal Agnone, purchasing instead a house in Palermo. Upon his death, most of his wealth went to that city.[228]

Understandably, the Mario debacle disillusioned many of the emigrants who had struggled to see a hospital established in Agnone. The New World efforts faltered.

The Emigrants' Impact

During the period from 1880 to World War I, emigrant remittances in their many forms provided much of the life blood of Agnone. The importance of this input is better appreciated when one considers that this was the period of the town's greatest cultural fluorescence, but one that coincided with a discernible, impending crisis in local, traditional economic activities. Though few of the emigrants were among the actual architects of Agnone's triumphs, there is little doubt that the achievements of the "Athens of the Sannio" period were in large measure capitalized by the diaspora.

7

The Consequences of Emigration, 1870–1914

Students of Italian migration are prone to divide the phenomenon into the old and the new. The latter refers to the massive post–World War II internal migration within the nation as well as to departures to other European countries, and I treat it in Chapter 9. The old migration, primarily transatlantic, antedates World War I, and its consequences constitute the subject of this chapter.

I have already presented some of the effects of overseas emigration from the standpoints of both the individual and the collectivity. I have noted that the human costs for many were high, and for some, intolerable. The emigrant risked his health, his personal security, and even his sense of purpose. The dangers were, of course, ameliorated somewhat as emigrants moved along established avenues, themselves becoming links in the town's chain migration as well as members of a colony in Agnone's far-flung diaspora. The majority of the emigrants managed only modest success in the New World, though a few experienced socioeconomic mobility well beyond anything to which they might have aspired had they remained in Agnone. Such persons became the role models, tantamount to winners of a lottery, that fueled the imaginations of other potential candidates for emigration.

On balance, one must assume that the emigrants perceived their decision to leave Agnone as a proper one, because in large measure it was

136

a matter of personal choice. While it may be true, as Bell has argued for other Italian communties faced with the same options,[1] that most Agnonesi eschewed the emigration alternative and stayed home, the sheer numbers of those who left (running well into the thousands) and the length of time over which they continued to do so (more than a century at this writing) underscores the importance of emigration and its consequences as the major issue in Agnone affairs since the late nineteenth century. If, as I have argued, the primary stimuli of the movement were poverty and social class deprivation, emigration once initiated could scarcely help but have a mighty impact on the very causes of its genesis.

Clearly, in the initial phases, the departures were regarded benignly by Agnone's establishment—the *galantuomini*—as a useful escape valve for the malcontent. Emigration was preferable to the alternative of brigandage. Once the movement developed momentum, there were, to be sure, those who raised the specter of economic and social chaos; but others were equally prone to view the emigrant diaspora as a target of opportunity. Accustomed to shaping the destinies of the peasants and workers, they believed that, with some effort, the loyalties of the mainly lower-class emigrants could be retained and orchestrated to the benefit of the town and, more to the point, its existing power structure. To the extent that emigration could be viewed as a local crisis, manipulation of the emigrant diaspora was regarded as the external solution. To appreciate the degree to which this approach proved simplistic and doomed to failure, one must consider the relevant developments in both Italy and Agnone between 1870 and 1914, or the end of the phase of the "old" emigration.

The Political and Social Climate

In the main, Italy's liberals heralded Garibaldi's victory. From their viewpoint the new national constitutional monarchy, with limited political enfranchisement, was preferable to either a broad-based democracy or the former Bourbon absolutism. There was, however, to be an immediate challenge to the new order. During the mid-nineteenth century, international socialism emerged as a viable force and the new political radicalism. Liberals were thereby cast in the conservative role, and in the first national parliament the real confrontation developed between them and the socialists.

Against this backdrop of national affairs, Agnone remained staunchly liberal. Ippolito Amicarelli, the first delegate to the national parliament from the electoral district of Agnone, possessed unequivocal liberal credentials. In terms of the political equation of the day, Agnone could be characterized as the most right-wing town in the Molise.[2] During the late nineteenth and early twentieth centuries, every deputy elected to Parliament from the area was of the right. This is all the more remarkable given that, in 1874, of the successful candidates from the seven electoral districts of the Molise, all but Agnone's were adherents of the left or center-left.[3] Under the system of limited political suffrage dictated by literacy and wealth, there were only 855 eligible voters that year in the nineteen communities in Agnone's electoral district. Of the 617 votes cast, the liberal candidate received 602.[4]

Agnone's liberal power establishment was not, however, united. Rather, it split into two factions that contested control of municipal affairs. To understand the nature of the division, it is first necessary to examine certain ramifications of the church-state confrontation in nineteenth-century Italy. Before the advent of liberalism, most priests were drawn from the ranks of the well-to-do. I have noted that many remained politically conservative and staunch supporters of the Bourbons. Once the *galantuomini* emerged as a dominant economic and political force, however, many of the younger generation of priests were recruited from their ranks and reflected their views. In Chapter 4, I noted the pedagogical activities of an extraordinary group of six young Agnonesi liberal intellectuals, five of whom were priests.

Garibaldi's triumph brought the church-state confrontation in Italy to a head and created an extreme crisis of conscience for the nation's liberal clerics. In 1862 nine thousand Italian priests petitioned Pope Pius IX, urging him not to break relations with the new government. No fewer than forty-four priests in Agnone signed the document.[5] When the effort failed, some of the signatories were so incensed that they renounced their vows. The Agnonesi Baldassare La Banca (who had worked in south Italy as an advance agent for Garibaldi's forces) and Giuseppe Nicola D'Agnillo both left the priesthood over the issue.[6]

Of equal interest, however, were the postures of those who opted to remain representatives of God while dedicating their daily efforts to the affairs of men. Like their more recent socially aware counterparts in the post-Pope John XXIII era of Catholicism, they found a mandate for social activism in the scriptures.[7] In Agnone, this was so much the case that, in the aftermath of Garibaldi's triumph, the liberal priests co-opted the critical leadership posts. Ipollito Amicarelli became the district's first elected deputy to the Italian Parliament,[8] and Giuseppe Tamburri became Agnone's mayor. Amicarelli was thirty-eight years of age, and Tamburri was only thirty-two. Meanwhile, the liberal priest Luigi Pannunzio, thirty years of age, founded a new, major, private boarding school in the town that was to dominate the educational scene for years to come.[9]

Arrayed against Mayor Tamburri was the older *galantuomo* businessman Francesco Saverio Sabelli and his followers. Tamburri held office from the unification until his untimely death in 1874. For the next thirty-three years, the mayor of Agnone was either Sabelli (1874–1881, 1892–1899) or Tamburri's philosophical successor, Giovanni Ionata (1882–1892, 1899–1907).

Throughout the late nineteenth century, then, the socialists were unable to mount a serious political challenge in Agnone. Rather, Agnone's civic affairs were dominated by the liberals, who were themselves divided into one faction of laissez-faire businessmen and landowners and another that, while adherents of the principles of free enterprise, manifested a strong social conscience. There are indications that the schism also occurred in part along gerontocratic lines, with the ranks of the business-oriented being more middle-aged, whereas those of the social activists reflected youthful and religious idealism.

The social activism of the Tamburri faction should in no way be confused, however, with a democratic sharing of wealth and power. Rather, their approach was entirely paternalistic. In a discourse to the town council in 1867, Tamburri called for creation of a technical school for the artisans as well as rural schooling for the *contadini* as a means of securing "the redemption of the plebes, equality of all before the law, and the foundation of free institutions."[10] At the same time, he believed that it was up to the *galantuomini* to show the way inasmuch as "the common people do not see, nor are they able to perceive, the future . . . we who have the obligation to improve them, do not however have to listen to them nor fear them. . . ."[11] The common people have the obligation to obey, just as we are obliged to instruct and benefit them."[12]

Progress depended on maintenance of class status quo. In 1882 the liberal priest Ascenso Marinelli authored a book entitled *Good Example in One's Town (Il buon esempio nel proprio paese)*, which consists of moral platitudes concerning the proper conduct of the various social classes. In discussing the *galantuomini* (referred to as *gentiluomini*), he notes:

> In a well-formed society, among the individuals comprising it, there will never lack all of those gradations and differences that we observe between poor and rich, plebe and nobleman, unlettered and educated, peasant and merchant. . . . If it were not so, the great social machine would not operate; and progress, that perfection of the individual and of mankind in general, would never transpire. Therefore, if one concludes that all of the great dissimilarity that we see in our midst is nothing more than the natural result of the human condition, it is also a providential state of affairs.[13]

Marinelli further believed that the lower classes should be resigned and impervious to appeals for radical social changes. In referring to manual laborers he states:

> Since they are the life and the strength of each nation, and the martyrs of its efforts, they must always be disposed to self-denial and self-sacrifice. Consequently, when a certain good example of flexibility and [subordination of] self-gratification is called for, the workers should give it, particularly in this day and age in which there is such abuse of socialist, internationalist, and nihilist doctrines.[14]

Baldassare La Banca penned a work dedicated to Agnone and entitled *My Testament* (*Il mio testamento*). In it he comments:

> At first there existed the proverb: the big fish eats the little fish. Now it is necessary to add that the little fish, through their greater numbers, eat the big fish. In medicine it is microbism, in society it is proletarianism that confirm the second proverb.[15]
>
> Being obligated to live under despotism, the despotism of the princes is preferable to that of the people, considering that the former gives rise to lesser injustices.[16]

It is against this philosophical backdrop that one can better appreciate the liberals' search for what might be labeled an "internal solution" to the crisis of emigration: the attempts to improve educational opportunity and to form mutual-assistance voluntary associations to alleviate the plight of the lower classes.

Mayor Tamburri's call in 1867 for both a technical and an agricultural school in the town went unheeded. Sabelli and his allies on the town council rejected the projects as being too costly.[17] Tamburri's proposals antedated the surge of emigrants from the town and were therefore largely devoid of obvious practicality. By the mid-1870s, however, the climate was more propitious, and a technical school actually functioned for three years before foundering.[18]

In 1885 Florindo Marinelli opened a new technical school in the town. Marinelli, a priest, had emigrated to America in 1873 and returned to Agnone some eight years later. Born in 1834, he was somewht younger than the Tamburri crowd but clearly their spiritual protégé. As a returned emigrant Marinelli perceived the necessity of halting the flow of personnel from Agnone's declining artisan trades.[19] The school began modestly, enrolling only 24 students in 1886.[20] By 1895, however, it was touted as one of the best of its kind in Italy and had become a source of civic pride.[21] That year, it enrolled 116 students.[22] By 1904 the institution had graduated a total of 1,195 students since its inception.[23]

Night schools for adult education were also popular. By 1883 such an institution was functioning in the town,[24] with an enrollment of 230 students.[25] Instruction was provided by teachers from the regular schools. The student body was comprised of working-class adolescents and adults. When the exams were given, it could be stated that "the results surpassed all expectations because all of those registered . . . gave evidence of modest worth in reading, writing, counting, etc."[26]

One of the instructors summed up the change in the attitude that schooling was the privilege of the elite by noting that

> if primary educational instruction, which is the basis of progress in modern times, is to strengthen the base of the grand social pyramid, it is abundantly clear that it is necessary and indispensable not only for those who dedicate themselves to professional studies, but also for the honest and hardworking laborer.[27]

In 1888 another night school for illiterates was inaugurated.[28] In 1885[29] and again in 1888, there were attempts to open a school to teach design to carpenters and stonemasons.[30] In 1908 two trade schools were functioning in the town. The Scuola di Disegno Applicato alle Arti was sponsored by the municipality and had fifty students in attendance.[31] The private Scuola Serale di Disegno Applicato alle Industrie enrolled

141

thirty-five students, and instruction was divided into woodworking, stonecutting, and metalworking.[32]

During the period 1877 to 1894, three private boarding schools were founded in the town. In 1877 Claudiano Giaccio founded a boys' school,[33] and by 1884 Cristina Serafini was operating a girls' boarding school (Convitto Serafini) that offered four classes at the secondary school level.[34] In 1881 Francesco Bonanni established the Convitto Vittorino da Feltre, which, by 1884, had 25 students.[35] In the ensuing decade the number of boarding students more than tripled to 80,[36] and by 1905 it had grown to 120 pupils.[37] The success of the baording schools was predicated in part on the fact that some parents in Agnone's diaspora began to send their children to the town to be educated.

The local educational base was broadened in other ways as well. By the turn of the century, there was a dramatic rise in student enrollment in the public elementary school. In 1899–1900 there were 436 pupils,[38] of whom a majority, or 222, were girls. Three years later there were almost 600 students in attendance.[39]

Not surprisingly, it was the peasants who received the least attention and benefit. In schooling, as in other contexts of Agnone society, peasants continued to be treated (or rather ignored) as if they were practically a lower form of life. Such attitudes notwithstanding, there were efforts made to improve agriculture through education, some of them aimed directly at the peasantry. By 1877 the two rural hamlets, Fontesambuco and Villacanale, had six grades of elementary schooling.[40] The quality was questionable, however, for in that year they closed for summer vacation without even bothering to give examinations.[41] A concerted effort to provide schooling to the *contadini* was not initiated until 1908, when the government founded schools in two rural districts of the municipality.[42]

It is, of course, impossible to determine the exact impact of schooling on emigration. One could speculate that the liberal attempt to retain potential emigrants by better preparing them to earn a living in the town's traditional enterprises simply backfired by broadening the student's horizons. What is certain is that the expansion of the town's eductional system coincided in time with the period of massive emigration. Whether it stemmed the tide or stimulated it must remain a moot point.

Formation of voluntary associations provided another possible means of deterring excessive emigration from the town. In 1868 it was again a young liberal priest, Francesco Iannicelli, who took the initiative and started the Società Operaia "Principe Umberto," or Worker's Society "Prince Umberto."[43] The purposes of the organization were to support Mayor Tamburri's political career, found a public butcher shop, and establish a regular municipal musical concert for the populace. Ippolito Amicarelli, absent in Naples, where he was headmaster of a private school, was made an honorary member. He hailed the new organization as a "school of moral and civil education and harbinger of a considerably better future in my birthplace."[44] In the words of Iannicelli, its founder, the organization would "combat and destroy the usuries of our Town, break those links which tie the debtor to the creditor, release the worker from the slavery of the master, rendering him free in speech and the vote."[45]

The original 160 members subscribed four-thousand liras. In 1869 the society opened the butcher shop, which lost a considerable amount of money. The following year Iannicelli emigrated to America, and the society became inactive. According to one observer, the society failed because of "the lengthy absence of Secretary Iannicelli, the premature death of the incomparable Mayor Tamburri, the emigration to America of many members, moroseness, and other causes."[46] In 1880, after his second sojourn in the New World, Iannicelli returned to Agnone and reorganized the society with 200 members.[47] In 1885 there was dissension in the membership and 140 members, including Iannicelli, seceded and founded their own group called the Mutuo Soccorso, or Mutual Aid.[48]

By this time the organizations had acquired banking characteristics, as their main function was to invest the funds advanced by the shareholders; but there was clearly an associational aspect as well. The Società Operaia, for example, held an occasional festival and selected a banner.[49] The group was represented at the funeral of a deceased member,[50] and on the last Monday of Carnival, the entire membership paid a visit to the cemetery to pray for their dead.[51] There was also a charitable mutual-aid aspect. In 1884 the original Workers' Society had a balance of 9,096.45 liras, which produced interest of 362.65 liras. Their annual report notes that the latter amount "will remain in the reserve fund for the exclusive benefit of indigent workers."[52]

It is difficult to determine the exact makeup of the Workers' Society, but its inspiration clearly came from the clique of socially minded liberal priests arrayed against the more conservative Sabelli faction. While the rank and file were workers employed in artisan workshops, many of the leaders were drawn from prominent liberal families. Paternalism was evident, if not a clear-cut patron–client arrangement.

Briggs argues that such workers' societies reflected an organizational capacity among the lower-class candidates for emigration, allowing them to transfer a certain associative spirit to their New World destinations.[53] Certainly the societies have provided a model, but unless the situation in Agnone was unique, the depiction of the workers as architects of their own destinies is considerably overdrawn.[54] That the workers' societies in Agnone were less a class phenomenon and more the creation of political factionalism is apparent in their subsequent evolution. The schism between the Società Operaia and the Mutuo Soccorso occurred along factional lines within the liberal ruling elite.

In 1886 the Workers' Society was reconstituted into a bank known as the Banca Cooperativa Popolare.[55] The new institution had 215 shareholders in 1887 and a total of 295 by 1894.[56] The driving force in the Banca Cooperativa Popolare was Giovanni Ionata, who, at the same time, was serving as mayor. The Mutuo Soccorso foundered, and in 1895 there was an abortive attempt by Ionata's political opponents to establish a new Banca Popolare Agnonese.[57] In 1899 they met with greater success in founding the Banca Sannitica.[58] The director of the new institution was a staunch Sabelli man.

Class Confrontation

Throughout the late nineteenth century, then, it was possible to foster the illusion that the liberal order could be perpetuated indefinitely. The *galantuomini* maintained a tight grip on the reins of local government; emigration served as an escape valve for lower class discontent; and the elite were even partially successful at manipulating the town's emigrant diaspora for their own purposes.

A perusal of the town records during the period suggests that social mobility in Agnone remained minimal. When registering births, deaths, and marriages, the record keepers continued to assign sons to their fathers' occupational categories. This procedure, however, masks a social development of considerable importance: the fact that while people found it difficult to change social categories, the categories themselves were undergoing redefinition. Specifically, peasants and manual laborers as a whole were experiencing upward mobility at a time when the artisan trades were disintegrating and the social prestige of the *galantuomini* was waning. Feedback of men, money, and ideas from transatlantic emigration was the prime factor in this realignment.

A particularly acute arena of class confrontation was local agriculture. Unlike some communities of the province where the land was concentrated in the hands of a few, in Agnone there was a substantial populace of landed *galantuomini*, and land was the favored investment of the successful artisan. Consequently, the nonagriculturalists of Agnone depended on the peasantry in a variety of ways. Not only did the *contadini* provide a clientele for professional services and artisan wares; they were the essential day laborers and sharecroppers on the fields owned by others.

At the same time, I have noted the nearly total exclusion of the *contadini* from the political process and the expanding educational system. Technical training and the cooperative movement were aimed almost exclusively at the artisans and manual laborers of the *cittadina*. The failure to draw the *contadini* into the "internal solution" for Agnone's emigration crisis doomed the effort to failure.

As early as 1885 *L'Aquilonia* was alarmed about the consequences of emigration for Agnone's agriculture. It predicted, "within a few years we will be left with fields uncultivated for lack of laborers."[59] The following year it stated:

The grape harvest . . . is about finished and is considerably inferior to that of the past year. Which is to say that for the last several years it goes from bad to worse. And meanwhile the direct taxes are paid, emigration grows, and our vineyards will end up remaining uncultivated, abandoned, unless the large proprietors induce Mantovan workers[60] to come . . . in the final analysis we will all have to go to work the vines.[61]

By 1895 there was the added problem that the dreaded disease phyloxia was decimating local vineyards.[62] By 1900 it could be said:

Our small proprietors (in Agnone there do not exist large landowners) find themselves between the hammer and the anvil, that is, between the extremely costly and at times absolutely scarce work force . . . the increased taxes and fiscal persecutions, the shameful usury of tithes and rents to be paid to moral and ecclesiastical entities . . . and on the other hand the scarce or null harvests. The good Agnonese landowner has not yet lost courage, and with heroic energy he has always continued to expose to risk his personal earnings and whatever few savings he has otherwise accumulated . . . and, to speak the truth, if the Agnonese proprietor was not so patriotic that, rather than ask just once for relief or a tax rebate, he emigrates to the most distant regions to earn money to send back here to pay taxes, the vast *agro* of Agnone would by now have reverted as a whole to the State.[63]

In 1901 there was an abortive attempt to import laborers. When, during a one-week period in April, more than one hundred of Agnone's workers emigrated, fifty-seven alarmed landowners pleaded with the authorities to create local incentives that would attract a minimum of fifty *contadini* to the town.[64] In 1902, as Gamberale notes:

Certainly the remittances of money have been and continue to be many, certainly Agnone's cash flow is maintained from this source . . . but the labor of our emigrants in Argentina, in Brazil, and in the United States constitutes an enormous mass of effort subtracted from our fields, and this enormous loss of labor translates into an enormous diminution in the harvests, which supposes an enormous loss of capital.[65]

In 1905 the *Eco del Sannio* noted bitterly:

Here the fields were prolific, and now they have become sterile; here industries flourished, and now they have almost disappeared completely; arts and letters also flourished, but no longer . . . if emigration has in a certain fashion saved us from misery, it cannot restore to us our lost advantages because many fields remain abandoned and others are cultivated badly; the small local industries can no longer sustain the competition of those of the large centers; and our workers, when they return from America with some savings, go in search of a more remunerative occupation and apply themselves to small-scale commerce.[66]

By the spring of 1907, however, it is clear that the remaining *contadini* were acting in concert as a confrontation was developing between the landowners and agricultural laborers. The *Eco del Sannio* editorialized:

Due to continuous emigration and to the severity of the last winter, it has not been possible to complete the work in the fields of this commune, the pruning of the olives and of other plants, and the hoeing of the vineyards.

How will it be possible to do the next chores of spraying the vines, not to mention the other hoeings and related tasks? The local *contadini*, organized among themselves, have redoubled the price of a day's labor with grave damage to the landlords. It is necessary that the owners unite as well in a league to resist the pretentions of the *contadini*. . . .

The proprietors would be well advised to see if we can attract from other towns as many laborers as are needed to attend to the aforementioned tasks, as these workers would be certain to find immediate employment here—and not of short duration.[67]

This prompted an immediate reply from a group of former *contadini* resident in Philadelphia. The following month they published a leaflet entitled "Voices from across the Ocean" and directed "To Our Exploiters" ("*Ai nostri sfruttatori*"). The open letter warned that such a land-owners' union would be met with increased militancy. The confrontational climate was clearly underscored in the closing statement:

We are, in society and in life, disposed to demolish this human scaffold which is full of hypocrisies and of intrinsic evils. This is our scope and our aim, and be reassured oh rubicund patrons and despicable clergymen, that we will never yield to your coalition, because the Proletariat is the factor that disposes of greatest forces, from production to [formulation] of tenacious propositions, and in the will to regain that which was usurped from it by the more powerful.[68]

In 1908 the mayor of Agnone, fearing grave shortages, prohibited the export of foodstuffs from the town.[69] At the same time, the weakened position of the landowners was being acknowledged publicly in the local press: "What will become of south Italy? Whoever has lived in these parts has been able to observe that . . . even the proprietors and those who are here called *galantuomini* (oh! irony of the word) have abandoned their houses and their possessions [in order to emigrate]."[70]

As labor became both scarer and dearer, and field abandonment more common, Agnone's agriculture underwent certain adjustments. One strategy of the landowner was to convert to less labor-intensive forms of cropping, such as animal husbandry and olive growing. In 1898 the *Eco del Sannio* reported that the livestock numbers of Agnone (and particularly those of cows) were increasing rapidly and becoming crucial to the economy.[71] In 1912 Ulisse Tirone, a powerful *galantuomo*, established a modern six-cow dairy with a bottling plant.[72] At the same time, proprietors were planting olive trees in grainfields and vineyards. The trees required relatively little labor compared to the wheat and grapes. In 1911 it was reported:

> From a well-made calculation it has been determined that in the *agro* of Agnone nearly 10,000 *tomoli* of olives were harvested, which have produced 600 quintals of oil.
>
> This production is more than satisfactory and is possibly greater than that of the grapes.[73]

The other strategy of the *galantuomini* and artisan landowners was simply to sell their holdings to peasant emigrants returning from abroad. U.S. dollars and Argentine pesos allowed the *contadini* to achieve what all of the abortive land reforms of the nineteenth century failed to accomplish. The peasants paid dearly, however, as land values soared.[74] Given the fact that, in the world view of the Agnonesi, landownership is socially prestigious, the peasant's stock rose accordingly, while the standing of the *galantuomini* declined.[75]

Gamberale observes:

> The peasant does not abandon our mountains with the intention of never seeing them again. He leaves his work and savings habits; he disembarks over there with these qualities, which he employs during his temporary exile. And, returned from exile to his native land, he buys a plot, a piece of land, and there for better or for worse he expends his sweat . . . fifty years from now the owners of our fields will be the peasants of today.[76]

As a member of the elite, Gamberale found this prospect appalling and potentially destructive of local agriculture. He believed the peasant to be too hidebound by tradition to initiate the changes required for modernizing the argrarian sector of Agnone's economy, which, as a liberal, he espoused.[77]

The successful returnee emigrant was a source of envy and concern for the *galantuomini*. Many emigrants developed a life style that was simply inconceivable within the confines of local society. The *galantuomini* were unaccustomed to dealing with "uppity" peasants and laborers with social pretensions, expensive tastes, and the wherewithal to indulge them. Some who emigrated from Agnone in humble circumstances returned several years later with a net worth beyond the wildest dreams of a locally rooted businessman, professional, or landowner.

For example, Michele Carosella, the son of an agricultural laborer, in 1881, at seventeen years of age, emigrated to the United States with his sister and brother-in-law. He first worked in the coal mines of Youngstown. When a friend was killed in a mining accident, he became a fruit vendor in a nearby city. Later he was a water carrier and a railroad worker. He joined a rail construction crew in Manitoba, and in 1887 he settled in Vancouver. Michele then returned to Agnone, where he renovated a house. He lost his savings, however, and mortgaged the house to reemigrate. He first worked in Canada in a German beer hall frequented by Italians. He then went to Youngstown, where he opened his own beer hall. Four years later he returned to Agnone with eight thousand dollars in savings, married, and then reemigrated to Youngstown. He opened a new bar and beer hall and made many successful real estate speculations before again returning to Agnone, where he lived out the remainder of his days as a man of leisure and means. He joined the elitist Circolo di Conversazione and became a prime mover in the efforts to construct the railway and a theater. On his death in 1913 an entire page of the *Eco del Sannio* was devoted to his obituary.[78]

A few emigrants were not above lording it over those who had never left the town. When the Italian government made Francesco Carlomagno of Belleville, Argentina a *cavaliere*, an Agnone newspaper noted: "We remind this gentleman that the honors he is receiving come from the government of Italy, which, during his return home last summer, he continually denigrated, making obnoxious comparisons between it and Argentina."[79] On another occasion the paper stated:

Remember those *certain signori* who, back from America, rich and depeasantized [*scafonizzati*], to holiday in the town where they were born and raised, allowed themselves, with vile discourtesy and evident ingratitude, to speak badly of Agnone and the Agnonesi, calling the former an extremely dirty town and labeling the latter uneducated.[80]

From the perspective of the *galantuomini*, then, the returnee represented a dangerous role model. His success was enviable in its own right and could only serve to fire the imaginations of other candidates for emigration. At the same time, he was little disposed to submit silently to the traditional constraints of Agnone society.

Some returnees aspired to inclusion in elite social circles. The more successful emigrants became members and prime movers of the prestigious Circolo di Conversazionee. When, in 1910, this organization constructed luxurious new quarters in Agnone, much of the funding came from Vincenzo Marinelli of Buenos Aires, the Cervone brothers of São Paolo, Domenico Antonelli and Daniele Michele of Youngstown, Filomeno Vitullo of Chicago, Paolo Borsella of New York, and Antonio Massanisso of Providence.[81] In 1911, Agnonesi resident in Argentina sent an embroidered banner to the organization.[82] Elegant receptions were held regularly in the *circolo* in honor of persons back from the Americas.[83] Clearly, by the first decade of the twentieth century, the economic and social position of the local *galantuomini* had been seriously undermined.

More ominously from the standpoint of the *galantuomini*, some returned emigrants became political adversaries of the liberal establishment and prime supporters of its newly emerging leftist opponents. By this time in Agnone, there were several rural schools, which, if they lacked the quality of those of the *cittadina*, did at least provide the *contadini* with rudimentary literary skills. Adult education programs were also initiated in the *cittadina* for the illiterate. Workers' children were attending elementary schools in increasing numbers. Consequently, the bases for lower-class participation in the political process were increasingly in evidence.

At times, pent-up lower-class frustrations boiled over into violence. By the turn of the century, practically every issue of the local newspapers reported criminal acts, and the town's elite was increasingly targeted.[84] In 1903 a physician was knifed by a young man who, at age thirteen, had lost an arm in an incident involving a letter bomb. He had later served a long prison term and returned to the town as twenty-five-year-old malcontent. He had gone about denouncing local officials, who obviously feared him. They had attempted to organize a public subscription to raise the money to send him to America, but he had refused to leave. Finally going beserk, in an apparently unprovoked attack, he almost killed the physician.[85] A year later a local lawyer, member of the powerful Tirone family, was deliberately ambushed and knifed by a young tailor.[86] According to the *Eco del Sannio*, after being imprisoned the assailant told others that

he was glad of what he had done and that he despised the landowners, the doctors, the lawyers, and the authorities, and that more
than anything he hated Doctor Cervone and the lawyer Tirone, both
of whom he had sworn to kill before the *festa* of San Cristanziano.
. . . [He further declared] that upon leaving prison he planned yet
to do to many others what he had *programmed* because many are
those who eat well and do not work, while he who lacks a *position*
cannot work or eat.[87] (emphasis theirs)

Neither man died of his wounds, but the *galantuomini* were beside
themselves with fear and outrage. They were quick to believe that both
attacks were politically motivated. The *Eco del Sannio* editorialized
against the assailants:

Ruthless enemies of work, the strongest foes of those who by their
labors live and feed themselves, drunken with false socialistic and
anarchistic ideas, in their alcoholic and degenerate mentality and
in the mania of purging the society of those who lead a life so different from theirs, they draw lots in vows of secrecy [to see] who must
strike the first blow. And in the busiest streets in plain daylight,
and habitually during a *festa*, they wound and destroy, and if they
do not kill, they put [their victims] in a bed of pain for many
months. Today the poor doctor who humbly brings his saving skills
to the suffering, who not infrequently with his generosity even extended them financial help; tomorrow the conscientious lawyer,
who walks the straight and narrow, studying the ways to best advise
his clients and defend their rights; another day the handsome and
vigorous young man who they in vain tried to lead down their own
path of perdition.[88]

The newspaper began a campaign to convince the government to establish a delegation of public safety in Agnone to increase the town's police
force, and within a few months the authorities acceded.[89] Eight *carabinieri* were stationed in Agnone to maintain public order.[90]

1908 was to be a critical year in the growing class confrontation in
Agnone. In May a new organization was formed by peasants and manual
laborers and called the Società di Lavoratori Indipendenti (Society of In-
dependent Workers); it was described as a "spontaneous movement of
the workers of the land."[91] That same month a local law student gave a
socialist lecture to a large audience.[92] In July the same orator gave a

speech to the town council entitled "Our Miseries: Causes and Remedies," which was subsequently published by the Socialist party.[93] The discourse inflamed passions as the young man accused the administration of factionalism and clientalism.[94] He upbraided the local landowners and businessmen for seeking to place their capital at usurious interest rates rather than investing it in riskier but dynamic sectors of the local economy.[95] He claimed that the illiteracy rate for the town was 70 percent.[96] He challenged the administration to take positive steps to improve the circumstances of the *contadini*, while at the same time exhorting the peasants to themselves form a consumers' cooperative to reduce their costs and modernize their operations.[97] Finally, he urged the lower classes to use the vote more effectively:

> Citizens, if we wish to lift ourselves out of our vile circumstances, if we wish to renew ourselves, it is indispensable to give to the vote its real value, its effective importance. Don't let yourselves be trailed to the urn like sheep to the fold in order to mark a name that is unweighed, unpondered, a name that does not represent a thing.[98]

The challenge fell equally upon both the Sabelli and Ionata factions, for in the municipal election held in July of 1907, the two slates had each won fifteen seats on the town council. Ionata had been replaced as mayor by Luigi Cremonese, a compromise choice drawn from the Sabelli slate.[99]

In September of 1908 the Società di Lavoratori Indipendenti inaugurated its banner, calling on the workers to unite and attacking the clergy (the bishop had refused them permission to have the banner blessed by a priest).[100] In November the organization sponsored an anticlerical address that was attended by "almost 200 *contadini*, artisans, and industrial workers."[101] In December, faced with a budding possibility of reformulation of Agnone's political equation and immobolized by the equal split of members on the town council, the Sabelli forces approached the Ionata people and proposed that the two camps resolve their differences. Though hailed in the local press, the idea was not realized.[102]

The following year May Day was celebrated for the first time in Agnone by some 175 people, who gathered to sing workers' songs.[103] The next month there was a well-attended conference on universal suffrage sponsored by "the nascent Agnonese Socialist party."[104] At the same time, the Società di Lavoratori Indipendenti organized a consumers' cooperative with its own butcher shop, grain storehouse, and general store. Ten thousand liras were pledged immediately.

At the end of 1911 a group of young people founded the newspaper *La lotta* (*The Struggle*) and initiated an attack on the policies and personages of the local administration. This was but the first of several twentieth-century confrontations between the gerontocratic establishment and young leftists. Giuseppe Sabelli, the founder and editor of the newspaper, was also, in 1911, the head of Agnone's Socialist party. In an editorial he stated: "We, the collaborators of this newspaper, are, in the main, young people, and it can be said that for the first time we enter the terrain of civil strife."[105]

By the second issue, *La lotta* could claim that one of the parish priests was circulating a petition condemning the newspaper as both socialistic and anticlerical.[106] Neither charge was unfounded inasmuch as the editor frequently championed peasants' and workers' rights and had published an open letter to the bishop chiding him on the spread of anticlericalism in the province.[107] Although midway through its first year of existence, *La lotta* ceased publication for financial reasons, the newspaper had its supporters. It started up again after fifty persons in Argentina collected 921 liras for it.[108]

In 1912 another newspaper, *Il rinnovamento*, made its appearance, carving out a middle-ground editorial position between the radicalism of *La lotta* and the conservatism of the *Eco del Sannio*. The new newspaper called for the electoral triumph of the artisans and *contadini*,[109] while it maintained that in Agnone, socialism, per se had little appeal.[110] It underscored the industriousness of the emigrants and the importance of their continued loyalty to the town, an attitude that could be undermined if Agnone developed a reputation for political radicalism.[111] *Il rinnovamento* also denounced the anticlericalism of *la lotta*.[112]

At the same time, *Il rinnovamento* leveled a scathing attack against the local political establishment. In condemning the social pretensions of some citizens, it noted:

> What aristocracy exists today in Agnone? Not an aristocracy of blood; Agnone's families have no genealogy. All, with no exceptions, appeared from invisibility to visibility, thanks to some professional person or even a priest. Agnone's "families" have had an astounding collapse; after one or two regenerations they plunge back again into obscurity, spent and physically, intellectually, and morally exhausted. Read Agnone's anagraphic registries of two or

153

three centuries ago. You will find surnames that no longer exist. What is the reason for this extinction, of this staying power which lasts for only two or three generations?

The discussion would be lengthy and the conclusions uncertain, but one cause may in fact be observed in our contemporary youth, which is born old and which lives decrepitly.[113]

In 1913 the three newspapers squared off over the national elections. Few Agnonesi favored the candidacy for Parliament of the incumbent Tommaso Mosca, the representative of the hated "Capracotta hegemony." Alessandro Marracino, Mosca's challenger and the candidate of the Socialist party, was, however, anathema to *Il rinnovamento* and the *Eco del Sannio*. Both newspapers supported the Agnonese Giovanni Piccoli.[114] *La lotta*, Marracino's champion in Agnone, regarded Piccoli as a spoiler. Bloc voting in Agnone for Piccoli destroyed Marracino's chances and reelected Mosca.[115]

During the election, representatives of both the Sabelli and Ionata factions met and agreed to back the candidacy of Piccoli.[116] Ionata himself, and a few of his followers, were, however, suspected of being Mosca supporters. On election night, when the Mosca victory became apparent, Ionata's home was assaulted by a disgruntled crowd, and he was forced to absent himself from Agnone for a period.[117]

By this time the emigrants had come to constitute a significant voting bloc in local elections. In 1913, of twenty-seven hundred registered electors in Agnone, six hundred were absent in the Americas.[118] That they were capable of collective political action was seen in the fact that committees were organized in Argentina and in the city of Chicago to promote the ill-fated candidacy of Prof. Piccoli. Both committees sent funds to Agnone for the campaign.[119] This political clout of the emigrants introduced a new element into local politics, one that, given the voters' overseas residence, was less susceptible to direct manipulation within the local system of political patronage.

In April of 1914 Cremonese resigned and Dr. Michele Cervone was elected mayor by the council. Cervone was a member of the *risveglisti* faction, the political heirs of Francesco Saverio Sabelli. He spoke of a rebirth for the town as defined in terms of past cultural and economic achievements. For the so-called reawakening (risveglio) movement, sanitary conditions in the municipal center took precedence over rural social conditions. Despite the fact that the town was already in the middle of a fiscal crisis, the mayor and council proposed to build a sewer and water system, resolving to finance it with increased taxes on landholdings. The stage was therefore set for confrontation between the new peasant proprietors and their old *galantuomini* nemeses.

Cervone came to power in the middle of peasant political activism emboldened by a new-found status financed by emigrant savings. The *Eco del Sannio* noted:

> Our *contadini*, and a few workers, wished to hold a demonstration hostile to the town government because of the increase in the property tax.
>
> The demonstration was preceded by the banner of the Circle of Independent Workers, who, a few days earlier, voted in good order for the communal administration! . . .
>
> We are truly surprised at the discontent of the *contadini*, who, being the most well-to-do class of the citizenry, should willingly submit to certain sacrifices for the good and benefit of everyone.
>
> It is they, the peasants, who are becoming the owners of the major part of Agnone's agricultural lands and who possess cash money, while the other classes of the citizenry are traversing a real crisis.[120]

Throughout the spring, there were continuing public demonstrations against the taxes. Curiously, *La lotta* sided with the administration, lecturing the peasants on the importance of meeting their civic duty as taxpayers.[121]

Agnone's problems attracted the attention of the government, and the authorities in Campobasso named a commission to review the situation. The local administration was exceedingly disturbed at the prospect. In March the *Eco del Sannio* noted:

> In Agnone the property base is subdivided between the peasants, the artisans, the merchants, and the so-called *galantuomini*. The most aggrieved are, without a doubt, the merchants, artisans, and *galantuomini*, who, in order to cultivate their fields, sacrifice a large part of the fruits of their labor. Even so, they have accepted the new sacrifice; the peasants on the other hand have rebelled and shout, "Down with the administration; we want the Royal Commission!" . . .
>
> The trend is inevitably toward a fratricidal class struggle.[122]

That same month the *contadini* formed their own political party to oppose the tax. The *Eco del Sannio* nervously lauded this move while cautioning the new group not to elect "egotists" or to try to take over more than their fair share of the administration. Almost wistfully, the newspaper acknowledged a major shift in the political alignments of the town:

And so the parties that before existed in Agnone should constitute only an historical recollection and a severe admonition for the future. For it is impossible to deny the evident fact the political parties in Agnone have been differentiated among themselves by personal sentiments, and never according to methods of administration.[123]

On April 20, 1914 Enrico Scapinelli, the royal commisstioner assigned to the Agnone investigation, issued a devastating report on the town's administration. His key criticisms were:

1. The town government was top-heavy with employees, most of whom were relatives, friends, or clients of persons in the adminstration.

2. Members of the town council had frequently, and in conflict of interest, awarded contracts to relatives and associates without going through the normal bidding process.

3. Council members profited personally from such critical and costly decisions as the trajectory of the railroad.

4. The members of the town administration had misused municipal property to benefit the Circolo di Conversazione, of which they were all members.

5. The town council had neglected Agnone's primary source of communal wealth, the fields and forests of the town commons (which were in a state of deterioration).[124]

6. The administration had lost several costly lawsuits initiated by its political opponents.

7. Services in rural areas were in a deplorable condition. Almost all municipal expenditures were made on improvements to the *cittadina*.[125]

This last issue was particularly explosive because the purpose of the new property taxes was to shift the tax burden onto the group that received the least benefit from public expenditures. That frustration was acute is reflected in the fact that the power company had to hire guards to patrol its lines because they were regularly cut by vandals.[126] Electricity was available only in the *cittadina*, making the power lines an onerous symbol for the inhabitants of the *agro*.

Meanwhile, political ferment among the peasantry continued. In early May a new political-action association, Circolo di San Nicola, was created. The membership was in its entirety made up of *contadini*.[127] Neither was the peasantry immune from the endemic Agnonese propensity for political factionalism. The following month the *Eco del Sannio* noted exasperatedly:

> Yet another association—Within a few days a new *circolo* will open on the Corso Vittorio Emanuele to accommodate those *contadini* who do not think like their colleagues in the *circolo* on the Largo S. Nicola. The members who have signed up are now numerous.
> Useless to comment![128]

In June the Scapinelli report was read publicly to a large audience, including many *contadini*. Predictably, it was roundly denounced by the *Eco del Sannio*, and just as predictably the Cirolo di San Nicola organized a demonstration highlighted with the general cry of "Viva il conte Scapinelli." The police were called in to break it up.[129] The following month an overflow crowd of more than two thousand people (primarily peasants) attended an organizational meeting for still another political association: the Circolo Popolare.[130]

In July there were municipal elections, which the *Eco del Sannio* heralded as among the most contested in Agnone's history. The newspaper abandoned its former pro-Ionata stance and upbraided his faction for pandering to the desires of the peasantry.[131] As of 1912 the *contadini* had been enfranchised and thereby constituted a potent new force in municipal affairs.[132] An exasperated *Eco del Sannio* accused the opposition slate of appealing "to the falange of enfranchised *contadini*, in large part illiterate and easily impressionable . . . persons who are not yet sufficiently evolved to participate in public affairs and who cannot be anything other than the blind instrument of those who manipulate them."[133] Each side presented twenty-four candidates, and the thirty with the highest vote total were to constitute the new council. Table 7.1 shows slates of candidates for municipal office by occupations.

On election eve thirty *carabinieri* and fifty infantry soldiers arrived in the town to maintain order. The elections were held without incident, and all twenty-four opposition candidates were elected. Mayor Cervone

Table 7.1. *Occupations of Candidates for Municipal Office, 1914*

Occupation	Administration slate	Opposition slate
Physicians	2	1
Artisans	3	6
Professors	1	0
Businessmen	6	2
Professionals	2	2
Landowners	2	1
Laborers	0	1
Peasants	8	11

Source: *Eco del Sannio*, August 17, 1914, p. 1.

barely retained his seat on the council, and Venancio Gamberale, the administration's candidate for a seat on the provincial council, was roundly defeated. The new council elected Ionata mayor. Although the emerging peasant-worker political coalition had tested its strength, it still had not managed to develop its own leadership. Rather, it rallied behind the treadworn candidacy of a man (Ionata) it regarded as the lesser of two evils.

In sum, the situation was critical. The peasants and workers were emboldened and organized; the *galantuomini* were fearful, yet still in partial control of the reins of authority. Clearly the social and political fabric of traditional Agnone society was shredded, but the outlines of a new order were far from discernible. At this moment, developments external to the town eclipsed local events. Italy and the rest of Europe entered the World War I, providing the Agnonesi with a rallying point, an issue that cut across class lines. Massive doses of patriotism gave the townspeople a new fixation, one that channeled local energies and forced the budding class confrontation into the background.

8

Fascism and Modern Decline

World War I and its aftermath represent a critical turning point in Agnone's history. For the duration of the hostilities, local political factionalism was suspended, and attempts to upgrade the town's cultural and economic life were abandoned. Energies were devoted almost exclusively to the support of the war effort. The two most active organizations were the Red Cross and the civil defense unit, Comitato di Preparazione Civile.[1]

As the conflict dragged on, there were many adverse effects on local life. In March of 1917 Mayor Ionata prohibited export from the town of wheat and wheat products.[2] By June there were acute shortages of wine and charcoal, and the bread was described as inedible.[3] Inflation was so rapid that it could be said that "the task of carrying on is a continual martyrdom."[4] A rising national debt forced the Italian government to intervene at the local level with increasing frequency. Extraordinary taxes and the sale of war bonds both drained resources from Agnone's economy. In 1917 the government commandeered a section of the town's communal forests for the navy.[5] Even personal property such as jewelry was collected for the war effort.[6]

In the final year of the conflict, Agnone incurred an additional burden. The town received many refugees from the war zones, and their care became a local responsibility. On one day alone, 110 people sought refuge in Agnone.[7] Many prisoners of war were also billeted in the area.[8]

Far and away the greatest toll was in terms of human life. To this day the route to Agnone's cemetery is lined with a seemingly interminable file of small markers, each a tribute to a fallen soldier. The town lost 177 young men in the conflict, no small sacrifice for a community of 10,000.[9] The return of veterans and prisoners of war,[10] many of whom were badly disabled, combined with the need to provide for hundreds of widows, orphans, and refugees, consumed almost all the collective energies of the townspeople. At a critical juncture in its history, Agnone was thus stripped of much of its resources and many of its potential leaders.

The Rise of Fascism

In the aftermath of the war, Italy was beset by monumental problems and considerable disillusionment. The toll of more than six hundred thousand killed and over one million disabled deeply scarred the national psyche. The nation's debt was staggering, the war having cost more than twice what the government had spent in the half century since unification.[11] Nationalist sentiment demanded that Italy be compensated territorially for its sacrifices in the winning cause. Italians were outraged when the terms of the Treaty of London, which promised Istria and parts of Dalmatia to Italy, were not implemented. Italy's allies sided with the nascent Yugoslavia in the negotiations, causing the Italians considerable diplomatic humiliation.[12]

Of equal importance was a renewed challenge from the political left. Italian Socialists were emboldened by the Bolshevik Revolution, and in the immediate postwar period they constituted a potent political and economic force. The years 1919 and 1920 are sometimes referred to as the "red years" and were a period of labor strife. By 1919 the Socialists controlled one-third of the provincial councils, many municipal governments, and 156 deputies in Parliament—the largest single voting bloc.[13] On the national scene, then, there was an accelerating confrontation between the workers and the discontented nationalists and war veterans. In street terms, the issues were runaway inflation, strikes, and lack of public order; and their resolution fueled Mussolini's rise to power.

Agnone was no exception. The budding class confrontation that characterized the town on the eve of the World War I made it clear that the lower classes were poised to challenge the *galantuomini* for control of the municipality. In mid-1917 Ionata died and was replaced by a member of his faction, the lawyer Raffaele Sabelli. Sabelli sought to appease the peasant activists and was quick to note that his "efforts would be expended in benefit of the town, and especially the hamlets of Villacanale and Fonte Sambuco."[14]

But the rather circumspect fashion with which political opponents dealt with each other through the war years dissipated once peace was restored. In January of 1919 the Circolo Populare outbid the Casino dell'Unione for a meeting place owned by the commune. A nervous *Eco del Sannio* commented, "We are witnessing the substitution of class hatreds for the former partisan ones, and those who foment and feed them for personal reasons are engaged in most contemptible behavior."[15]

There were immediate signs of political polarization in the town. The Circolo Popolare called for formation of a *federazione regionale dei lavoratori del Molise* to improve workers' conditions. A skeptical and patronizing *Eco del Sannio* questioned, "Have our peasants and workers the intellectual and moral maturity for such new forms of life?" When the new federation became a reality, the newspaper lectured its members on democratic action:

> Our Jacobins in 1799 were ardent proponents of democratic ideas in the face of Bourbon tyranny. Our workers do not have amongst us tyrants to combat. They—and principally the peasants—are [now] the dominant class, and there is neither person, nor family, nor class in our midst who plans or intends to oppress them, or who could do so.[16]

In May of 1919 the *Eco del Sannio* noted: "Disillusionment is increasing out of all proportion because of the exorbitant prices of goods."[17] That summer the newspaper editorialized, "The rising cost of living is felt here more than elsewhere because our town is eminently agricultural and should be a place where the foodstuffs of prime necessity are sold at less scandalous prices."[18]

It was at this time that the war veterans formed a group, called the Fascio di Combattimento, that threatened to take unusual measures against inflation in order to head off popular revolution. It was headed by

161

Michele Cervone, Agnone's former mayor on the *risveglisti* slate. The *Eco del Sannio* lent its approval, stating, "In times of exceptional events, exceptional remedies!"[19]

Meanwhile, the Socialists were also organizing. In January 1920 a new socialist organization for young people, Circolo Andrea Costa, was founded in the town. The newspaper nervously proclaimed that a red dictatorship was to be detested as much as a black or white dictatorship and that totalitarianism of any stripe was anathema to the Agnonesi. By the following summer there was a socialist organization functioning in Villacanale, and party spokesman were regularly conducting political rallies in Agnone.[20]

It was about this same time that Agnone's railway workers initiated a strike that was to last for several months and all but paralyze the local economy. The strike triggered a public demonstration against the workers and a call for their dismissal.[21] Tensions in the town were aggravated by the adverse news of Italy's frustrated attempts to acquire the city of Fiume. In September the *Eco del Sannio* editorialized in favor of Italy's claim,[22] and shortly thereafter Agnone's war veterans held a public demonstration to protest the nation's reversals in the negotiations.[23]

Control of municipal government provided a primary battleground between the contending factions. In January of 1920 Mayor Sabelli, reelected only one hundred days earlier, resigned his post. He contended that Agnone had become ungovernable owing to excessive partisanship. He was unable to get a working majority on the town council when only ten council members were carryovers from his past administration, whereas six new members were from his old political opposition and ten were of the new peasant activists.[24] As the councilmen bickered, Agnone's municipal budget ran sixty-two thousand liras in the red.[25]

In the fall of 1920 there were new municipal elections in the town. One slate of candidates, presented by a new Democratico-Sociale party, was headed by Francescopaolo Covitti. Covitti, although an ex-goldsmith, was a defender of peasant interests and director of the primarily peasant Circolo Popolare. The slate was also supported by the Circolo di Lavoratori Indipendenti, essentially an artisan workers organization. The second slate was fielded by Agnone's Socialist party.

To the extent that the former political factions were still viable, they contested control of the Democratico-Sociale party. An attempt was made within the party to head off a complete peasant takeover. Cervone argued, successfully, that the slate should contain eight peasants, eight workers, and eight professionals. Covitti rejected this attempt by the old *risveglisti* to retain a modicum of power.[26] The final electoral list consisted of thirteen *contadini*, nine artisans, and only two *galantuomini*. In a gesture to the growing influence of the war veterans, six ex-combatants were included. The Socialist party presented its own slate consisting of thirteen *contadini*, ten artisans, and only one *galantuomo*, the lawyer Salvatore Pannunzio (who was its leader and also its candidate for a seat on the provincial council).

Several comments are in order. At this juncture neither the extreme left nor the extreme right was capable of monopolizing political power in Agnone. The Democratico-Sociale slate was rather middle-of-the-road in makeup. The fact that it was backed by both the Circolo Popolare and the Circolo di Lavoratori Indipendenti suggests that the Socialists lacked majority support among Agnone's peasants and workers. That the right was gaining in strength, while remaining a minority force, is seen in the inclusion of the six war veterans on the slate. The Risveglisti were excluded from municipal government but occupied a powerful position within the ranks of the Fascio di Combattimento. The fact that the Socialist party fielded a full complement of candidates meant it was emerging as a major factor in local politics.

All twenty-four of the Democratico-Sociale candidates were elected by a comfortable margin. The results were viewed, nonetheless, with concern by the old guard. The Socialist candidates showed surprising electoral strength. Pannunzio defeated the Democratico-Sociale candidate for Agnone's seat on the provincial council. The *Eco del Sannio* nervously attributed this to strenuous campaigning rather than to socialist conviction within the electorate.[27] Equally appalling to the newspaper was the class makeup of the new council, which consisted of fourteen *contadini*, ten artisans, and only four professionals and merchants. In reporting the results the newspaper noted: "Our peasants and workers are now in power; they must demonstrate that they know how to use it. . . . In this period of transition Agnone's soul is disoriented."[28]

Covitti, named mayor by the new council, faced an immediate crisis. Agnone's fiscal problems were so acute that a royal commission was appointed to study them. In December the commission's report was issued; it required the council to increase taxes on consumers' goods and real estate. At the same time, the town was ordered to divest itself of certain nonessential landholdings and sell off large tracts of timber stands on the commons. Despite its deficits, Agnone was authorized to seek a loan to finance public works projects as a means of ameliorating the high local rate of unemployment. The commission's findings triggered acrimonious public debate between Mayor Covitti on the one hand and both the Socialists and conservatives on the other.[29]

Clearly, then, during the first two years of the postwar period, Agnone experienced severe political and economic crisis. As the town entered the year 1921, inflation was rampant, unemployment high, and the critical rail link with the outside interdicted by a strike. Additionally, municipal finances were in a shambles, and there was the immediate prospect of sharply increased taxation. A three-cornered political struggle had all but precluded the possibility of consensual political efforts to resolve the problems.

It was at this point that local affairs took an ugly turn for the worse as the Socialists and Fascists, both emboldened by growing organizational strength, resorted to violence. In January of 1921 the new Circolo Giovanile Socialista began to function in Agnone, and one section enrolled two hundred members and acquired its own meeting hall.[30] Almost immediately there was trouble, as a group of Fascists seized and burned their red flag. The *carabinieri* were called in to separate the two groups. The Socialists assaulted the police in their attempts to get at their tormenters and were themselves forcibly routed down Agnone's side streets.[31] The *Eco del Sannio* noted that whenever the Socialists from Villacanale came to Agnone to attend a party meeting, they were armed with clubs and were threatening in their mannerisms. They had beaten one man outside their meeting hall.[32]

During the spring the Fascists increased their verbal attacks on the left. The Fascio di Combattimento counted over two hundred members plus many sympathizers.[33] In April the organization formed an antisocialist political coalition that fielded a slate of candidates in the provincial elections.[34] Cervone presented his candidacy for deputy to Parliament. Although he was unsuccessful, the *Eco del Sannio* heralded this as a hopeful sign and an opportunity for all Agnonesi to unite against the threat of communism.[35]

Meanwhile, in May the Fascists attacked a Socialist meeting, entering the hall, where they seized three red flags and a portrait of Lenin. "Socialist infiltrators" in the Fascist ranks were beaten with clubs.[36] About the same time, there were blows and gunfire in Villacanale as the Fascists assaulted another Socialist gathering. Apparently the latter gained

164

the upper hand, for the *carabinieri* had to constrain Agnone's Fascists from setting out for the hamlet to retaliate.[37] The situation was so tense that violence was to be expected as a matter of course whenever Fascists and Socialists met in the streets.[38]

The year 1922 was critical in that the balance of power tilted toward the Fascists. To be sure, there was still organizational activity by the left, such as the inauguration in Fontesambuco of a workers' association with 120 members;[39] yet there were signs of fatigue among the moderates and the Socialists. Peasant demonstrations against new taxes undermined the power base of Covitti's administration,[40] and the mayor temporarily resigned his office.[41] When the Circolo Popolare, of which Covitti served as director, met to elect officers, it failed to assemble the necessary quorum of one hundred of a total membership of more than four hundred.[42]

Meanwhile, the Fascists were gaining strength. In May they held a huge rally in Agnone that was well attended and without incident. Cervone praised Mussolini and denounced the *"socialcommunisti"* for misleading the working classes.[43] Shortly thereafter there were new street clashes between Fascists and Socialists that left one person knifed, one beaten, and six Fascists in jail.[44] In August *squadristi* from Agnone went to Campobasso to confront and coerce striking railroad workers.[45]

Squadrism is the term for the groups of young Fascists organized as paramilitaries who bullied anyone critical of the party. In the Alto Molise, Agnone was famed as the focus of squadrism. Agnone's squads sometimes paid nocturnal visits to suspected Socialists in other towns, rousting them out of bed, beating them with clubs, and forcing them to ingest large amounts of castor oil.

In the fall of 1922 Mussolini emerged as Italy's national leader. The *Eco del Sannio* noted: "Finally, we have a government! Let it be for the pacification of passions, for the restoration of public order, for the respect of the laws and the discipline of labor. By a fortunate coincidence fascism has come to power."[46] After Mussolini's victory legitimized the movement at the national level, Agnone's Fascists became image conscious. In late 1922 they laid claim to being the advance guard in the entire Molise in the struggle against the Bolshevists.[47] In a burst of concern over their reputation for lawlessness, the newly created Sezione Fascista Agnonese purged a part of its membership for excesses.[48] The concern was short-lived.

For Agnone's Fascists, 1923 was a year of considerable activity and success. Large rallies, of which the major theme was the restoration of patriotic sentiment among the youth became the order of the day.[49] In February forty disabled veterans formed an association and announced their public support of fascism.[50] By March, Fascist *squadristi* were conducting joint patrols with the *carabinieri*, engaging in house searches, and arresting suspected Socialists.[51] Membership in the Sezione Fascista Agnone climbed to 450 (even Mayor Covitti joined), and the organization took over the meeting hall of the Casino dell'Unione.[52] That same month a section of the Gruppo "Balilla," or youth vanguard of the Fascist party for young men between eight and thirteen years of age, began to function in Agnone.[53] In May a Fascist section was inaugurated in Villacanale.[54] In the early summer Cervone was a member of a Fascist delegation from the Molise that met with Mussolini himself.[55]

By autumn the Fascists were sufficiently emboldened to make a bid for control of municipal government. The *Eco del Sannio* initiated a campaign against the administration and invited the Fascists to join in a general housecleaning.[56] Covitti's power base in the town council eroded quickly, and by year's end he retained the loyalty of only nine council members. The newspaper called for his resignation.[57]

Meanwhile, Covitti and his supporters launched a counterattack within the ranks of the Fascists. Covitti had joined the local *fascio* and, as Agnone's mayor, became a director. He threw his support to Giuseppe Marinelli, the young *segretario politico* (political secretary, the highest office in any Fascist section). In late 1923 Marinelli and the board had Cervone expelled from the party.[58] Cervone challenged Marinelli to a public confrontation and vote of the local membership.[59] He was victorious by a landslide,[60] emerging as Agnone's new political secretary. A defeated Giuseppe Marinelli characterized his loss as the "victory of the old clientalism over fascist youth. . . . It was not Cervone as a person who prevailed but rather the interests of family and social castes."[61]

A few days later Mayor Covitti resigned his office, attributing the decision to pressure from Cervone.[62] The new mayor was Raffaele Sabelli, the man who had held the post before Covitti in 1917–1920. By this juncture the office was largely a figurehead; real political power in Agnone rested with the political secretary of the Fascist party. In April of 1924 the *Eco del Sannio* remarked approvingly concerning upcoming provincial elections:

> The actual electoral campaign that will begin in a few days . . . is considerably different from ancient and recent ones held in Agnone. The force and the merits of fascism, the profound esteem for the *Duce* and the head of the government, the lack of a true and hardened opposition give to this electoral campaign a serene and trustworthy aspect.[63]

Although the Fascists were in effective control of local government, there was still potential for dissent. The press was not, as yet, totally subservient to the Fascist party line. On one occasion Agnone's Fascist section worked successfully to replace the local correspondent of the powerful newspaper *Il mattino*.[64] Then, too, there were still organizations that had the potential for antifascist opposition. As Agnone entered the year 1925, the Circolo Popolare, headed by ex-mayor Covitti, had 600 members, and the Circolo di Lavoratori Indipendenti had 220. By contrast, the Sezione Fascista Agnonese had only 350.[65] It was at this point that the Fascists began systematically to preempt any possible source of opposition.

In early 1925 Cervone was elected head of the Circolo di Conversazione.[66] Shortly thereafter, the Fascist party, again concerned with its violent image, reorganized and purged some of its members.[67] In March of 1926 there was a complete internal revamping of the party. Cervone was dismissed from his political secretary's post in disgrace. Venanzio Gamberale (the unsuccessful candidate for the provincial council in 1914 on the *risveglisti* ticket) was elected to the office. The *Eco del Sannio* remarked that "squadrism is over and it should be over."[68] As Gamberale assumed his post, he gave a special salute to the *contadini*. At the same time, he announced that the provincial authorities had decreed abolishment of the Circolo Popolare. The Fascists urged the peasants to accept loss of their association, maintaining that the rank and file in the *circolo* were good people but that the leaders were insidious.[69] The following year the new *Circolo Fascista Lavoratori Agnonese* was formed, and the Circolo di Lavoratori Indipendenti was abolished by the authorities.[70]

By 1927 there was some kind of Fascist organization for just about every person in Agnone. In May a women's section of the party was created.[71] A Fascist union for artisans was also started.[72] In June a section of the Associazione Nazionale Italiana Fascista was inaugurated in the town and dedicated to the "fascistization of the schools."[73] That same month the Federazione Fascista di Commercianti, or Fascists merchants' association, began operations in Agnone.[74] In July a local voluntary militia was organized in the town.[75] The next year a local section of a Fascist youth organization began to function.[76]

The impossibility of organizing effective political opposition is underscored by the results of the 1929 national plebiscite on fascism. In Agnone 92 percent of the registered voters cast ballots, and *all* were in favor of the Fascist program. In the entire Molise only nineteen no votes were cast.[77]

If, during the decade after World War I, the Fascists managed to seize all political power in the nation, their success was not due entirely to the fears engendered by their strongarm tactics. They had influential allies in their rise to power. One of the crucial factors was a rapprochement between Mussolini and the Vatican that culminated in the concordat of 1929. Before that agreement, relations between the church and the Italian government were officially belligerent. Despite considerable anticlericalism, there was, however, a strong strain of Catholic sentiment in the nation that Mussolini sought to win over to his cause.

In Agnone, from the outset, there was a close relationship between the Fascists and the clergy. In 1921 when the town's Fascist section was inaugurated, its first official function was the blessing of its pennant in a ceremony held in the Church of San Emidio.[78] Fascist oratory was regularly laced with appeals linking patriotism and religious sentiment. As fascism gained strength in Agnone, the church began to prosper. In 1924 the bishop of Trivento announced plans to refurbish the Monastery of San Berardino and install there a summer retreat for his seminarians.[79] He was feted and honored when he visited the town.[80] More than two hundred thousand liras were raised for the project, much of it in Agnone itself.[81] In 1926 the pastor of the parish of San Biase stated during a religious ceremony, "Glory to the leader of Italy, to Benito Mussolini, the man chosen by Providence who restored to us this racial pride, who returned us to the source of greatness."[82]

The *Eco del Sannio* began to report regularly on local religious activities, and Agnone was once again providing religious vocations for the diocese.[83] In the late 1920s and early 1930s, there were several building projects in the town designed to improve the church's patrimony. The

Monastery of San Francesco was refurbished;[84] three churches were re-modeled;[85] and the Church of San Biase was provided with a new altar.[86] In 1928 a new Catholic youth organization was founded in the parish of San Nicola, and Agnone's political secretary was made an honorary member.[87]

The majority of the clergy in Agnone were in favor of the concordat. The parish priest of San Emidio published a pamphlet lauding the event.[88] Some clergy were outspoken defenders of the Fascist order and members of the party as well. In the aftermath of the agreement, religion was taught regularly in the schools.[89] In a discourse on fascist culture in the educational system, one official in Agnone noted: "The instruction of our religion, reminding the young of sublime examples of goodness, sacrifice, and purity, converts the school into a spiritual organism in which, in harmony, the supreme conquests of the nation are joined to the ideals of the superior forms of life."[90]

The Fascist Order

At both the national and the local levels, the Fascists sought to defuse potential discontent with an appeal to past and present national glories. Of greatest significance to the Italians and the world as a whole was Mussolini's imperial dream, which prompted Italy's colonial adventure in Africa, its intervention in the Spanish Civil War, and its involvement in World War II. In preparation for his foreign adventures, Il Duce initiated new population policies. On the one hand he discouraged emigration; on the other he encouraged Italians to marry young and have many children. Procreation became a national goal. Families with the greatest number of offspring were awarded prizes.[91] The *Eco del Sannio* regularly reported census figures and long-range projections of national demographic trends.[92] A Mother's and Children's Day was decreed, and on that occasion, prizes were awarded in Agnone to the youngest married couples.[93]

Mussolini also initiated a new agricultural program. Italy's dependence on food imports seriously limited his options in international affairs. Therefore, the Fascists used many techniques to increase production. Short-term courses for the *contadini* were held regularly in places like Agnone.[94] In 1926 an agricultural extension agent was appointed in the town to service Agnone and surrounding communities.[95] In 1928

Mussolini made a personal appeal to Italy's agriculturalists, which was published in the *Eco del Sannio*.[96] Within a few days Cervone addressed a large rally attended by seven hundred of Agnone's *contadini* and exhorted them to higher production.[97] The government increased the incentives by offering prizes[98] and by establishing a pension program for the peasants.[99] By the early 1930s the national effort was christened "the Grain Battle,' and the press regularly reported on Italy's total production and its declining imports.[100] Mussolini ingeniously set one province off against the others in the effort to increase the yield. The campaign was so successful that by 1933 the nation had reduced its imports by 90 percent and was all but self-sufficient.[101]

At no other time in its history has Agnone been farmed as intensively. Forests were felled, massive amounts of rock removed, and the tiniest of plots scratched out of a difficult landscape. By 1929 Agnone had a total of 7,397 hectares of land under plow agriculture,[102] compared to only 2,534.23 hectares in 1970.[103] As marginal lands were brought under cultivation, however, yield declined. In 1929 the wheat harvest averaged only 8.3 quintals to the hectare compared to over 9 quintals during the previous five-year period.[104] The costs were enormous in other respects as well. Agnone's communal forests have never fully recovered; the steepest of hillsides still bear the scars of the "Battle."

In 1934 Italy was put on a war footing. The *Eco del Sannio* noted that there was a paramilitary or military unit for every Italian male between the ages of six and fifty-five years.[105] By the following year several Agnonesi were serving in Italy's East African war,[106] and there were some casualties.[107] Shortly thereafter, other soldiers from Agnone were fighting in Spain.[108] Although the newspaper emphasized military glories and refrained from publishing any unfavorable news, in 1937 there was one brief local item, titled "Vandalism," that suggests that not all of the townspeople were behind the war effort: "In Remembrance Street several window fronts containing the photos of the glorious war dead were broken, and other similar profanations committed."[109]

Beset with economic problems and exhorted (even in the bedroom) to work for the greater glory of the nation, the citizen of the Fascist order required outlets. These, too, were provided by the system. In Agnone, as elsewhere, they took the form of physical recreation and folklore. By the late 1920s, features on the importance of physical culture began to appear regularly in the *Eco del Sannio*.[110] By 1929 winter sports were being organized in nearby Capracotta.[111] That same year a sports facility was constructed in Agnone, and the Dopolavoro organization established a municipal soccer team.[112] A few months later the Associazione Sportiva Agnonese was formed to foment interest in soccer and cycling.[113] In succeeding years Agnone's teams competed widely throughout the Molise and parts of the Abruzzo.

At the same time, Agnone's religious and folk heritages were both revived and embellished under the Fascists. In 1929 the procession of Corpus Domini was reinstituted by the Circolo Giovanile Cattolico.[114] When, the following year, the procession of San Cristanziano was not held,[115] there were protests and the festival was restored. In 1929 a harvest festival, Sagra dell'Uva was instituted on an annual basis. It was held in the Piazza del Plebiscito of the town, and everyone wore traditional peasant dress.[116] Another folkloric event was the Fiaccolata di Natale, in which on Christmas Eve peasants converged on the *cittadina* bearing lighted torches in honor of the Christ child.[117] It was also at this time that Agnone's special dialect first received serious literary attention. The newspaper began to publish verse in the local idiom.[118]

Such rhetoric, diversions, and bursts of organizational energy notwithstanding, the Fascists were to learn that it is easier to criticize than to remedy the ills of a nation. They were able, by decree, to resolve labor strife and excessive emigration; other questions, such as inflation, were not as amenable to government directives. Despite repeated price controls and efforts to punish speculators, the cost of living soared throughout the 1920s. In Agnone, for example, bread sold in 1924 for 1.65 liras per kilo.[119] Less than two years later it was selling for 2.30 liras per kilo, a price rise on the order of 39 percent.[120]

Fiscal crises at the national level were felt locally. Periodically, and with considerable fanfare, the government sold bonds to help liquidate Italy's enormous foreign debt. One such effort in 1927 drained, 2,806,100 liras from Agnone's economy alone.[121] It is interesting to note, however, that of this total, only 3,000 liras were raised in Villacanale, a former stronghold of socialist sentiment.[122] In 1929 Agnone was in the midst of one of its endemic budgetary deficits, and it was necessary for the town authorities to double property taxes and impose new levies on consumers' goods.[123] In Italy, as elsewhere, the effective cure for inflation was the Great Depression; in January of 1931 municipal taxes were reduced and bread was valued at 1.40 liras per kilo.[124]

Furthermore, there are indications that even before the depression there was a grave economic crisis in at least some sectors of Agnone's economy. In early 1929 some of Agnone's artisans petitioned for exemption from certain taxes on the grounds of "the present economic conditions and because of unemployment which for some workers and workshops has lasted for several months."[125] Included on the list were fifty-eight people who were either invalided or unemployed. In 1931 unemployment remained a major problem and was exacerbated by a steady stream of returnees from the Americas, where the Great Depression had a particular impact on the immigrant population.[126]

Agnone's cultural and civic life languished under the Fascist administration. Fascism discouraged diversity of opinion, and few were inspired to take pen in hand. Consequently, during the Fascist years, Agnone's long tradition of producing literary figures was essentially broken. In the same vein, every public performance, regardless of its purpose, was tinged with fascist oratory. When even a musical concert became a Fascist rally, the climate was scarcely conducive to the arts.

Although not solely attributable to Fascist mismanagement, during the 1920s and 1930s several of Agnone's key civic institutions did crumble and collapse. By 1922 the crown jewel of the town's educational complex, the Scuola Tecnica, was in a grave crisis owing to lack of students and lax instruction.[127] The following year the status of the school was downgraded to that of Scuola Elementare.[128] A chagrined *Eco del Sannio* urged public support of the new institution, but in its first year of operation it was in deep trouble. Only eighty students attended classes, whereas the former institution had enrolled as many as two hundred.[129] The following year the school was on the verge of closing, as it had only forty-four students in all.[130]

In 1923 the railroad was in serious economic difficulty. As a short branch line, its market was too limited for it to prosper. Attempts (unsuccessful) were initiated to extend the system to Vasto and Atessa.[131] The next year the directors threatened to close down operations unless the government provided a 100,000 liras subsidy.[132] The request for assistance was reiterated in 1928,[133] and in 1931 train service was curtailed because of operating losses.[134] In 1935 the railroad had a 149,292 liras deficit,[135] and the following year it was on the verge of bankruptcy.[136]

Agnone's banks were likewise in serious straits even before the depression. In 1927 the deposits in the Banca Operaia began to decline,[137] and in August of 1929 it curtailed services and dismissed several employees.[138] By 1932 both banks were practically without reserves, and there was a run by the depositors.[139] In November of that year the Banca Sannitica was in receivership.[140] The Banca Operaia survived until late 1936, when it, too, was closed.[141]

I have noted that the newspaper *Eco del Sannio* was openly supportive of the national goals of fascism and tolerant of the personal excesses of local Fascists. It was not, however, willing to ignore the decline of the town. In 1936 it published the impressions of emigrants returned from Argentina to visit Agnone after many years absence: "They have come to see Agnone again, which gave them quite a painful impression because they found it quite different from when they first left. That is, when all was a fervor of the arts, of the professions, of every possible activity."[142]

Throughout 1937 and 1938 the newspaper pressed the administration on a number of local issues, including the poor state of Agnone's roads, problems in the schools, and the lamentable lack of a hospital for the Alto Molise.[143] At the same time, the newspaper was itself in deep financial trouble, in part because New World subscribers were often remiss in paying their subscriptions.[144] In 1938 it announced it would have to charge for running birth, death, and marriage notices.[145] In December of that year the *Eco del Sannio* ceased publication. Its financial problems notwithstanding, the key reason was that the local authorities had come to regard the newspaper as a thorn in their sides.

With the demise of the newspaper, the last potential source of criticism of the Fascist order was removed. Indeed, Agnone had become the apotheosis of fascism in the Molise. *Squadristi* from the town were the scourge of surrounding communities. A number of political prisoners from other parts of Italy were placed under "town arrest" in Agnone. It could be stated with accuracy the "the first Fascio di Combattimento in our province was that of Agnone and, without fear of lying, we can in good conscience affirm that Agnone has been the cradle of Molise fascism."[146]

Viewed against the backdrop of the town's history, it is not at all surprising that fascism would strike such a responsive chord in many Agnonesi. Agnone was the former stronghold of liberalism in the province, which meant that the Socialists enjoyed only tardy and moderate successes there when compared to other areas. Agnone's Fascists saw themselves as direct descendants of the town's liberal leaders. The Fas-

cist leadership was recruited from the risveglisti movement of the pre–
World War I political period. At a political rally one Fascist orator thus
cloaked the movement in the mantle of Agnone's liberal heritage:

> Agnonese patriotism is not recent patriotism. It revealed itself in
> 1799 when Libero Serafini suffered martyrdom for the Nation; it
> revealed itself in 1848 when the school of Ippolito Amicarelli,
> Francescoantonio Marinelli, Giuseppe Nicola d'Agnillo, and other
> illustrious citizens inculcated in the souls of the youth hatred for
> the oppressor; it revealed itself in 1860 and in 1866 when so many
> young Agnonesi joined Garibaldi's legion; it revealed itself in 1886
> when Giovanni Tirone, at Dogali, shed his youthful blood for the
> Nation; it revealed itself in the recent war with the 200 dead and 40
> invalided that Agnone offered to the Country. [147]

Modern Decline

It is ironic that Agnone, after serving as the cradle of fascism in its region, suffered relatively little during World War II. As the Allied armies
advanced, the German defenders of the Alto Molise elected to make
their stand near Pescopennataro, Capracotta, and San Pietro Avellana,
which were leveled by artillery fire. Agnone escaped virtually un-
scathed, although the retreating Germans destroyed the railroad. The
Agnonesi did, however, pay a considerable price in war dead and prisoners. Individual townspeople died while serving in the Axis forces in
other parts of Italy, North Africa, Greece, Germany, and Russia. Larger
numbers spent the war interned in England, the United States, or
Germany. The exact figures are difficult to determine. For obvious reasons the Agnonesi do little to commemorate World War II in either
speech and ceremony or brass and stone.

In any event, at the conclusion of the war, in Agnone (as in the rest of
Italy), discretion demanded repudiation of fascism. On March 18, 1945
a pro-Allies rally was held in the town, and the Agnonesi collected a
large sum of money for the partisans. [148] Agnone's new mayor denounced the Fascists in the strongest terms:

> Never has a more fearful tragedy befallen our beautiful and unfortu-
> nate country! For twenty years Italy has been dissipated by a gang

of adventurers, deceived by superpatriotism, who, after having committed with impunity the most bold-faced robberies, after having deprived the nation of all of its fruits of liberty . . . have bartered away in the world the country's honor and fortune, thrusting it, out of foolish imperialistic insanity, into the hurricane of iron and fire that has transformed our land into a desert of devastation and death. Our bold youth has either been crushed or scattered throughout the world; millions of citizens have been left without a roof and suffer cold and hunger.[149]

In the aftermath of the war, Italy faced a political vacuum. After two decades of fascism and the demoralizing war years, the political infrastructure of the nation had to be reconstructed practically from scratch. Fascism and socialism were both anathema to the victorious Allies, so it was the Christian Democratic party, a broad centrist coalition of disparate forces, that prevailed. In 1946 the prime minister de Gasperi presided over a national referendum on the monarchy. While the Molise and the Mezzogiorno favored retaining it, the electorate as a whole voted in the Italian Republic.

As the prostrate nation entered the postwar era, the Allies had a vested interest in rebuilding the economy, if only to effect political stability for the fledgling democracy. Fueled by foreign aid, the government intervened in many areas of Italian life on an unprecedented scale. Numerous programs were launched, designed to provide new social, educational, and medical services to the populace.

While it is clear that Agnone's traditional sources of economic strength and civic pride were largely dissipated, the national political climate itself provided the town with a new range of opportunities. There was an abundance of financial aid earmarked for national development that was being dispensed in large measure through clientalistic political networks. Any town with representation in high places had an edge in the competition for government aid. Consequently, during the postwar era, Agnone benefited considerably from the fact that it produced two key political figures, Remo Sammartino and Bruno Vecchiarelli.

From 1953 to 1968 Sammartino sat as a deputy in the Italian Parliament. Beginning in 1968 he served two terms in the Senate. That same year, Vecchiarelli, mayor of Agnone, won the seat in the Parliament vacated by Senator Sammartino. He still occupies it at this writing. Thus, during much of the postwar period, of the Molise's total of two senators and four deputies, Agnone claimed one of each, giving the town political representation all out of proportion to its economic importance or population size. In trumpeting the election victories of 1968, one newspaper underscored a question being asked only half-jokingly throughout the province: Is Agnone the capital of the Molise?[150]

By the early 1950s Agnone was alive with government-funded building projects. In November of 1950 the town received fifteen million liras from the Ispettorato Centrale della Ricostruzione to rebuild private residences and twenty million liras from the Ministry of Public Works for construction of a school in Villacanale.[151] The following month an orphanage opened in the town financed by the Ministry of Public Assistance.[152]

In 1951 the Cassa per il Mezzogiorno, a governmental agency designed expressly to assist the Italian South, began to function. By June of that year the Agnonesi had under consideration a plan to bring electric power to the rural areas.[153] Work had also begun on a new sporting field,[154] and on a pediatrics clinic[155] both financed by the state.

For Agnone, 1952 was a banner year. In March construction on a new post office was begun.[156] On April 1 the townspeople realized a long-standing goal, for on that day a new hospital opened its doors.[157] Although the original Sabelli donation (made in 1887) had gone toward the project, it was mainly financed from an 11,400,000-lira government grant.[158] Thus, political influence had succeeded where past efforts to mobilize local and emigrant support had failed. In 1953 government largesse continued, as parliamentarian Samartino announced a 100,000-lira grant for Agnone's orphanage.[159] That same year, several private businesses were either begun or modernized.[160]

The early 1950s, then, was a time of optimism in Agnone, stimulated by the illusion that the town was renewing itself.[161] Nor was the upbeat spirit restricted to projects involving bricks and mortar. Rather, the Agnonesi attempted to rekindle the town's former cultural initiatives. In 1950 a new newspaper, *La fucina*, made its appearance.[162] Events such as musical recitals were organized. Efforts were begun to reopen the Biblioteca La Banca.[163] In 1951 Agnone hosted a huge eucharistic conference attended by many bishops.[164] There were also initiatives to reconstitute such voluntary associations as the Circolo di Conversazione,[165] a Catholic workers' organization,[166] a federation of agriculturalists,[167] and an artisans' group.[168]

176

Similarly, the Agnonesi employed a mixture of private initiative and government assistance to restore and extend the town's role as an educational center of regional importance. In 1945 there was an abortive effort to found a lycee, or private secondary school, in the town.[169] That same year, a new technical school also began operations.[170] In 1956, for example, the struggling lycee was made a state school.[171] That year its total student body was 31 students. In succeeding years it grew impressively. It is now housed in a new government-financed structure.[172] During the academic year 1972–1973, enrollment stood at 220 students. In 1959 Agnone acquired two other state technical schools, one for girls and the other boys, both geared to provide occupational training.

Such initial successes notwithstanding, on balance, the postwar period has been one of waning vitality for Agnone. By the late 1960s and early 1970s, a series of developments on the national and local scenes conspired to create new political and economic crises in Agnone. The Christian Democratic initiative in Italian politics lost much of its momentum. Support for both the left and right was growing, and the party itself was riven with internal dissent, splintering into myriad *correnti*, or currents. The unstable, cliff-hanging nature of Italy's postwar democratic experiment is by now legendary. Increasingly, the Christian Democratic survival is due more to an ability to forge coalitions and dispense favors than to ideological appeal.

Given all this, the postwar political climate in Agnone (as elsewhere in Italy) is permeated by cynicism. On the local scene the situation is further exacerbated by the fact that, out of a sense of expediency, many people have had to shift their political allegiance radically. I attended a town meeting in 1973 at which a frustrated Communist student blurted out, "We all know who in this room exchanged their black shirt [symbol of fascism] for a white one [symbolic of the Christian Democrats]." He was shouted down, not because he was wrong, but because he was stating the unmentionable. Scathing critiques of clientalistic democracy may be found in the poems "La libberta" ("Liberty"), Dun Frangiscandonie" ("Don Francescantonio"), and "La mucrazia" ("Democracy") written in Agnone's local dialect.[173]

If for the first two decades after the war, state projects secured through the political influence of Agnone's local politicians provided the major driving force in the local economy, by the early 1970s much of the initiative was dissipating. By that time, the town had its hospital, a new post

office and town hall, and most of its schools were housed in new facilities. It was increasingly difficult to justify new, major government-
financed projects.

At the same time, the pillars of the traditional local economy—agriculture and artisanship—have all but collapsed in recent years. Ecological factors alone militate against a healthy agricultural system in
Agnone. Harsh climate and difficult topography make plow agriculture a
marginal activity at best. Attempts to modernize cultivation are further
frustrated by a problematic land-tenure system. During the late nineteenth and early twentieth centuries, emigrant remittances permitted
Agnone's peasants to capitalize their long-standing dream of owning
land. The landlords were beset on the one hand by an acute labor shortage (itself the result of emigration) and on the other, by rising peasant
purchasing power that inflated land values all out of proportion to a
field's intrinsic agricultural worth.[174] So the *galantuomini* sold out,[175]
but in so doing they divided their estates, for most emigrants were only
in a position to acquire a few plots at a time. Yields were also affected
adversely because the peasant, prone to expend all his savings acquiring
the land itself, then lacked the necessary capital to maintain and improve it.[176]

These developments accelerated the centuries-old process of fragmentation of landownership in the town. Furthermore, the divisive effects of
the partible inheritance system were exacerbated once virtually all of
Agnone's fields became influenced by marriages and deaths in the town's
peasantry. Thus, whereas in the 1816 property register, Agnone's land
base was divided into 7,838 individual plots, in the modern register formulated in the 1950s there are 41,753 holdings. In the two decades following, there has been considerable additional parcelization.

Felt frustrations among the peasantry are evident and are sometimes
expressed in spectacular fashion. During the postwar period, Agnone's
peasants, on one occasion, assaulted the local Land Registry Office,
where they destroyed the land-tenure records used for taxation (a futile
exercise because there were copies in Isernia). A more successful tactic
has been the peasants' recent refusal to pay the religious tithes that theoretically remain in effect against the fields. The clergy continue to record
the mounting arrears but are powerless to enforce their collection.

During the postwar period, then, few people in Agnone have believed
that local agriculture is viable in a world increasingly dominated by
modern agribusiness. Local reformers and government agents talk wist-

fully of restructuring the agricultural system of the Alto Molise by consolidating landholdings and converting them to livestock pasturage, but the statistics on the fragmentation of land tenureship in Agnone testify to the enormity of the task. The peasants have few illusions. Unable and, in many cases, unwilling to recruit their sons and daughters to what they regard as an anachronistic and dying way of life, many peasants in Agnone today expend their resources helping their offspring to acquire a university career or to emigrate permanently. Among the Agnonesi as throughout much of rural Italy,[177] the postwar period has seen discernible aging and feminizing of the agricultural work force. Faced with a labor shortage and waning capabilities, the peasant family abandons its more marginal holdings and eventually the entire farmstead. Today much of Agnone's *agro* is either cultivated badly or not at all.

The artisans have experienced their own crisis despite successful attempts to organize,[178] to hold exhibits of their wares in Agnone and elsewhere,[179] and to solicit government assistance in the form of pension plans and low-interest loans.[180] There have even been some spectacular postwar highpoints in the history of Agnone's artisanship. For example, in 1965 the artisans' association of the Molise donated to the pope a bell made in Agnone, which became the official bell of the Second Ecumenical Council.[181]

The signs of collapse in the artisan sector of Agnone's economy were abundantly clear, however, as early as 1950.[182] In 1956 it was contended that only a well-conceived artisans' school could save the tottering industries.[183] New legislation designed to alleviate the artisans' plight was greeted with brief spurts of optimism, but the decline continued unabated.[184] By the mid-1960s the best thing that could be said for the artisans' prospects was: "It is important not to have illusions. Only a small artisan complex is possible, and for it to survive it must produce goods of such artistic value that they will be much sought after."[185]

Table 8.1 details the magnitude of the decline of Agnone's artisan trades. The 639 artisans in the 1901 census represented 16.48 percent of the male population fifteen years of age and over. The 94 artisans in the 1971 census constitute only 3.51 percent of Agnone's adolescent and adult males in that year.[186]

There is another sense in which Agnone's artisans are now in crisis. Like the peasant, the craftsman is now loath to recruit young people into his trade. Today, very few of Agnone's artisans have an apprentice. Social legislation in 1950 required artisans to pay apprentices a minimum

179

Table 8.1. *Agnone's Artisans: 1901 and 1971 Compared*

Kind of artisan	Number in 1901	Number in 1971
Coppersmith	116	14
Goldsmith	145	1
Ironsmith	68	19
Tailor	60	19
Shoemaker	144	6
Carder	10	1
Carpenter-cabinetmaker	70	30
Clocksmith	4	2
Bell maker	4	2
Hemp dresser	18	0
Totals	639	94

Sources: Comune di Agnone, "Elenco delle famiglie e delle persone censite il 10 febbraio, 1901," passim; "Censimento di Agnone," passim.

Note: The 1901 census lists men sixty-five and over according to their lifelong occupations; the 1971 census lists them as simply "retired." Thus, in the former case, artisans are included in my figures who would be excluded in the latter case, making the magnitude of the decline somewhat overstated. I have elected not to correct for this difference inasmuch as it reflects a behavioral reality. That is, before the implementation of government pensions, the elderly artisan frequently remained active until death; today he retires.

wage, an expense that many were unable to bear.[187] Consequently, the remaining practitioners are largely middle-aged men, bitter at their lot but fearful of changing professions. In the words of one, "I can't make a living with my copper, but it is the only trade I know." In 1971 the mean age of Agnone's artisans was forty-four years, and among coppersmiths, for example, the mean was forty-seven. Though there was one twenty-year-old, the second-youngest coppersmith was thirty-six.

To the litany of local economic problems may be added the fact that, by the late 1960s, Italy's postwar economic miracle had dissipated. Rampant inflation and unemployment were endemic throughout the nation. The latter was a particularly explosive issue in that the postwar experiment in mass higher education had produced large numbers of overtrained young people, many of whom were politically radicalized and alienated.

In places like Agnone, where, during the postwar years, the private sector of the economy had all but collapsed, the situation was critical. For many years, the town's politicians have been under considerable pressure to provide public employment for their followers. Consequently, the system of political patronage in Agnone today has just about probed the outer limits of the capacity of public institutions to absorb menials and doormen. One disgusted informant summed up Agnone's present sad state by saying, "We have become a town of janitors!" Similarly, there are limits to the possibilities for dividing such positions as teaching posts into part-time positions for a surfeit of applicants.

In the 1971 census between 400 and 500 Agnone residents were on a government payroll in some capacity. Dozens more were eligible for government aid as invalids; 239 men and 315 women were drawing retirement pensions.[188] Yet despite this magnitude of government subsidization of the economic life of the town, fully 91 men in their active years and 60 women were unemployed and in search of work. In 1973 it could be claimed that Agnone was in grave, immediate need of two hundred new jobs.[189]

All these developments have served to create new factionalism in Agnone's body politic. Beginning in the late 1960s many idealistic young people, frustrated by their lack of opportunity and disillusioned by local political clientalism, began to agitate for reform. In part, they were also reflecting the position of the growing left-wing opposition to Christian Democratic hegemony in national and local affairs. In Agnone this movement crystallized in an organization called the "Gruppo 38" (as there were 38 founding members).

Initially, the local political establishment observed these developments nervously, content occasionally to lecture wayward youth[190] while applauding such humanitarian efforts as the Gruppo 38's collection of funds for earthquake victims in late 1970.[191] By 1971 it was clear that a major confrontation was brewing. In the summer of that year, the Gruppo 38 organized a program whereby many students lived with rural Agonone families in order better to understand peasant problems.[192] *La fucina* denounced the organization in the strongest terms, accusing some of its membership of being "Maoist."[193]

In 1973 Agnone's young leftists went on the offensive by founding a new newspaper called *Piazza del tomolo*. The publication wasted little time in attacking the local political establishment.[194] In pointed fashion, the paper asked:

181

Why does the D.C. [Christian Democrats] have the power? It was obtained in the postwar period through the sellout of the interests of the popular classes to large capital whose only purpose is to maintain and augment profit. And the D.C. intends fully to maintain itself as it has up until now, ignoring and damaging the interests and the aspirations of the workers, the peasants, and the students. Consequently, it is necessary that everyone realize these facts and that the struggle against the D.C. become progressively more incisive.[195]

In sum, the economic crises of the postwar era rapidly translate into a political crisis of considerable magnitude. In this, the town is far from alone; rather, it is a microcosm of the Italian nation as a whole, and particularly of mountainous, rural regions ill-suited for either the siting of industry or the implementation of modern agribusiness. There is also a sense, however, in which the issues are perhaps felt more profoundly in a community such as Agnone. For the Agnonesi must conduct the debate of contemporary failures and frustrations against the backdrop of a perceived illustrious past. As if local decline were not galling enough, the townspeople are further confronted with the striking postwar successes of rural centers such as Isernia and Campobasso. Table 8.2 details demographic trends in the three communities for the postwar era.

Thus, during the postwar period, the populations of Isernia and Campobasso have almost doubled while that of Agnone has declined by one-third. Between 1971 and 1979 the town's population remained stable, but this was a period of considerable economic retrenchment both in Italy and in the countries that have traditionally hosted Agnonese immigrants. Once conditions improve in the receiving areas, renewed emigration seems likely.

Agnone's decline as a regional servicing center is not to be measured solely in terms of the town's own demographics. Rather, over the past century, the population of Agnone's hinterland has actually declined more than that of the town itself. Between 1871 and 1971 the combined population of the eighteen satellite communities (see Table 2.1) was almost halved from 45,130 to 27,385.

A further modern-era irony undercutting Agnone's economic vitality should be noted. Not only has the town's hinterland clientele contracted sharply in absolute numbers; Agnone's control over regional marketing has loosened considerably. Motorized transportation now facilitates fre-

Table 8.2. *Postwar Populations of Agnone,*
Isernia, and Campobasso

Town	1951	1961	Percentage change	1971	Percentage change	1979	Percentage change
Agnone	9,509	7,831	− 17.65	6,481	− 17.24	6,484	0.00
Isérnia	10,976	12,308	+ 12.14	15,575	+ 26.54	19,121	+ 22.77
Campobasso	28,387	33,798	+ 19.06	41,889	+ 23.94	47,316	+ 12.96

Sources: ISTAT, *Popolazione residente e presente dei comuni ai censimenti dal 1861 al 1961*, pp. 291, 293; idem, *Primi risultati provinciali e comunali sulla popolazione e sulle abitazioni*, pp. 124–125; idem, *Popolazione e movimento anagrafico dei comuni*, pp. 115–116.

quent visits of villagers of the Alto Molise to larger cities such as Isernia, Campobasso, Chieti, and even Naples and Rome. Agnone's small-scale merchants are simply unable to compete with urban department stores. Conversely, Agnone's market is easily penetrated by motorized, itinerant jobbers who specialize in discounting particular product lines, much to the chagrin of local purveyors.

Given the collapse of Agnone's traditional economic activities, there has been considerable local soul-searching and brainstorming for possible new initiatives. Tourism was viewed as a particularly attractive possibility. As early as 1950 the natural beauty of the Alto Molise was being extolled in the local press as a surefire tourist attraction.[196] In 1955 the Agnonesi formed a nonpartisan citizens' group called "Pro Agnone" to stimulate the local economy, in part by increasing tourism.[197] In 1963 a local dentist founded a newspaper, *Turisport*, devoted exclusively to touting the recreational potential of Agnone and the Alto Molise. Writing in 1965, one observer noted that "tourism is the factor of fundamental importance in determining the economic rebirth of Agnone."[198]

Unfortunately for the town, the promise of significant income from the tourist sources has proven chimerical. On a number of criteria, Agnone comes temptingly close to being a tourist attraction, but not quite. The old part of the town is photogenic but not nearly so as many other Italian cities. While there are artistically noteworthy structures, altars, effigies, and so on in Agnone, none is sufficiently famous to attract the traveler. In natural resources, the area is similarly marginal. While the town has some beautiful wooded areas, it is the dense forest of nearby Pescopennataro that attracts the camper. Topographically, Agnone is located just below the critical altitude for developing winter sports. It is the higher town of Capracotta that benefits from a ski resort.

The other major initiative in the postwar period has been the major lobbying effort by Agnone's politicians to ameliorate Agnone's physical isolation. I have noted the long-standing tradition of attributing Agnone's economic problems to the lack of adequate transportation. Some thought that if Agnone's highway connection with the rest of the nation could be improved, prosperity would automatically follow. It is fair to say that the proponents experienced remarkable success in acquiring the means without securing the ends. Much of Senator Sammartino's political career was devoted to construction of a modern road system for the Alto Molise. Today, Agnone is perched between two of the tallest highway bridges in Italy and the world. The new system has reduced travel time between Agnone and Isernia to about half an hour. At this writing, no new industry has located, nor is rumored to be about to locate, in Agnone. Rather, the only tangible result of the road system to date is the facilition of the commute of a growing number of Agnonesi who work in Isernia. Becoming a bedroom community for the provincial capital is scarcely the satisfactory future envisioned by Agnone's boosters.

9

The New Emigration

From a variety of standpoints, emigration from Agnone between 1870 and World War I differed markedly from that of subsequent years. The "old" emigration was largely unfettered. That is, there were a minimum of restrictions on immigration in the New World receiving areas and only a modicum of state control on emigration from Italy. The latter was directed mainly at ensuring at least a measure of humane conditions during the emigration process, rather than controlling the actual magnitude of departures.

For communities like Agnone, transatlantic emigration provided an economic alternative at a critical juncture in their history when more than a century of pronounced population increase had translated into a declining standard of living. It also provided an escape valve for the political malcontent alienated by the tensions of nineteenth-century political developments on the Italic peninsula. The abolishment of feudalism, the struggle between the Bourbons and liberals, the unification of the nation, and the rising challenge from socialism had produced a plethora of false starts and broken promises. The outpouring of the huddled masses, beset as it was with its own set of problems, did provide the hope of a new beginning to the individual and the alleviation of certain economic and social problems in the sending communities. In the case of Agnone, I have noted the extent to which support from the emigrant diaspora helped sustain a burst of civic energy that gave the town a splendid Indian summer before it plunged into the maelstrom of the Fascist years and the winter of modern decline. There is a sense in which the new emigration was both a cause and a symptom of the town's demise as a significant urban place. The details are the subject of this chapter.

Restricted Migration

World War I brought the massive and largely unregulated old emigration to a virtual standstill. The hostilities made the crossing hazardous, while at the same time, the prime candidates for emigration (males in their productive years) were enlisted into the Italian armed forces. As Italy did not enter the fray until late in 1914, 133 people managed to emigrate that year from the town (113 to the United States and 20 to Argentina). During the next four years only an additional 145 emigrants went out to the New World (120 to the United States, 14 to Argentina, and 11 to Canada).[1]

Writing in the postwar period (1923), Jannone claims, somewhat hyperbolically, that the migration rate in the Molise was higher than in other parts of Italy and that in many towns more than 50 percent of the populace had departed.[2] In Agnone, however, though emigration resumed, it did not acquire its prewar magnitude (see Table 9.1). Only in 1920 did the number of emigrants in any one year surpass 175.

It should be noted, however, that reference is only to "legal" emigrants, those who obtained valid exit visas. Apparently there was an active underground movement as well. In 1924 four Agnonesi were arrested in Naples for attempting to leave illegally. They had paid another Agnonese eighteen thousand liras to make the arrangements.[3] The following year, a man was arrested in Agnone for defrauding clandestine emigrants.[4]

The postwar figures reflect an interesting shift in choice of destination. For the first two decades of the twentieth century, Agnone's emigrants preferred North America. Between 1921 and 1927 the emphasis shifted to the southern hemisphere. During that period, 757 Agnonesi emigrated to Argentina and Brazil, while only 226 departed for either the United States or Canada.

In large measure, growing anti-immigration sentiment in the United

Table 9.1. *Agnone Emigration, 1919–1927, by Destination*

Year	Argentina	United States	Canada	Brazil	Europe	Africa	Totals
1919	15	83	10	0	2	0	110
1920	8	178 + 45[a]	6	0	5	0	242
1921	48	27	1	0	1	1	79[b]
1922	139	25	5	2	4	0	175
1923	129	38	2	6	0	0	175
1924	138	22	3	2	4	0	169
1925	63	14	4	2	1	1	85
1926	126	31	2	2	4	0	165
1927	98	49	3	2	4	0	156
Totals	764	512	36	16	25	2	1,356[b]

Source: *Libri dei passaporti*, Archivio Comunale di Agnone, 1919–1927.

[a] Destination listed as "North America" and might thus include some traveling to Canada.

[b] Includes one traveling to Mexico.

States accounts for this change. In 1917 the U.S. Senate prohibited entry to immigrants who were illiterate.[5] During the early 1920s the United States implemented a system of national-origins immigration quotas that had a strong anti–southern European bias. By 1924 the *Eco del Sannio* proclaimed that emigration to the United States was all but foreclosed.[6] Whereas, for example, in 1922 the Italian quota was set at 42,057,[7] in 1925 only 3,845 Italian nationals were to be admitted, and in fact only 2,690 visas were actually issued.[8] The magnitude of the curtailment may be appreciated if one considers that, between 1899 and 1922, 584,905 north Italians and 3,128,592 south Italians entered the country.[9]

In the history of Italian emigration, 1927 represents a critical juncture. The Mussolini government abolished the Commissariato Generale dell'Emigrazione and placed severe restrictions on the Italian citizen's right to leave. Henceforth emigration was to be restricted to destinations that furthered Italy's political goals (meaning the nation's African colonies) or that reunited separated nuclear family members.[10]

In 1928 there were only sixty-five emigrants from Agnone. Table 9.2 reflects Agnone's emigration for the period between 1929 and 1945. Clearly, with the exception of the brief three years between 1935 and

Table 9.2. *Agnone Emigration, 1929–1945, by Destination*

Year	Argentina	United States	Canada	Brazil	Europe	Africa	Totals
1929	7	0	1	0	0	0	8
1930	5	4	3	1	0	0	13
1931	1	2	0	0	0	0	3
1932	3	0	0	0	0	0	3
1933	3	0	2	0	1	0	6
1934	7	2	0	0	0	3	12
1935	68	65	2	0	0	0	258[a]
1936	22	79	16	0	4	2	124[b]
1937	225	73	15	0	6	2	329[c]
1938	3	1	5	0	0	4	13
1939	18	4	3	0	0	8	33
1940	5	0	0	0	1	3	9
1941	3	0	0	0	0	2	5
1942	14	0	3	0	0	1	18
1943	1	0	0	0	0	0	1
1944	0	0	0	0	1	0	1
1945	1	0	1	0	0	0	2
Totals	386	230	51	1	13	25	838

Sources: *Libri dei passaporti*, Archivio Comunale di Agnone and emigration files, Comune di Agnone.

Note: There is a record linkage problem that may have slightly inflated the statistics (particularly for the 1935–1938 period). In some instances it is impossible to determine if the same person is listed both in the passport book and on a card in the emigration file.

[a] Includes 61 listed as "South America" and 62 as "North America."

[b] Includes 1 to Chile.

[c] Includes 5 to "abroad" and 3 to Uruguay.

1937, when restrictions on departures were temporarily eased, emigration from Agnone was reduced to a trickle. For fourteen years of that seventeen-year-period, transatlantic departures from the town averaged only nine persons annually.

The New World Agnonesi

The curtailment of emigration from Agnone between 1914 and 1945 had considerable impact on the town's diaspora. The first casualties were the emigration agencies on both sides of the Atlantic. By 1915 the Marinelli agency in Buenos Aires had failed.[11] The Mastronardi agency in the same city survived a bit longer, but after 1918 ceased advertising in the pages of the *Eco del Sannio*. At the same time, because of the hostilities, Agnone's religious ceremonial life was suspended, and no overtures were made to the New World Agnonesi for donations in support of the religious *feste*.

On the other hand, the war effort and its aftermath constituted the bases for a new appeal to the emigrants. For example, the Agnonesi of Youngstown had earlier raised funds to support Italy's Libyan campaign (1911–1912), and in 1915 they organized a committee to raise money for the current Italian war effort.[12] As Agnone's casualties mounted, the diaspora provided assistance. In 1917 relief funds for the town's orphans were established in Argentina;[13] Jersey City, New Jersey;[14] and Trail, British Columbia.[15] The following year, a substantial amount of money was raised in Youngstown and distributed with considerable ceremony to forty-four widows and ninety-eight orphans in Agnone.[16]

During the euphoria of the postwar period, there was considerable interest in Agnone in memorializing both the victory and the war dead. Projects along these lines were to strike a particularly responsive chord among the grateful emigrants. In 1919 a Festa della Pace, or Peace Festival, was organized to honor the military. While only 606.10 liras were collected for it in Agnone, the committee received 687.10 liras from the United States and 1,527.00 liras from Buenos Aires.[17]

That same year, Luigi Gamberale organized a campaign to honor Agnone's war dead with a stone monument,[18] and the committee issued an appeal to the New World Agnonesi.[19] In 1920 a fund-raising committee for the project was formed in New York City,[20] and donations totaling 786.69 liras were sent in from Argentina.[21] The Youngstown colony provided an additional 3,496.00 liras.[22]

The following year the New York City committee made the stunning announcement that it had raised 50,554.75 liras, including 25,000.00 liras from Michelino de Menna and 8,000.00 liras given by Nicolo de Menna. Donors were from the New York City area; Philadelphia; Providence; Jersey City; Elmira, New York; Detroit; Springfield, Massachusetts; and Cool Creek and Pueblo, Colorado. The organizers tweaked the Ohio colony for not joining this common effort.[23] About the same time, the Youngstown Agnonesi underscored their growing independence by forming their own committee to solicit funds for a separate plaque to commemorate Agnone's war dead. They managed to collect 3,571.00 for the project.[24]

By 1923 funding for the monument was secured. That year 53,000 liras reached the committee from Argentina.[25] That the project was preeminently an "American" effort is seen in the fact that only about 10,000 of the liras were raised for it locally.[26] After considerable wrangling and procrastination, the imposing stone structure was constructed in the town's Piazza XX Settembre and inaugurated in September of 1927.[27] Today it is the monumental anchor of new Agnone.

Another project of considerable magnitude and duration that involved the emigrants as well was the construction of a theater. In 1911 thirty-two locals each subscribed 500 liras to purchase shares in the enterprise. Gamberale then wrote to the Agnonesi of Buenos Aires asking them to redirect their 12,803-lira fund for the defunct hospital to the new endeavor.[28] Ruggiero di Paola of Buenos Aires personally donated 12,000 liras with the stipulation that the theater pay 300 liras annual subsidy to the Asilo Infantile.[29] By 1916 the structure was almost completed, and Gamberale donated certain of his book royalties to the project.[30] Nevertheless, it was not until 1922 that the theater was finally inaugurated,[31] and only after the two local banks resolved its financial difficulties.[32] The theater, christened the Politeama Italo-Argentino, began to function at precisely the time when Agnone's cultural life, buffeted by Fascist strictures, was entering decline. After a lively operetta season in 1923, it came to be used primarily as a cinema.

During the postwar period, relations between Agnone and its diaspora reacquired their earlier forms. During the war years the newspaper rarely mentioned the emigrants with the exception of publishing an occasional death notice. It is clear, however, that the cocitizens retained a strong stake in the town's civic life. In 1919, of the 3,391 registered eligible voters for the municipal election, 716 were residing overseas.[33]

By 1918, funds in the form of bank deposits were once again flowing into the town from abroad. That year the Banca Sannitica received 179,449.60 liras from the New World, including 69,120.00 liras sent from Youngstown.[34] Six years later, emigrant remittances to the same bank amounted to 709,682.22 liras.[35] The annual report stated:

> We have received from bankers, our correspondents across the ocean, sums to be placed directly in deposit in our bank, sending to America the respective passbooks.

> This method of many of our emigrants who withdraw large sums
> from their hoards and savings to send to us to be deposited . . .
> demonstrates the predilection of our emigrants always to maintain
> good economic relations with their beautiful homeland.[36]

It is harder to determine the extent to which emigrant remittances played
a part in the operations of the Banca Operaia because such funds were
not listed separately in its annual report. The bank prospered, however,
during the early 1920s and closed the year 1924 with 5,267,465.78 liras
on deposit in savings.[37]

By 1922 the *Eco del Sannio* had reinstituted an *Americhe* section that
regularly reported on emigrant activities. It gave particular attention to
events such as the graduation of Francesco Massanisso from Harvard
Medical School;[38] Agostino Sammartino from the school of medicine at
Columbia University;[39] Alfredo Borgini from the medical school in Cordoba, Argentina;[40] and Felice Buoscio from the law school at the University of Chicago.[41]

Illustrious returnees from the New World were officially honored by
the town. In 1925, when Michele di Menna, donor of twenty-five thousand liras for the war dead monument, paid a brief visit to Agnone, he
was given receptions by the Circolo di Conversazione, Circolo di Lavoratori Indipendenti, Sezione Mutilati di Guerra, Asilo Infantile, and the
directors of the elementary schools.[42]

Both collectively and individually, New World Agnonesi resumed a
philanthropic stance toward the town. In 1922 money was raised in
Youngstown, New York City, Detroit, and Jersey City to assist poor students in Agnone with their educational expenses.[43] More than half the
funds to restore the bell tower of the Church of Maiella were raised in the
New World.[44] On occasion, people in South America made individual
donations to the Asilo Infantile.[45] The Sammartino and Piccione families of Mendoza, Argentina, donated a building site in Agnone for construction of a hospital.[46]

When the religious *feste* were reinstituted, the New World Agnonesi
were quick to resume their role as patrons. In 1920, of the 6,494.90 liras expended in celebrating the *festa* of the Madonna della Libera,
4,846.00 liras were raised in the Americas.[47] In 1925 only 979 liras
were donated in Agnone for the *festa* of Maria SS della Cintura, whereas
4,163 liras and 1,610 liras, respectively, were raised in North and South
America.[48] Throughout the late 1920s and early 1930s, the emigrants

consistently surpassed the Agnonesi in their support of the town's *feste*.[49]

Given the fact that the *Eco del Sannio*, through predilection and circumspection, seldom spoke ill of fascism, it is difficult to determine how Agnone's emigrants perceived the town's fascist interlude. While many were probably disappointed, it is clear that this was not true in every case. In 1928 Gaetano Piccione returned to Agnone, where he was touted as the founder in Mendoza of one of the first Italian Fascist sections ever established abroad.[50] Piccione had raised over four hundred thousand liras in Argentina for diasbled veterans, of which he had donated ten thousand himself. In 1930 Giuseppe Santarelli of Argentina sent a bronze medallion to Agnone's Fascist section.[51] In 1936 Agnonesi resident in New York City and Youngstown paid homage to Agnone's Fascist political secretary.[52] Shortly thereafter, despite world condemnation of Mussolini, the colony of Youngstown celebrated the Italian victory in Abyssinia.[53]

There was one other development in the diaspora that deserves mention. By 1935 it was claimed that there were several thousand Agnonesi residing in the Youngstown area. In February of that year more than 200 of them came together to form a social club, which they called the Club Agnonese.[54] By April the membership had grown to 350.[55] The following year the organization was ridden with factionalism.[56] By September of 1937 membership had declined to 40 persons, so the club ceased operation.[57] After considerable chiding by the *Eco del Sannio*, the Club Agnonese of Youngstown was reconstituted in early 1938.[58] By April it had 140 members,[59] and in September it initiated a membership drive with a goal of 500 members.[60]

On balance, then, during the 1914–1945 period, the emigrant diaspora continued to play a significant if somewhat diminished role in Agnone's civic life. At the same time, curtailment of emigration combined with the return to Italy of many former emigrants during the Great Depression meant that the town's overseas colonies were both aging and dwindling.

Postwar Emigration

With the cessation of hostilities at the end of World War II, conditions were again propitious for emigration. A defeated and prostrate Italy of-

Table 9.3. *Destinations of Transatlantic Emigrants from Agnone, 1946–1972*

Destination	Males	Females	Totals
Argentina	747	671	1,418
Canada	742	629	1,371
Australia	70	57	127
United States	55	56	111
Brazil	11	4	15
South Africa	6	8	14
Chile	0	1	1
Mexico	1	0	1
Paraguay	1	0	1
Totals	1,633	1,426	3,059

Source: Emigration files, Comune di Agnone.

Note: There are sufficient difficulties with the sources so as to preclude regarding the figures as a completely accurate summary of all transatlantic emigration from the town during the period in question. These include linkage problems within the municipal records, the fact that some individuals emigrated more than once, while others who eventually emigrated overseas had a brief prior change of residence elsewhere in Italy and therefore appear in the Agnone sources as internal (within Italy) migrants. Furthermore, because the Italian government has not maintained the former controls, such as requiring the emigrants to obtain a license, many have gone without leaving a trace in local official records. For example, today there are a few Agnonesi in Caracas; yet not a single person was listed in my sources as opting for Venezuela.

fered a bleak economic panorama for its citizenry. Democratization of its government gave Italy new standing with the community of nations, and antifascist anti-Italianism abated. The war years had eliminated the Great Depression. Consequently, there was a renewed spurt of transatlantic emigration from Agnone. Table 9.3 details the destinations of its 3,059 transatlantic emigrants for the period 1946 to 1972.

Several comments are in order. In the first five years (1946–1950), 113 people, or only 3.69 percent of the total in Table 9.3, managed to emigrate overseas. During the next several years, it almost appears as if Agnone's transatlantic emigration had come full cycle. That is, Argentina was initially favored by the Agnonesi before being eclipsed in the late nineteenth and early twentieth centuries by the United States. In the early 1950s the South American country again became the preferred destination.

Despite the fact that fully 46.36 percent of the Agnonesi sampled above elected Argentina, the movement there was largely limited to the decade of the 1950s. With Europe's conomy still in a shambles, many were willing to emigrate; for the average person, however, there were serious difficulties. The United States and Canada emerged from the war with the problem of reabsorbing the returning soldiers into their economies. Hence they continued their restrictive immigration policies. Most of the exceptions were aimed at alleviating the suffering of displaced persons and other war refugees.[61] Argentina, on the other hand, implemented a liberal immigration policy, and one that did not discriminate against nationals of former Axis countries. Italians, in particular, flocked to the South American nation in large numbers (461,832 from 1947 until 1957).[62]

Of the 1,418 Agnonesi emigrating to Argentina between the years 1946 and 1972, 1,014, or 72 percent of the total, did so between the years 1951 and 1958. As conditions improved in Italy and Argentina entered a period of social unrest, the South American nation's attractiveness waned. By the late 1950s many of Argentina's new European immigrants had departed the country. That nation's latest experiment in fostering economic development through immigration was a failure.[63]

Canada received almost as many Agnonesi during the postwar period as did Argentina: 1,371, or 44.82 percent of the total in Table 9.3. Before World War II, Canada had pursued a restrictive immigration policy designed to favor British and northern European immigrants, limit southern European ones, and exclude nonwhites altogether. In the postwar period there was continued emphasis on British immigration; but during the early 1950s, restrictions on the entry of other Europeans were liberalized considerably.[64] Potential Italian immigrants were required to have close relatives already living in Canada willing to sponsor them.[65] While posing a difficulty, it was not nearly as problematical as it might have been. During the first two decades of the twentieth century, Canada permitted several thousand Italians into the country, primarily to provide the labor force for expansion of its railway network. Most of the Agnonesi mentioned earlier who settled in Trail, British Columbia, entered in that fashion. There were also Agnonesi in the eastern provinces. According to one source, in the year 1923 several Agnonesi entered Canada clandestinely and settled in Leamington, Ontario.[66] So the bases for chain migration from Agnone to Canada were in place when the new rulings went into effect.

Between 1946 and 1965, 307,356 Italian nationals entered Canada. Of this total, the large majority, or 253,053, came during the 1950s.[67] Beginning in the middle of the decade (or just about the time Argentina lost its attraction), large numbers of Agnonesi began to opt for the North American nation. In 1957 alone, 264 Agnonesi entered Canada. Although Canada continued to attract the townspeople throughout the remainder of the period 1946–1972, 766 people (or 56% of the total 1,371 Canadian emigrants) left Agnone between the years 1956 and 1962.

Another development that requires comment is the departure of 127 Agnonesi for Australia. As a part of the British dominion, Australia had historically restricted immigration according to its White Australia Policy. In practice, exclusion of nonwhites meant swarthy southern Europeans as well. Consequently, before World War II, only about 56,000 southern Europeans had settled in the country throughout its history.[68] After the conflict, Australian attitudes shifted radically. Shaken by the recent Japanese challenge to their sovereignty, desirous of quickening economic growth, and beset by acute labor shortages, successive Australian governments have pursued an aggressive policy designed to increase the national population 1 percent annually through immigration alone.[69] Thus, between 1947 and 1974, Australia received a net gain of 534,860 southern Europeans, of whom the largest single contingent (271,608) were from Italy. This makes Italians the second-largest ethnic group (after the British) in Australian society today.[70] Assisted-passage plans and active recruitment by Australian agents who guaranteed employment in such labor-starved industries as sugar have managed to establish a new thrust of Italian emigration within a relatively short time. From the perspective of the Agnonesi, Australia during the postwar period ranks behind only Argentina and Canada as their preferred overseas destination.

Finally, the United States, which was once the favored destination of Agnone's emigrants, has played a minor role as a potential receiving country during recent years. Throughout the postwar period the American nation has continued a restrictive immigration policy with respect to the unskilled. In 1950 Agnone's newspaper editorialized against U.S. immigration legislation.[71] Most of the Agnonesi who have been successful in entering the country were effecting family reunions.

European Migration

After World War II, then, overseas emigration regained a modicum of its former significance for the Agnonesi, but during the same period it has had to vie with two new alternative destinations for potential emigrants from the town. Beginning in the late 1950s and continuing into the mid-1960s, Italy experienced strong economic recovery. As government-sponsored development programs and consumerism swept the nation, north Italy's industries boomed.[72] The resulting demand for workers proved attractive to many south Italian migrants.

During the same period Italians found ready employment in other Western European economies as well. Labor-starved Switzerland welcomed temporary foreign workers, and Italy's entry in 1957 into the Common Market gave her citizens access to manual and semiskilled employment in France, Belgium, and Germany. This movement of Italian workers to neighboring European countries is not a new pattern; it dates from the late nineteenth century and by World War II had involved several million people.[73] For the Agnonesi, however, it is largely a postwar phenomenon.

During the period 1957 through 1965, 969,332 Italians entered Switzerland, 625,865 went to Germany, and 450,521 chose France.[74] In Germany, for instance, during the 1960s of all southern European workers (including Greeks, Spaniards, Turks, Portuguese, and Yugoslavians), Italians were by far the largest group, ranging from a low of 134,900 workers in 1963 to a high of 391,300 in 1966.[75] Table 9.4 details the movement of Agnonesi to Western European countries between the years 1946 and 1972.

Thus, during the postwar period, of all the Western European countries, France has attracted the largest contingent of Agnonesi (61.02% of the total in Table 9.4) followed by Germany and then Switzerland. The town's Western European emigration was far from evenly distributed throughout the period. In 1967 alone, 109 Agnonesi went to France, 36 to Germany, 26 to Switzerland, and 5 to Belgium. These 176 emigrants represented 24.86 percent of the total for the 1946–1972 period. During the years 1967, 1970, and 1972, 230 Agnonesi went to France, which represented 53.24 percent of Agnone's French emigration during the entire period. Between 1970 and 1972, 92 Agnonesi went to Germany, which is 60.13 percent of the German emigration.

Table 9.4. *Emigration from Agnone to Western European Countries, 1946–1972*

Destination	Males	Females	Totals
France	237	195	432
Germany	86	67	153
Switzerland	41	33	74
Belgium	24	19	43
England	4	2	6
Totals	392	316	708

Source: Emigration files, Comune di Agnone.

Note: As with Table 9.3, and for the same reasons, the figures should not be construed as a completely reliable total of all Agnonesi emigrating to Western Europe during the period.

Finally, Belgium merits mention. As early as 1950 the local newspaper was publishing information on how to enter that country.[76] Several Agnonesi availed themselves of the opportunity to work in coal mining there. Some returned with major disabilities, including black lung. Consequently, Belgium has in recent years fallen into disfavor with the townspeople.

Table 9.5 reflects the emigration of Agnonesi to other parts of Italy. It is interesting to note that of the 2,271 Agnone-born internal migrants, only 486, or 21.40 percent of the total, opted for the industrial north. The cities of Rome and Naples together accounted for 29.19 percent of the migrants. Other communities in the Molise, and notably Isernia and Campobasso, accounted for 28.75 percent. In sum, almost four out of five of Agnone's internal migrants during the period 1946–1972 selected either Rome or a destination somewhere in south Italy.

There are some general comments to be made about postwar emigration from Agnone. If the three postwar currents (transatlantic = 3,059 people, inter-European = 708, and intra-Italian = 2,271) are summed, a total of 6,038 people departed Agnone for residence elsewhere between 1946 and 1972. This represents an average of 223 departures annually over the twenty-seven year-period. In terms of absolute numbers, there were fewer emigrants from the town than during the peak years of pre–World War I emigration; yet when one considers that by the

Table 9.5. *Agnone-born Migrants to Other Areas of Italy, 1946–1972*

Destination	Males	Females	Totals
Other Molise	274	379	653
Rome	281	276	557
Naples	52	54	106
Other south Italy	214	255	469
Central and north Italy	255	231	486
Totals	1,076	1,195	2,271

Source: Emigration files, Comune di Agnone.

Note: For the purposes of this analysis, only people born in Agnone are included. I chose to exclude those born elsewhere to factor out the transients such as students and *carabinieri* who spend a relatively brief period in the town but who are, nevertheless, represented in local emigration records.

post–World War II period the town's population was reduced, the magnitude of emigration vis-à-vis Agnone's population base was similar.

In one critical respect, however, the new emigration differs from the old, namely, in the sex ratio of the migrants. Whereas near the turn of the century, the emigrant from Agnone was typically a young adult male, after World War II there is considerable balance between the sexes. Of the 6,038 people represented in Tables 9.3–9.5, 3,101, or only 51.36 percent are male. During the postwar period, then, female emigration and the departure of entire family units have become considerably more common. This is not to say, however, that the pattern of single, male emigration is entirely gone. When destination implies the search for employment, the male ratio rises slightly. Thus 53.38 percent of Agnone's overseas emigrants are male, as are 52.37 percent of the Western European emigrants and 52.47 percent of the north Italian migrants. It is when other migration motives enter in, such as the desire for education or special health care, that the ratio shifts. Thus, less than half (47.38%) of Agnone's migrants within south Italy are male.

A new figure may be discerned within the ranks of Agnone's postwar emigrants, that of the short-term sojourner. These are people who seek employment in either north Italy or neighboring Western European countries. Many of the Agnonesi who went to north Italy with the intention of settling permanently have returned disgruntled. The south Italian worker encounters considerable discrimination in the north. For

Table 9.6. Legal Residents Absent from Agnone at the Time of the 1971 Census

Place of Residence	Employment		As a family dependent		Study		Military service		Medical care		Tourism		Unspecified		Totals	
	M	F	M	F	M	F	M	F	M	F	M	F	M	F	M	F
Germany	105	1	0	0	0	0	0	0	0	0	0	0	0	0	105	1
Switzerland	49	5	0	1	0	0	0	0	0	0	0	0	0	0	49	6
France	12	0	0	0	0	0	0	0	0	0	0	0	0	0	12	0
South Africa	2	0	0	0	0	0	0	0	0	0	0	0	0	0	2	0
Canada	0	3	0	0	0	0	0	0	0	0	1	3	0	0	1	6
Argentina	0	1	0	0	0	0	0	0	0	0	0	0	0	0	0	1
Australia	1	0	0	0	0	0	0	0	0	0	0	0	0	0	1	0
United States	0	0	0	0	0	0	0	0	0	0	1	0	0	0	1	0
Rome	23	7	2	4	12	9	4	0	2	11	1	3	0	1	44	35
Naples	5	2	0	0	8	15	1	0	3	2	4	1	0	0	21	20
Other Molise	6	3	0	0	6	6	0	0	2	2	2	5	0	0	16	16
Other south Italy	16	3	5	3	3	6	7	0	3	3	1	6	0	0	35	21
Central and north Italy	39	6	3	7	16	8	18	0	1	0	0	2	0	0	77	23
Totals	258	31	10	15	45	44	30	0	11	18	10	20	0	1	364	129

N = 493

Source: "Censimento di Agnone."

many Agnonesi, to be treated as a second-class citizen is too high a price to pay for economic opportunity.

As for the other Common Market countries, few Italians have entered them with the intention of settling permanently.[77] Rather, the migrant tends to set a personal goal. In this respect he is predisposed to accept a circumscribed social life and, at times, barrackslike living conditions in order to maximize savings and shorten his sojourn. At the same time, he is highly vulnerable because he is the first to face layoff during economic slumps.[78] The German phrase for the immigrant laborer, *Gästarbeiter*, or guest worker, neatly sums up the tenuousness of his position.

I conclude this discussion of the magnitude of emigration in postwar Agnone by analyzing the 1971 census data. Table 9.6 details the numbers of Agnonesi who at the time of the census were residing elsewhere but who continued to maintain official residence in the town. Of note is the large disparity between males ($N = 364$) and females ($N = 129$). In contrast to the diachronic analysis that sampled those who had completed the process of severing legal residence in the town, this synchronic approach details those in the process of making their decisions. In this profile, it is possible to appreciate the extent to which, at any one time, there were solitary Agnonese men away from the town on a work sojourn. It is only after a decision to leave Agnone permanently that they would send for their dependents.

Finally, it should be noted that, during the decade of the 1970s, migration from the town has slowed considerably. An unfavorable world economy has adversely affected all of the traditional destinations of Agnonese emigrants.

The Demographic Consequences

Between the years 1809 and 1977, there was an excess of 17,212 births over deaths in Agnone.[79] From 1809 to the 1870s the town's population grew from about eight thousand to the twelve thousand range. The latter figure is approximately halved at present after a century of emigration. Stated differently, on balance, between 1809 and 1977 (but primarily since the 1870s), almost twenty thousand people emigrated from Agnone permanently.[80]

But Agnone's current demographic crisis is not limited to simple population loss alone. Rather, the makeup of the remaining inhabitants has experienced modification detrimental to the town's continued vitality. While many Agnonesi have sought opportunity elsewhere, for the inhabitants of the town's more impoverished hinterland, Agnone itself proved economically attractive. Between 1945 and 1972 a total of 603 people from Agnone's hinterland (as defined in Table 2.1) applied for residency in the town. Whereas in the 1901 census, fully 92.48 percent of all residents of Agnone's *cittadina* had been born in the municipality,[81] by 1971 the figure had declined to 81.23 percent.[82] Today, approximately 1 in 5 residents is an outsider, and the proportion of outsiders among the economically active adult population is considerably greater. Where, formerly, loyalty to birthplace was an important ingredient in mobilizing support for civic projects, the growing proportion of newcomers within the populace makes such appeals increasingly less effective. Many of the new residents are not only unconcerned by Agnone's decline but are actually bemused by it. The Agnonesi are not particularly loved within the region.

During the twentieth century, Agnone's population has undergone another metamorphosis as well, in that it has aged considerably. Figures 9.1 and 9.2 compare those in the 1901 and 1971 censuses for whom age is specified.[83] In the year 1901, 30.18 percent of all Agnonesi were under fifteen years of age. By 1971 the figure had declined to 23.96 percent. Conversely, in 1901 only 33.26 percent of the townspeople were forty years of age, whereas by 1971 42.58 percent of all Agnonesi had completed their fortieth birthday.

Gone are the former peasant and artisan patrilineally extended joint families with several active adults and myriad children—domestic groups easily capable of providing many candidates for emigration while at the same time ensuring local social continuity. Today's household often contains a solitary individual or a middle-aged couple living alone, unwilling to leave their birthplace, yet unable to ensure its survival.

By using their emigrant savings, peasant families acquired most of the available land base. No longer landed and faced with the recent economic misfortunes of Agnone and the Alto Molise, many *galantuomini* opted to exercise a professional career elsewhere in Italy. Gone, then, are most of those families of the past who, for all their rapaciousness, did provide Agnone with capital, initiative, and a sense of purpose.

Nor has the peasant agriculturalist prospered either socially or

Figure 9.1. *Age Profile of the Population of Agnone in the 1901 Census*

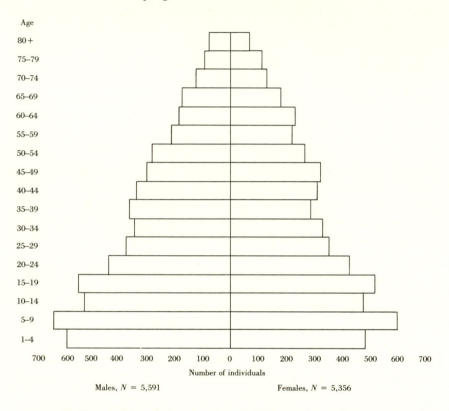

Males, *N* = 5,591   Females, *N* = 5,356

economically on his newly acquired holdings. According to one observer, perceived social class deprivation continues to play a major role as a motive for Agnone's *contadini* to emigrate:

> Even though many are willing to ascribe the exodus from the countryside to purely economic reasons, in reality it derives from a patent but unconfessed phenomenon—the desire of the peasant to enter the social order on the equal basis that corresponds to his rights. Such an entry in the social arena was always denied to the peasant because he was regarded as pertaining to a different and inferior class, to a subspecies of mankind. The hoe was and is his pillory and penance, and the peasant now seeks with vehemence to break away from it. For that reason, emigration is, in a most evident and concrete manner, the revolt against the hoe.[84]

Figure 9.2. *Age Profile of the Population of Agnone in the 1971 Census*

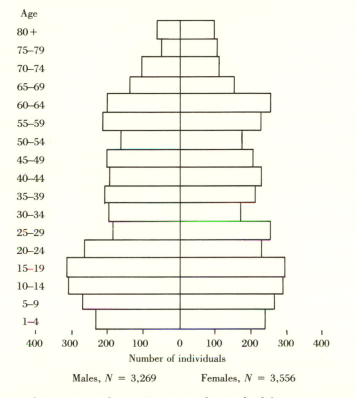

Males, *N* = 3,269   Females, *N* = 3,556

In several instances, then, a peasant who worked for years as an emigrant before returning to Agnone to acquire land has subsequently abandoned his hard-earned property to reemigrate. Writing of the situation in 1964, one observer noted:

> Whoever takes the trouble today to visit any of Agnone's peasant neighborhoods, Fontesambuco for example, sees many semiruined and abandoned farmhouses, with collapsed roofs and open doors and windows banging in the wind, while weeds take over in the rooms. One has the impression that war rather than emigration had passed through.[85]

Of the 842 male *contadini* over fifteen years of age resident in Agnone's *agro* in 1971, 133, or 15.80 percent, were absent and employed elsewhere as workers. These included 56 in Germany, 33 in Switzerland, and 11 in France. Thus, in 1971, 1 out of every 8.42 adolescent and adult Agnonesi peasant males was employed outside of Italy in a neighboring Western European country.

While difficult to measure, there is one final sense in which Agnone's vitality has diminished. I have argued that, at the outset of transatlantic emigration, the candidates were drawn from the ranks of those least suited to compete effectively within the local society and economy—the disaffected, unpropertied, and excess members of large peasant and artisan households. Since World War II, however, the selective thrust is noticeably reversed. Today it is the better educated and ambitious person who leaves the town. Although the point should not be overemphasized, it seems clear that the local populace is now a kind of residual category comprised inordinately of the aged, the lame, and the less imaginative.

The Waning Diaspora

I have noted that from the late nineteenth century until World War II, the two-way transfer of people, wealth, and ideas between the town and its diaspora was one of the most important features of Agnone's social and economic life. During the recent postwar period, and despite a recrudescence of emigration, the influence of the diaspora on local life has waned considerably.

To be sure, in the first decade after the war, the New World Agnonesi responded in their usual fashion to the town's appeals. When the hospital project was initiated, the mayor urged the emigrants to send donations.[86] By the summer of 1950, Argentine pesos and United States and Canadian dollars were pouring in.[87] More than three thousand dollars were raised in Youngstown alone.[88] Subsequently, individual donors in Youngstown made large contributions,[89] and a committee was formed in Caracas to collect money for the project.[90] Meanwhile, funds were raised in the New World to restore a church in Fontesambuco,[91] and in 1951, a committee of Agnonesi in Buenos Aires sent 115,400 liras to parliamentarian Sammartino to be used as he saw fit for the good of the town.[92]

The diaspora also continued to influence Agnone's political and religious life. In 1953 the Agnonesi of Buenos Aires supported Sammartino's candidacy for the Italian Parliament.[93] In 1955, of the money collected for the *festa* of the Madonna della Libera, 245,467 liras were raised in the Americas, compared to only 163,370 liras in the town.[94]

Similarly, a personal tragedy publicized in *La fucina* could elicit a charitable response among the emigrant diaspora.[95]

Another development worthy of note is the effort, beginning in the mid-1960s, of one of Agnone's parish priests to minister to the emigrants. On two occasions he has visited Agnone's Canadian colonies, where he solicited considerable funds for the reconstruction of the Hermitage of San Onofrio (a church in Agnone's *agro*), where he annually celebrates the Day of the Emigrant.[96]

There has also been a spurt of associational activity in the diaspora. In 1950 the Pro-Agnone Committee was formed in Buenos Aires.[97] In 1952 a women's club called the Club Femminile Agnonese began to function in Youngstown.[98] Two years later the Agnonesi of Springfield, Massachusetts, founded the Società Agnone del Sannio.[99] By the mid-1960s a social club called the Lega Agnonese was functioning in Montreal. That year, over five hundred Agnonesi attended one club affair, and the practice of annually crowning a young woman Miss Agnone was instituted,[100] a practice continued as recently as 1972.[101] Meanwhile, in Leamington, Ontario, there was a sizeable Italian colony, the major part of which came originally from Villacanale.[102] In consort with other Italians, many Agnonesi began the Club Roma of Leamington. In 1973 that organization crowned its own Miss Agnone.[103]

While the recent colonies were manifesting associational energy, there were, however, ample signs that the older ones had lost their campanilistic orientation toward the town. In Buenos Aires, for example, the energies of the remaining Agnonesi were diluted with those of other Molisani in the Centro Molisano Monforte.[104] In 1968 a woman from Agnone visited the Club Agnonese of Youngstown and reported that "the assurance that in Youngstown there exists a Club of the Agnonesi has deepened my feeling of being a citizen of Agnone; but I must note that the young children, some of whom do not know or speak our beautiful language, have lost interest."[105] Within a few years the Youngstown organization was disbanded.

On balance, during the postwar period, the importance of Agnone's overseas diaspora in the ongoing life of the town has declined. To cite one simple indicator, by the year 1967, 455,240 liras were raised in Agnone for the *festa* of the Madonna della Libera, or more than three times as much as the 134,524 liras sent from the diaspora.[106] In part, this simply reflects generational erosion in the oldest and most developed colonies. At this writing, the concentrations of Agnonesi resident in the United States have received practically no new emigrants from the town for almost half a century. The same may be said, up to a point, for Argentina, for many of the postwar emigrants to that nation subsequently returned to Italy.

Nor were the emigrants particularly successful in transmitting their commitment to Agnone to their descendants born in the New World. What, for the emigrant, remained a profound loyalty to birthplace translated for his son or daughter into simple curiosity about ethnic heritage. The return visit of the emigrant was akin to a pilgrimage; for his offspring, it was a holiday.

There has been considerable discontinuity, then, between the town's earlier emigration and the new emigration that followed World War II. It may be said that Agnone's overseas diaspora today consists of colonies that are on the one hand too ancient and atrophied and on the other too recent and underdeveloped to play a significant role in the town's present. To use a medical metaphor, at the same time that Agnone's civic institutions are becoming arthritic, its former transatlantic arteries are aging and hardening.

Yet there is still a sense in which emigration and its consequences continues to permeate the life of the town. Today's emigrant is largely spared the heartrending prospect of years of separation from loved ones. Even the person who opts for an overseas destination has rapid mail and intercontinental telephone service to ameliorate his sense of separation. Modern air transportation places him within a day's travel of Agnone from anywhere in the world. The migrant who remains in Italy or Western Europe has even greater contact with the town. The proliferation of the automobile means that Agnonesi living in other parts of south Italy can return on weekends. People living further away in north Italy or other Western European countries are prone to spend their annual vacation in Agnone (usually during the month of August or the Christmas holidays).

A stroll through the streets of the *cittadina* provides constant reminders of the importance of Agnone's emigratory tradition. One passes the carpentry shop of the man who earned his stake in Venezuela. In the nearby piazza four brothers have their individual businesses, financed with their Australian savings. A fifth brother continues to live in Adelaide, and their three married sisters reside in Sicily, Naples, and

Africa, respectively. An old man approaches to test his halting English on the American visitor. After many years in Youngstown, he has returned to Agnone, where he is able to stretch his U.S. social security checks.

The store front on the right, which doubles as a travel agency, posts the round trip airfares to New York, Boston, Montreal, Toronto, Vancouver, Buenos Aires, and Caracas for clients interested in visiting their relatives abroad. There is a small coffee bar owned by a man who spent several years in Chicago; next to it is a restaurant operated by an ex-peasant who lost his health in the bowels of a Belgian coal mine.

A middle-aged woman appears and speaks bitterly of her husband, who went to the United States many years earlier and decided to remain there despite her refusal to join him. He later returned and took their children away to America as well, arguing that she had become mentally unbalanced. Now she lives alone and has grown desperate in her solitude. She pours out her story to anyone willing to listen, but over the years the volunteers have dwindled.

Finally, one comes to a stately stone building. Constructed near the turn of the century, it is a veritable architectural monument to emigrant success. To be sure, it was the first residence in Agnone to have steam heat. Over the lintel hangs a stone effigy of the American Indianhead penny, a fitting escutcheon of the emigrant's pursuit of wealth. At the head of an impressive stairway, there is a sitting room. Emblazoned on the ceiling is a large painting containing four portraits. Mazzini and Garibaldi, heroes of Italian unification, share the canvas with George Washington and Karl Marx—a juxtaposition of symbols that in the context of this story requires no explanation.

10

Conclusion

For more than a century, emigration and its feedback have profoundly shaped the lives of the Agnonesi. They were the first in their region to incur the risks and explore the opportunities of transatlantic travel. I have shown how several factors in Agnone's remote and recent history preconditioned the townspeople for emigration. There was the feudal heritage in which all of the town's social classes used physical mobility as an economic strategy. This, coupled with the town's role as a regional marketing, religious, educational, and administrative center, lent Agnone a cosmopolitan air. The medieval Agnonese did not fit the stereotype of the serf, bound to the soil, subservient to authority, citizen of a closed community and exponent of a circumscribed world view.

There is much in this image of feudal distinctiveness that presaged the townspeople's strong commitment to nineteenth-century liberalism. Agnone became the primary redoubt of liberal thought and practice in the Molise. Over time, then, the town became a stage upon which the triumphs and tragedies of the liberal social order were played out in stark fashion. By the second half of the century, the townspeople were polarized into two contending camps. The *galantuomini* justified their monopoly of power and wealth by invoking the liberal tenet of free enterprise. The less advantaged experienced perennial poverty, occasionally venting their frustration in riots and brigandage. It was at this time that Italy became involved in transatlantic emigration. Not surprisingly, many underprivileged Agnonesi were prime candidates.

If one were to select a single term with which to characterize attitudes about emigration and all that it supposd for the townspeople and their community, it would be *ambivalence*. For the peasant or manual laborer, emigration held out the prospect of bettering his lot by virtue of permanent settlement elsewhere or accumulation of significant savings with which to return to Agnone. Yet, for the nineteenth-century emigrant, the personal privations were considerable as he ran the gamut of experiences from unscrupulous agents and a surely unpleasant and sometimes perilous transatlantic crossing, to entry into a foreign land where his lack of skills and formal education was exacerbated by a language problem. The psychological costs of the prospect of prolonged separation were considerable, given the strong emphasis in south Italian society on loyalty to family and birthplace.

For the elite, the successes of the emigrant diaspora provided a new resource to be controlled and orchestrated to benefit the town. Here too, however, the costs proved high once there were insufficient tillers of the fields of absentee landlords, and nouveau riche returnees began to challenge the privileges and political hegemony of the ruling *galantuomini*.

By the turn of the century, the town's emigrant diaspora extended into disparate corners of the globe. The feedback of diaspora capital underwrote a burst of cultural and civic activity in Agnone while forestalling its economic collapse in the face of inexorable twentieth-century pressures. The relief of course proved temporary. No amount of money could salvage an economy based on peasant agriculture and artisan manufactures, both becoming anachronistic in an emerging world of agribusiness and industry. Nor could sheer enthusiasm and a spur railroad line outweigh the adverse effects of the budding realignment of south Italy's communications and transportation infrastructure, developments that would ultimately eclipse Agnone as a significant urban place.

As the external pressures on the town mounted, internal political pressures increased as well. Agnone's strong liberal establishment successfully forestalled the challenge of international socialism throughout much of the late nineteenth century, but this very success seemed to increase the virulence with which the new philosophy ultimately penetrated the body politic.

Consequently, the town entered the twentieth century riven with internal dissension and class conflict, poised on the brink of economic

209

disaster. As if the lack of local solutions to seemingly irreconcilable problems were not enough, other events in the form of two world wars sandwiched around a disastrous Fascist interlude and leavened by the Great Depression hastened the process of decline.

Both war efforts sapped local energies considerably, absorbing the town's resources and its youth. The Fascist years polarized the townspeople into two contentious camps. In many respects this represented old wine in new bottles, inasmuch as the Socialists championed the cause of the poor and the peasants, while the Fascists were the self-proclaimed torchbearers of Agnone's liberal tradition. Their confrontations, whether in the streets, the town hall, or the voluntary associations, made Agnone all but ungovernable.

The Great Depression of the 1930s occurred, then, at a time when the townspeople's capacity for collective action was at an extremely low ebb. Consequently, most of Agnone's institutions, the sources of former civic pride and local initiative, withered away. The two local banks, several voluntary associations, and many of the town's schools had all disappeared by the time the retreating German army dynamited the railroad—the last physical vestige of the Athens of Samnium.

Possibly more tellingly, the global conflicts and restrictive Fascist emigration policies largely interdicted Agnone's relations with its emigrant diaspora. From 1914 to 1945 few Agnonesi managed to emigrate, so the town's New World "colonies" were not being rejuvenated. As the former emigrants became increasingly adapted to their host countries and their offspring matured into functional citizens of New World societies, emigrant orientation to Agnone diminished and thereby deprived the town of yet another source of its former vitality.

During the post–World War II period, Agnone flourished briefly by virtue of circumstantial political influence and patronage. The outer limits of this "new initiative" were quickly determined, however, and the underlying economic, social, and political crises remained.

At the same time, there was recrudescence of emigration, the thrust of which shifted to new destinations: Australia, Switzerland, the Common Market countries, and north Italy. Temporally, the movement is too recent to provide the town with a new significant emigrant diaspora comparable to the one that supported Agnone's former glories. Furthermore, the new emigration depletes a very different kind of population base. During the late nineteenth and early twentieth centuries, Agnone had roughly twice as many people as today, and their age profile was broadly based. The town was therefore capable of providing several hundred emigrants annually without completely compromising its future. Many young adults left, but others returned; and a considerable number of Agnonesi never left at all. Today, however, it is the rare young person who has not departed or does not contemplate doing so. Agnone, then, is on the brink of becoming a community of the middle-aged and elderly, precluded, on biological grounds alone, from sustaining even its currently sharply reduced populace for another generation. The pessimism of the townspeople is reflected in their sense of malaise when discussing the future. It assumes tangible form in crumbling dwellings, churches, and convents as well as in closed artisan workshops and abandoned fields.

There is, of course, the temptation to conclude by predicting that the town will continue an unabated slide into oblivion as individuals emigrate permanently to escape a stagnating economy and society. It may well be, however, that in evaluating Agnone today, an analogue of the long-distance runner is appropriate. While the Agnonesi show many physical and spiritual signs of fatigue, the race goes on. Who is to say that the town will not get its second wind? Such does not appear likely from the internal evidence alone; yet, the townspeople are not, nor have they ever been, the sole architects of their destiny. A presently unpredictable piece of favorable legislation, the decision by the government or a factory owner to locate a plant in the town, or the growing disillusionment in Italy with urban life might trigger a chain of events that could restore to the Agnonesi their lost sense of purpose.

Broader Implications

The townspeople currently evaluate their collective experience in highly personal terms. Perceptions of past failures, present circumstances, and future opportunities must be weighed carefully as each person activates a particular life strategy while participating in collective responses to Agnone's current challenges. Few Agnonesi are motivated, though, to ponder the philosophical issues posed by the town's historical plight.

For the student of history and society, however, there are many implications in this case study of emigration and deurbanization in one small, south Italian hill town. Some are substantive, others, more methodological and theoretical. Several of the more salient issues may be treated under the following rubrics:

Urban processes and deurbanization. It might be argued that anthropologists acquired their interest in urban studies by following peasants and tribesmen into the city. That is, the new concern grew out of the fact that the world's explosive urban growth feeds in large measure upon a general rural exodus. A truly massive defection from the peasant and tribal ways of life is one of the more notable patterns of the twentieth century. Thus, it has become increasingly artificial to conduct synchronic studies of traditional societies. Unless his effort is quite consciously an exercise in salvage ethnology, today's social anthropologist is practically forced to abandon the discipline's classic concern with the *state of being* for the more problematic study of the *process of becoming*.

It is in meeting this new challenge that the subdiscipline of urban anthropology emerged and currently flourishes. Today's anthropologist is as likely to study a neighborhood, occupational, or ethnic group in one of the world's cities as a self-contained island or tribal culture. Furthermore, even those who focus on the little community are forced to consider its external networks, networks that almost inevitably terminate in urban centers. Feedback from city to village is likely to provide even the more traditional anthropological study with an urban anthropological dimension.

In writing the social history of the twentieth century, social scientists have given considerable attention to the closely related phenomena of industrialization, modernity, and urbanization. Whether dealing with the urban sociology of the developed nations or the urban anthropology of the Third World, the emphasis is on the burgeoning center—the city on the move. Because in such cases population increase inevitably outstrips the city's national growth rate, the question of in-migration assumes considerable importance. The perspective of the urban center as magnet for a nation's internal migrants and international emigrants is well developed in the literature.

There is, however, a relevant social process that has gone practically unnoticed by the urban anthropologist, namely, deurbanization (see Benedict for a notable exception[1]). The explosive recent growth of the world's metropolises has not been solely at the expense of peasant and tribal societies. Rather, there are cities, classically the preindustrial city described by Sjoberg,[2] that have lost their initiative, raison d'être, and much of their populace. Agnone is one such urban place: today, a small, insignificant town that, nevertheless, possesses a brilliant history as a former artisan, cultural, religious, educational, marketing, and administrative center of considerable regional importance.

Benedict, in his study of deurbanization of Ula, an Anatolian community, emphasizes that urban processes may only be understood if the town is viewed "as a regional mediating center reflecting the region in which it is located."[3] As in Ula, Agnone's history of decline must be measured in adverse developments in the town's various hinterlands, not just in events limited strictly to the center itself. An understanding, then, of the nature of deurbanization as a function of the redefinition of the interrelationship between an urban place and its several hinterlands is essential to a rounded view of urban processes. This treatment of Agnone's urban decline is intended as a contribution to this highly underdeveloped area of the social science literature.

Rural exodus and migration. While it is possible to regard Agnone as an urban center and to detail its recent history in terms of processes of deurbanization, it is equally true that the community has a significant rural dimension in its makeup. The *contadini* did and do constitute by far the largest single group in the populace, and the town's isolated, mountainous geographical setting makes it a part of the Italian countryside. Agnone's recent depopulation is therefore part of the larger twentieth-century rural exodus apparent in both Italy and much of the rest of Europe.

Within Italian national life, there is possibly no issue of greater importance than the stark economic and social disparities between the North/Center and the South, and the attendant interchange of people and capital between them.[4] Rampant urbanization and industrialization of the industrial triangle Liguria, Piedmont, and Lombardy, as well as that of cities like Rome and Naples, have attracted the attention of Italian social scientists and social reformers alike.[5] The impact of literally millions of internal rural migrants upon the nation's cities is now well documented,[6] as are the migrants' frequently lamentable living circumstances.[7] The published studies range from macrostructural overviews of entire regions,[8] to detailed analyses of single migrant neighborhoods[9] and anecdotal treatments of the migrant as an individual.[10]

Parelleling this interest in the city-as-receptacle is a somewhat less extensive literature on the impact rural–urban migration has had on the

Italian countryside. Here, most of the research remains largely macro-structural, leaning heavily on published governmental statistics.[11] The results suggest that, throughout Italy, depopulation is most pronounced in the more mountainous districts;[12] the mean age of the remaining population is increasing;[13] the agricultural work force is becoming feminized;[14] and there is general constriction in the local economic infrastructure as former activities are discontinued and rural communities become increasingly dependent on migrant remittances and government subsidies.[15] As we have seen, much in the recent trends of Agnone's history support these conclusions.

There is a sense, however, in which the above literature presents a simplistic, almost one-dimensional view of rural exodus in Italy. The urban sociologist is struck by the cohesiveness of the migrant community, and particularly the extent to which the migrants of a neighborhood or apartment building are from the same village or cluster of villages.[16] Viewed from Milan, it is easy to conclude that Milan is *the* alternative to the peasant way of life for the inhabitants of a particular village.

The Agnonesi resident in the capital of Lombardy could be studied from this perspective and would themselves provide an example of the process and effects of a pattern of chain migration. Few strike out for the North without some contacts and assurance of assistance, usually from kinsmen.

Once the rural exodus question is examined from the viewpoint of a donor community, however, and framed in broad historical terms, its true complexity becomes apparent. In the case of Agnone I have shown that, for at least the past century, there has been massive out-migration to a plethora of destinations. The town's historical and contemporary diaspora thus encompasses five continents, several European countries, and many urban centers in both north and south Italy. I have also shown that the migrants are drawn differentially from Agnone's social classes and that their motives for migrating vary over time in response to shifting economic, social, and political factors both internal and external to the local society. Similarly, the effects of emigration on the town varied markedly from period to period. Nor did they ever constitute a clear-cut blessing or bane. Rather, the drain on local resources and the countervailing feedback from the emigrant diaspora represented a constantly shifting interplay of costs and benefits.

Viewed against this backdrop, three conclusions may be derived from the Agnone data, conclusions that, though not unique, are currently underdeveloped in the migration literature. First, migrant choice making is far from a simple rejection of "traditional" life in a stagnating rural context. Rather, the potential migrant formulates his life strategies by opting from an array of readily available alternatives. In the case of the Agnonesi opting for Milan today, more is entailed that the decision to leave Agnone. Just as important, the outcome reflects a resolution *not* to go to Montevideo, Montreal, or Munich.

Second, for the individual, migration is more of a process than an event. The many studies of migrant adaptation and assimilitation in a host society are, of course, sensitive to this point. Similarly, there are many studies of reemigration as migrants return to their place of origin.[17] A theme that is underdeveloped in the literature is that of the "multiple migrant." That is, in the case of Agnone, one finds people regularly employing mixed migratory strategies. Indeed, there are examples of individuals in Agnone today who have sojourned abroad, worked in north Italy, and resided elsewhere within the Molise. It is only when such complexity is taken into account that the true nature and significance of migration ploys both for the individual and his community become apparent.

Third, it is critical to note that the departure of each individual changes the equation, that is, the circumstances and opportunity structure, for those who remain behind. A family loses a member, a field its tiller, a patron his client, a merchant his customer, a priest his parishioner. At the same time there is one less person making demands on the local resource base. Finally, to the extent that the migrant maintains ties with his family of orientation and his childhood peers, remitting information and funds, his natal community acquires new resources and widens its window on the world. The concatenation of the decisions and actions of many migrants over time led to the kinds of discernible social, economic, and political changes I have detailed in this study, yet it is important to note that there is a sense in which no two migrants ever left the same "Agnone."

In sum, microanalytical approaches to the rural depopulation issue, like this one, are absolutely essential if future policymakers are to make informed decisions. Clearly, as Italy probes the outer limits of urban living as a tolerance human environment on the one hand, while villages crumble and vast reaches of the Italian countryside lie fallow on the other, such questions cease to be academic.

Capital formation in post-colonial Western Europe. There is a final major issue that is more suggested than addressed (or resolved) by the Agnone data, namely, the nature of capital formation in nineteenth- and twentieth-century European economies. Much scholarship, most recently synthesized in the brilliant treatise by Wallenstein, has been expended in the effort to understand the emergence of the modern capitalist order in the West.[18] The elaborate interplay of colonial expansion, development of trading networks into noncolonized corners of the globe, and attendant industrialization of several European economies is well documented. For the colonial era, whether the subject be that of state policy regarding economic relations between the metropole and its client colonies,[19] or the role of banking houses[20] and trading companies,[21] it is easy to appreciae and even quantify the magnitude of the transfers of capital and other resources between Europe and the rest of the world.

Of less direct concern, however, has been the impact of the massive nineteenth- and twentieth-century transatlantic migration of millions of Europeans. The phenomenon has, of course, been far from ignored. The penurious and lamentable social and economic conditions of emigration Europe's huddled-masses have been described from the standpoint of Old World deprivation, travails during transit, and difficulties encountered in the New World receiving areas.[22] Similarly, it would be impossible to write the postcolonial social and economic histories of countries like the United States,[23] Canada,[24] Argentina,[25] and Australia[26] with out giving considerable weight to the immigration factor. But the related question of the significance of the movement for Europe's sending areas has received far less attention, and the analyses there are tend to be largely negative and simplistic. That is, the transatlantic emigration is frequently analyzed as a kind of escape-valve response to natural disasters such as crop failures, man-made calamities such as wars, or subtler forces such as overpopulation.[27]

This microanalytic study of the causes and consequences of emigration in one small, south Italian hill town from the inception of the transatlantic option to the present demonstrates the extent to which the movement represented much more than a unidirectinal transfer of men and resources from one setting to another. Rather, it created an ongoing dialectic between receiving and sending areas. Furthermore, while the forces did not assume such tangible form as colonial administrators and troops, the concatenation of New World activities by millions upon millions of Old World emigrants provided countries such as Italy with considerable capacity to "capture" a portion of New World wealth.[28] Indeed, in the case of Italy, transatlantic emigration began shortly after the birth of the modern Italian state. Between 1871 and 1971 almost twenty-six million Italians emigrated abroad, and over half returned to Italy.[29] It is impossible to understand the configuration of modern Italy without taking into account the consequences of this massive movement and feedback of men, money, and ideas from abroad.

Finally, when one considers that in Italy, as elsewhere in Europe, the majority of transatlantic emigrants were drawn from rural districts, assessment of the impact of emigration forces a reevaluation of the relationship between the urban-industrial and rural-peasant sectors of the nation. It is easy to treat the recent history of rural Europe in terms of twentieth-century developments that have undermined the viability of peasant agriculture and artisanship, resulting in considerable rural depopulation. The passing of a particular life style should not, however, be equated with the disappearance of a rural–urban dialectic within a nation.[30] That rural migrants to the city have provided much of the manpower for twentieth-century urbanization and industrialization in countries like Italy is well documented. By focusing on the illiterate, confused country bumpkin as he seeks to cope with the complexities of Milan (as well as the social problems that the collectivity of ill-prepared rural migrants poses for the city), it is easy to overlook the broader question of to what extent does the industrialization of north Italy depend on capital formation by emigrants in the rural sectors of the nation? For the past century emigrant remittances and the savings of returnees have provided an enormous infusion of wealth into Italian economic life. Similarly, the rising expectations of the emigrants and their increased ability to satisfy them provide much of the dynamism in modern Italian consumerism.

Such, then, are some of the issues posed by this work. Although they cannot be resolved within the context of the study of emigration from a single community, I would contend that they may not even be adequately addressed without many such studies. It is the role and responsibility of the anthropological historian to pose, and provide detailed, micro-analytical treatment of, such broader issues as all social scientists collaborate in the enterprise of understanding human behavior.

Notes

Preface

1. William A. Douglass, *Echalar and Murelaga*.

2. Lawrence Rosen, "Language, History and the Logic of Inquiry in Lévi-Strauss and Sartre," p. 286.

3. I. M. Lewis, "Introduction," p. x.

4. M. I. Finley, "Anthropology and the Classics," p. 113.

5. Peter Laslett and Richard Wall, *Household and Family in Past Time*; Jack Goody, Joan Thirsk, and E. P. Thompson, *Family and Inheritance*; Alan Macfarlane, Sarah Harrison, and Charles Jardine, *Reconstructing Historical Communities*; Kenneth W. Wachter, Eugene A. Hammel, and Peter Laslett, *Statistical Studies of Historical Social Structure*.

6. Alan Macfarlane, *The Family Life of Ralph Josselin, an Eighteenth Century Clergyman*; Anton Blok, *The Mafia of a Sicilian Village, 1860–1960*; Joel M. Halpern and Barbara Kerewsky Halpern, *A Serbian Village in Historical Perspective*; Richard P. Horwitz, *Anthropology toward History*; Emmanuel le Roy Ladurie, *The Peasants of Languedoc*; idem, *Montaillou*.

Chapter 1

1. From the term *campanile*, or bell tower, reference being to the fact that everyone within earshot of the same *campanile* shares common interests.

Chapter 2

1. Within the region of the Molise, Agnone ranks third in size behind Guglionesi (10,073 hectares) and San Martino in Pensilis (10,171 hectares). Cf. ISTAT, *Annuario statistico dei comuni italiani*, pp. 422–430 passim.

2. ISTAT, *Secondo censimento generale dell'agricoltura*, p. 36.

3. John Davis, "Town and Country," p. 173; idem, *Land and Family in Pisticci*, pp. 9–10; Sydel Silverman, *Three Bells of Civilization*, pp. 1–11 and passim.

4. "Censimento di Agnone."

5. Indeed another name for the piazza is Piazza del Tomolo.

6. ISTAT, *Primi risultati provinciali e comunali sulla popolazione e sulle abitazioni*, pp. 124–125.

7. ISTAT, *Popolazione residente e presente dei comuni ai censimenti dal 1861 al 1961*, pp. 124–125.

8. *Atti del consiglio provinciale di Molise*, pp. 199–203.

9. For a similar treatment of social class in another community of the Alto Molise, cf. Leonard W. Moss and Stephan C. Cappannari, "Estate and Class in a South Italian Hill Village."

10. "Onciario dell'università della città di Agnone," passim.

11. Calculated from the *stato di anime*, or parish censuses, of Agnone's seven parishes.

12. *La città di Agnone*, pp. 28–29.

13. "Censimento di Agnone," passim.

14. "Onciario," passim.

15. Calculated from the *stato di anime* records of Agnone's seven parishes. It is, however, doubtful that all practiced. Among the elite of the nineteenth century it was prestigious to become lettered in the law irrespective of one's subsequent professional commitments. It seems clear that many of Agnone's "lawyers" actually devoted their labors to managing property, speculating in commodities, and controlling local politics.

16. *Città di Agnone*, pp. 28–29.

17. "Censimento di Agnone," passim.

18. Ascenso Marinelli, *Memorie patrie con alcune biografie di uomini illustri agnonesi*, p. 52.

19. It should be noted that since publication of Edward C. Banfield's *The Moral Basis of a Backward Society* the social scientific literature has emphasized the importance of the nuclear family in south Italian society. Elsewhere I argue that such was not the case for Agnone (*see* William A. Douglass, "The South Italian Family").

Chapter 3

1. E. T. Salmon, *Samnium and the Samnites*, p. 1.

2. Ibid., pp. 18–19.

3. Ibid., pp. 50, 126–136.

4. Ibid., p. 133.

5. Ibid., pp. 61, 119.

6. Ibid., p. 143. Nor is its value underestimated by the modern Agnonesi. While the original Oscan tablet is today housed in the British Museum, the local bellworks makes a bronze reproduction that is sold as a memento of the town. Since the discovery, Agnone has always had its own antiquarians who scour the rural areas for new finds and who both study and contribute to the literature on Samnite history. For example, Domenico Cremonese, *Congetture sulla tavola osca di Agnone.*

7. Flavio Biondo, *Italia illustrata*, p. 399.

8. Cesare Orlandi, *Delle città d'Italia e sue isole adjacenti*, pp. 123–124.

9. Francesco Sacco, *Dizionario geografico-istorico-fisico del regno di Napoli*, p. 16.

10. Custode Carlomagno, *Agnone dalle origini ai nostri giorni*, p. 86.

11. Remo Nicola de Ciocchis, *Agnone*, pp. 101–102.

12. Ascenso Marinelli, *Memorie patrie con alcune biografie di uomini illustri agnonesi*, pp. 10–11.

13. Salmon, *Samnium and the Samnites*, p. 271n.

14. Il Comitato della Provincia, *La provincia di Molise nelle nuove circoscrizioni amministrative*; Francesco d'Ovidio, *Nel primo centenario della provincia di Molise*; Gaetano Amoroso, *Il Molise in una circoscrizione regionale.*

15. Carlomagno, *Agnone*, p. 116.

16. Giovanni Antonio Summonte, *Historia della città e regno di Napoli*, vol. 1, pp. 417–418.

17. Ascenso Marinelli, *Memorie patrie*, pp. 16–17.

18. Ibid., p. 17.

19. Giambattista Masciotta, *Il Molise dalle origini ai nostri giorni*, vol. 1, p. 36; Ricciarda Simoncelli, *Il Molise*, p. xi.

20. Masciotta, *Molise*, p. 36.

21. Filippo la Gamba, *Statuti e capitoli della terra di Agnone*, p. 13.

22. A. Ludovico Antinori, "Corografia," pp. 70, 75; Vincenzo Aloi, *Memoria da presentarsi al supremo tribunale della regal camera di S. Chiara . . . ,* p. 6; Ascenso Marinelli, *Memorie patrie*, pp. 18–19; G. Vincenzo G. Ciarlanti, *Memorie historiche del Sannio*, p. 320.

23. Summonte, *Napoli*, vol. 2, pp. 165–166.

24. Ciarlanti, *Memorie historiche del Sannio*, p. 358.

25. Ibid., p. 379; Antinori, "Corografia," p. 76.

26. Biagio Aldimari, *Historia genealogica della familia Carafa*, p. 122.

27. *Università* is the medieval term for municipality.

28. La Gamba, *Statuti e capitoli*, p. 15.

29. Ibid., p. 16.

30. Ibid.

31. Orlandi, *Delle città d'Italia*, p. 125.

32. Ibid., p. 127.

33. Antinori, "Corografia," p. 78.

34. Ibid., p. 79.

35. Ibid., p. 80.

36. Ibid.

37. A. Ludovico Antinori, *Raccolta di memorie istoriche delle tre provincie degli Abbruzzi*, p. 273.

38. Antinori, "Corografia," p. 84.

39. Ibid.

40. Ibid., p. 86.

41. La Gamba, *Statuti e capitoli*, pp. 115, 120.

42. Ibid., p. 98.

43. Ibid., pp. 81–169.

44. Ibid., p. 119.

45. Antinori, "Corografia," p. 79.

46. Ibid., p. 80.

47. Ibid., p. 79.

48. Ibid., p. 84.

49. "Stato conforme si ritrova l'università di Agnone. . . ."

50. "Ragioni per il regio fisco coll'ill'"; "Memoria senza autore a sensa titolo riguardante il principe di Santo Buono ed il duca di Castel di Sangro"; Antinori, "Corografia," pp. 87–95; Odoardo Ciani, *La città di Agnone e la sua cronistoria*, pp. 33–35; Chieti, January 7, 1789.

51. Ascenso Marinelli, *Alcune biografie di uomini illustri agnonesi*, p. 63.

52. Ibid.

53. Chieti, June 23, 1788.

54. La Gamba, *Statuti e capitoli*, passim.

55. "Onciario dell'università della città di Agnone," passim.

56. La Gamba, *Statuti e capitoli*, pp. 225–226.

57. Ibid., pp. 231–232.

58. Ibid., pp. 227–228.

59. Ibid., pp. 229–230.

60. Ibid., pp. 225–226.

61. Ibid., p. 230.

62. Ibid., p. 200.

63. Ibid., p. 191.

64. Ibid., pp. 191–192.

65. Ibid., p. 190.

66. Ibid., p. 211.

67. Ibid., p. 233.

68. Julius Klein, *The Mesta*.

69. Giuseppe Mª Galanti, *Della descrizione geografica e politica delle Si-*

cilie, vol. 1, p. 517.

70. Guglielmo Josa, "Il caseificio nomade nell'Italia meridionale," p. 4.

71. Galanti, *Della descrizione*, p. 519.

72. "Squarciafoglie pecore, anno 1597–1598," passim.

73. La Gamba, *Statuti e capitoli*, pp. 233–234.

74. Antinori, "Corografia," p. 79.

75. La Gamba, *Statuti e capitoli*, p. 142.

76. Derived from an examination of *surviving* legible parchments in the Biblioteca La Banca of Agnone; many such documents were either destroyed or are illegible, so the actual number of such purchases is probably greater.

77. La Gamba, *Statuti e capitoli*, p. 103.

78. Ibid.

79. Ibid., p. 111.

80. Ibid., p. 110.

81. Ibid, pp. 113–119.

82. For example, "Ragioni per l'università della città d'Agnone con li magnifici fratelli Fioriti"; Naples, March 13, 1782; March 16, 1782; "Per li fratelli di Nicola, e D. Aloisio Fioriti della città di Agnone contro l'università della città sudetta."

83. One *tomolo* = .3086 hectares.

84. "Città di Agnone, i demani comunali," pp. 3–11.

85. Galanti, *Della descrizione*, p. 196; Masciotta, *Molise*, vol. 1, p. 142.

86. La Gamba, *Statuti e capitoli*, pp. 224, 243, 247.

87. Ibid., pp. 184–185.

88. Ibid., p. 186.

89. Ibid., pp. 217–219, 237–239.

90. Ibid., p. 220; Catherine E. Boyd, *Tithes and Parishes in Medieval Italy*, provides a detailed analysis of the phenomenon; for my purposes here, it is of limited use in that it refers primarily to the situation in central and northern Italy.

91. La Gamba, *Statuti e capitoli*, pp. 220–221.

92. Ascenso Marinelli, *Memorie patrie*, pp. 54, 59–60.

93. Antinori, "Corografia," p. 81.

94. Indigo Velez de Guevara, *Nova situatione de pagamenti fiscale delli carlini 42. . . .*

95. "Lib. I. S. Visita 1615–1675," passim.

96. "Onciario," passim.

97. "Inter universitatem civitatis anglonis et Ῑˢlem Pnpēm Stⁱ Boni," p. 507.

98. In the kingdom of Naples throughout most of the eighteenth century, adult males were paid twenty *grane* daily for work in the fields. Women and children received ten *grane* (one hundred *grane* = one ducat). Cf. Ruggiero

Romano, *Prezzi, salari e servizi a Napoli nel secolo XVIII (1734–1806)*. Agnone documents from the period reflect the same wage scale.

99. "Inter universitatem," p. 620.

100. "Città di Agnone," p. 11.

101. Lorenzo Giustiniani, *Dizionario geografico ragionato del regno di Napoli*, p. 76.

102. Sacco, *Dizionario*, p. 16.

103. Antinori, "Corografia," p. 74.

104. Ciarlanti, *Memorie historiche del Sannio*, pp. 336–338.

105. Orlandi, *Delle città d'Italia*, pp. 127–140, passim.

106. Ascenso Marinelli, *Memorie patrie*, pp. 61–63.

107. Angelo Tirabasso, *Breve dizionario biografico del Molise*, p. 154.

108. Ibid., p. 19.

109. *Enciclopedia italiana*, p. 565.

110. Masciotta, *Molise*, vol. 3, pp. 59–61.

111. Tirabasso, *Breve dizionario biografico del Molise*, p. 259.

112. Ascanio Mancinelli, *Floridum opusculum hic inde a tot pomariis a recollectum*. . . .

113. Masciotta, *Molise*, vol. 3, pp. 61–62.

114. Tirabasso, *Breve dizionario biografico del Molise*, p. 68.

115. Orlandi, *Delle città d'Italia*, p. 124.

116. Ibid., p. 132.

117. Ibid., p. 140.

118. Instruction was probably in the form of private tutelage, a system that, I show, persisted into the nineteenth century. The majority of instructors were undoubtedly religious, although in the "Onciario" a number of leisured people bore the title *magistero*, or teacher. In 1760, for example, the sole elected public *mastro di scuola* was the rector of the parish of San Emidio (Chieti, July 13, 1760). Unfortunately, it is impossible to determine from the "Onciario" census the number of such outside students present in Agnone in 1753 because only those with official residence or property in the town were included.

119. Orlandi, *Delle città d'Italia*, p. 129.

120. Velez de Guevara, *Nova situatione*, pp. 19, 20, 76.

121. Partially destroyed document in "Provincia di Molise anno 1813."

122. In her seminal article on the feudal administration of the Molise in the twelfth and thirteenth centuries, Jamison notes, "No doubt there was infinite variation in the adjustment of rights from place to place": Evelyn Jamison, "The Administration of the County of Molise in the Twelfth and Thirteenth Centuries," p. 18.

Chapter 4

1. Giuseppe Mª Galanti, *Descrizione del contado del Molise*, pp. 27–28.
2. Ibid., p. 29.
3. Ibid., p. 15.
4. Ibid., pp. 18–32 passim.
5. Ibid., p. 18.
6. Abate Longano, *Viaggio dell'abate Longano per lo contado del Molise*, p. 24.
7. Ibid., p. 31.
8. Ibid., p. 34–35.
9. Ibid., p. 107.
10. Ibid., p. 82.
11. Ibid., pp. 87–90.
12. Ibid., pp. 91–93, 97.
13. Luigi Gamberale, *Notizie sui fatti di Agnone nel 1799*, pp. 18–19.
14. Jack F. Bernard, *Italy*, pp. 345–346.
15. Giovanni Zarrilli, *Il Molise dal 1789 al 1860*, pp. 14–15.
16. Longano, *Viaggio dell'abate Longano*, p. 31.
17. This interpretation runs counter to that of Antonio Genovesi, "Il problema della terra," who maintains that the absenteeism of the aristocracy created a deleterious vacuum by leaving decision making in the hands of disinterested overseers and uneducated peasants.
18. Zarrilli, *Molise dal 1789 al 1860*, p. 37.
19. Giovanni Zarrilli, *Il Molise nel declino del regno borbonico*, p. 5.
20. Naples, February 16, 1810.
21. Naples, January 1, 1812.
22. Ibid.
23. V. Dandolo, "Discorso su i danni della soverchia divisione de' fondi," pp. 63–64.
24. Undated letter appended to Naples, January 1, 1812.
25. Chieti, July 4, 1761.
26. Chieti, July 5, 1761.
27. Campobasso, December 29, 1768.
28. Chieti, July 19, 1777; August 4, 1777.
29. Chieti, August 8, 1781.
30. Chieti, August 9, 1781.
31. Ascenso Marinelli, *Memorie patrie con alcune biografie di uomini illustri agnonesi*, p. 96.
32. Gamberale, *Notizie sui fatti*, pp. 7–8.
33. Ibid., pp. 9–10.
34. Ibid., p. 7.

35. Custode Carlomagno, *Agnone dalle origini ai nostri giorni*, p. 216.
36. Gamberale, *Notizie sui fatti*, p. 11.
37. Ibid., p. 16.
38. Ibid., p. 17.
39. Carlomagno, *Agnone*, p. 217.
40. Ascenso Marinelli, *Alcune biografie di uomini illustri agnonesi*, pp. 90–91.
41. Gamberale, *Notizie sui fatti*, pp. 18–19.
42. Ascenso Marinelli, *Memorie patrie*, p. 97.
43. Carlomagno, *Agnone*, p. 218.
44. Ascenso Marinelli, *Alcune biografie*, pp. 101–116.
45. *Eco del Sannio*, July 25, 1894, p. 1.
46. Ascenso Marinelli, *I miei racconti*, pp. 33–43.
47. Ibid., pp. 38–39.
48. Campobasso, November 8, 1827.
49. Campobasso, December 3, 1860.
50. "Catasto vecchio di Agnone," passim.
51. Giambattista Masciotta, *Il Molise dalle origini ai nostri giorni*, vol. 1, p. 283.
52. Ibid.
53. Ibid., pp. 283–284.
54. Ibid., p. 284.
55. Campobasso, December 27, 1815.
56. Campobasso, December 31, 1839.
57. Masciotta, *Molise*, vol. 1, p. 285.
58. Campobasso, December 3, 1809.
59. Campobasso, November 12, 1812.
60. Campobasso, November 12, 1811.
61. Campobasso, August 28, 1821.
62. Campobasso, September 26, 1835.
63. For example, Campobasso, April 13, 1831; December 17, 1836.
64. "Atti per la vendita del grano, granone, vino mosto di ragione di queste chiese pel corrente anno 1852."
65. Nicola Marinelli, *La chiesa e l'ex-convento di Maiella in Agnone*, p. 18.
66. Campobasso, January 31, 1812.
67. For example, Campobasso, May 23, 1812.
68. Campobasso, October 2, 1821.
69. "Di stato d'introito ed esito del monastero d. S. Chiara di Agnone."
70. "Libro de' conti del pbte monastero di Santa Chiara di questa città di Agnone," passim.
71. Ibid.
72. Campobasso, October 8, 1816.

73. Campobasso, November 15, 1823.

74. Campobasso, June 15, 1812.

75. Campobasso, September 2, 1838.

76. Campobasso, February 28, 1817.

77. Zarrilli, *Il Molise dal 1789 al 1860*, pp. 80–81, 162–163.

78. *L'Aquilonia*, May 2, 1885, p. 3.

79. Ibid., January 1, 1887, p. 4.

80. "Catasto vecchio di Agnone," passim.

81. *Citta di "Agnone*," p. 11.

82. Giustino Fortunato, "Il problema demaniale," p. 164.

83. "Statistica-popolazione, provincia di Molise, anno 1814"; "Provincia di Molise, statistica-popolazione anno 1845."

84. *Il giornale d'intendenza della provincia di Molise anno 1838*, pp. 409–413.

85. "Lista degli eligibili del comune di Agnone redatta a seconda del circolare. . . ."

86. Campobasso, July 28, 1821.

87. Campobasso, August 28, 1816.

88. Campobasso, November 1, 1817.

89. Cf. documents in the Fondo Intendenza del Molise, Busta 211, in the Archivio di Stato di Campobasso.

90. Campobasso, August 3, 1811.

91. Campobasso, October 27, 1814.

92. Campobasso, January 18, 1814.

93. Campobasso, August 8, 1820.

94. "Esercizio 1827, ruolo per transazione pel dazio pel macinato descritto nell'art^o dello stato."

95. Campobasso, n.d. (ca. 1835).

96. Campobasso, n.d. (ca. 1833).

97. "Città di Agnone, i demani comunali," p. 11.

98. "Provincia di Molise anno 1813."

99. "Statistica stato di popolazione, provincia di Molise, 1830."

100. "Provincia di Molise anno 1813."

101. "Statistica stato di popolazione."

102. "Provincia di Molise, statistica-popolazione anno 1845."

103. "Atti di morte, comune di Agnone, 1820–1829; 1885–1892," passim.

104. Oscar Handlin, *The Uprooted*, p. 25.

105. Alfred W. Crosby, Jr., *The Columbian Exchange*, pp. 177–188.

106. Campobasso, September 21, 1811.

107. "Provincia di Molise anno 1813."

108. *Stato di anime* records in the parish archives of San Emidio and San Antonio Abbate.

227

109. "Statistica stato di popolazione."
110. Alessandro Serafini, *Sul colera del 1837 in Agnone*, p. 12.
111. "Provincia di Molise, statistica-popolazione anno 1845."
112. "Onciario dell'università della città di Agnone," passim.
113. "Provincia di Molise, distretto d'Isernia."
114. ISTAT, *Secondo censimento generale dell'agricoltura*, p. 36.
115. "Città di Agnone," p. 11.
116. "Stato delle pecore del 1834."
117. Campobasso, June 8, 1822.
118. Campobasso, June 15, 1850.
119. As a grain measure, 1 *tomolo* = 55.5 liters.
120. "Comune di Agnone, censimento-notizie statistiche, 1838."
121. Campobasso, August 21, 1821.
122. "Stato delle anime della chiesa parrocchiale di S. Emidio di questa città di Agnone. . . ," passim.
123. Ibid.
124. "Atti di morte," passim.
125. For minors, the documents list the occupation of the father; women are designated by husband's profession.
126. Campobasso, August 1, 1814.
127. Campobasso, September 25, 1816.
128. Campobasso, May 11, 1817.
129. Antonio Arduino, *Agnone, paese di suoni antichi*, unpaginated.
130. Campobasso, June 30, 1817.
131. *Aquilonia*, April 17, 1884, p. 1.
132. Carlo Barbieri, "Riposte su de' quesiti statistici fatti da S. E. il sig^r ministro dell'interno," unpaginated.
133. Ibid.
134. Ibid.
135. "Statistica-popolazione"; "Provincia di Molise, statistica-popolazione anno 1845."
136. D. Benedetto Cantalupo, *Stato economico-morale del contado del Molise*, p. 11.
137. Ibid., p. 25.
138. Ibid., p. 11.
139. Giuseppe del Re, *Descrizione generale della provincia del Molise*, p. 108.
140. Nicola de Luca, *Condizioni economiche ed industriali della provincia di Molise nel 1844*, pp. 24–26.
141. Ibid., pp. 29–30.
142. Ibid., p. 29.

143. Ibid., p. 30.

144. Ibid., pp. 30–31.

145. Cantalupo, *Stato economico-morale*, pp. 11–12.

146. Nicola de Luca, *Condizioni economiche ed industriali*, p. 37.

147. Campobasso, September 21, 1811.

148. Campobasso, August 10, 1818.

149. Campobasso, September 14, 1817; December 10, 1817.

150. Naples, n.d. (ca. 1834).

151. "Stato de' maestri e maestre primarie, maestri secondari e privati, n° degli alunni. . . ."

152. Calculated from figures given in "Statistica stato di popolazione" and "Provincia di Molise, statistica-popolazione anno 1845."

153. "Specchio della istruzione della provincia di Molise, che si ha dalle scuole primarie. . . ."

154. Giuseppantonio Savastano, *La forza educativa pensieri pratici*, pp. 5–8.

155. Luigi Gamberale, *Il mio libro paesano*, p. 130.

156. Ascenso Marinelli, *I miei racconti*, pp. 46–48.

157. Ibid., p. 47.

158. Gamberale, *Il mio libro paesano*, p. 5.

159. Ascenso Marinelli, *I miei racconti*, pp. 48–49.

160. Ibid., p. 64.

161. Ibid., pp. 73–74; Gamberale, *Il mio libro paesano*, p. 5.

162. Gamberale, *Il mio libro paesano*, p. 45.

163. Ibid., p. 46.

164. Ibid.

165. Ibid., p. 4.

166. Ibid., p. 10.

167. Ibid., p. 6.

168. Ibid., p. 11.

169. Ibid., p. 16.

170. Baldassare La Banca, *Ricordi autobiografici*, pp. 12–13.

171. Ibid., pp. 23–24.

172. Gamberale, *Il mio libro paesano*, p. 160.

173. Ibid., p. 175.

174. Ibid., p. 187.

175. Ibid., p. 226.

176. Ibid., pp. 108–109.

177. Ascenso Marinelli, *I miei racconti*.

178. La Banca, *Ricordi autobiografici*, p. 31.

179. Ibid., pp. 34–41.

180. Ibid., pp. 42–58.

181. Nicolino Marinelli, *Luigi Gamberale (1840–1929)*, pp. 18–19.

182. Gamberale, *Il mio libro paesano*, pp. 159–180.

Chapter 5

1. Gianfausto Rosoli, "L'emigrazione di ritorno," p. 235.

2. Giustino Fortunato, "L'emigrazione e le classi dirigenti."

3. Robert F. Foerster, *The Italian Emigration of Our Times*, p. 98.

4. John S. MacDonald, "Italy's Rural Social Structure and Emigration"; idem, "Some Socio-economic Emigration Differentials in Rural Italy, 1902–1913"; idem, "Agricultural Organization, Migration and Labour Militancy in Rural Italy."

5. Edward C. Banfield, *The Moral Basis of a Backward Society*.

6. For example, Herbert J. Gans, *The Urban Villagers*, pp. 203–204; Constance Cronin, *The Sting of Change*, p. 85; Humbert S. Nelli, *Italians in Chicago, 1880–1930*, p. 5.

7. Joseph Lopreato, *Peasants No More*, p. 80.

8. Josef J. Barton, *Peasants and Strangers*, p. 47; John W. Briggs, *An Italian Passage*, p. 9.

9. Briggs, *Italian Passage*, pp. 37–64.

10. Ibid., pp. 15–36.

11. Rudolph M. Bell, *Fate and Honor, Family and Village*, pp. 181–189.

12. Ibid., p. 180.

13. Ibid., p. 15; Oscar Handlin, *The Uprooted*, pp. 152–180.

14. This is a position with which I am in essential agreement; cf. William A. Douglass, "Peasant Emigrants."

15. Lopreato, *Peasants No More*, pp. 47–48.

16. Bell, *Fate and Honor*, p. 193.

17. Leopoldo Franchetti, *Condizione economiche ed amministrative delle provincie napoletane, Abruzzi e Molise—Calabria e Basilicata*, pp. 4–5.

18. Ibid., pp. 21–22.

19. Ibid., p. 27.

20. Giovanni Zarrilli, *Il Molise dal 1860 al 1900*, p. 11.

21. Ibid., p. 10.

22. Ibid., pp. 46, 98.

23. Ibid., p. 83.

24. Ibid., p. 80.

25. Ibid., pp. 134–135.

26. In particular Campobasso, May 1, 1860; October 1, 1860; December 22, 1869. My account is a composite reconstructed from several (sometimes

conflicting) versions. The interested reader is referred to buste 91–94 in the Fondo Brigantaggio Processi of the Archivio di Stato di Campobasso.

27. Il conte Viti, *Discorso sulla inaugurazione del monte de' pegni di Agnone*, pp. 8–11.

28. Giovanni Zarrilli, *Il Molise dal 1789 al 1860*, p. 161.

29. "Processo relativo all cospirazione ed attentata avenuti per oggetti di distruggere e cambiare. . . ."

30. Ibid.

31. Campobasso, January 13, 1862.

32. Campobasso, March 13, 1863.

33. Campobasso, May 31, 1862.

34. Campobasso, July 29, 1862.

35. Campobasso, March 22, 1863.

36. *L'Aquilonia*, August 1, 1888, p. 1.

37. Custode Carlomagno, *Agnone dalle origini ai nostri giorni*, p. 237.

38. *Aquilonia*, November 16, 1884, p. 3.

39. Ibid., July 16, 1886, p. 3.

40. Bell, *Fate and Honor*, pp. 151–177, 193.

41. *Aquilonia*, January 1, 1884, p. 1.

42. *Popolazione presente ed assente per comuni, centri, e frazioni di comune*, pp. 66, 83.

43. This apparently represents the numerical pinnacle of Agnone's population. It was at this juncture that many Agnonesi became involved in transatlantic emigration, initiating population decline that continues down to the present.

44. Sidney Sonnino, "La crisi agraria"; Antonio de Viti de Marco, "Gli effetti del protezionismo"; Bell, *Fate and Honor*, p. 192.

45. Foerster, *Italian Emigration of Our Times*, pp. 90–93.

46. *Aquilonia*, February 16, 1884, p. 1.

47. Giambattista Masciotta, *Il Molise dalle origini ai nostri giorni*, vol. 1, p. 341.

48. *Eco del Sannio*, December 24, 1908, p. 2.

49. Ibid., December 10, 1898, p. 3; February 25, 1900, p. 2.

50. *Aquilonia*, July 9, 1884, p. 3.

51. *Eco del Sannio*, October 25, 1897, p. 2.

52. *Aquilonia*, July 16, 1888, p. 3; *Eco del Sannio*, September 10, 1897, p. 1.

53. *Eco del Sannio*, October 25, 1898, p. 2.

54. Ibid., August 10, 1897, p. 2; *Aquilonia*, July 9, 1884, p. 3.

55. "Stato delle condanne forestale compilato nell'anno 1863."

56. Juan A. Alsina, *La inmigración europea en la República Argentina*. Though much was made of the activities of emigration agents and the need to control the unscrupulous ones (cf. Fortunato, "Emigrazione e le classi

dirigenti"), I am unable to document their direct influence or involvement in Agnone during the 1870s. Contemporary and near-contemporary accounts from the town are silent on this issue, suggesting that Agnone's first emigrants were not recruited.

57. For example, Banfield, *Moral Basis*; F. G. Friedmann, "The World of *La Miseria*"; Joseph Lopreato, "How Would You Like to Be a Peasant?"; idem, *Peasants No More*; idem, *Perchè emigrano i contadini*.

58. Joseph Lopreato and Janet E. Saltzman, "Descriptive Models of Peasant Society," pp. 138–141.

59. *Censimento degli italiani all'estero 31 dic. 1871*, p. cxxvi.

60. Giovanni Florenzano, *Della emigrazione italiana in America comparata alle altre emigrazioni europee*, p. 146.

61. Ibid., table A.

62. Guglielmo Josa, "L'emigrazione nel Molise," p. 5.

63. Ibid., p. 7.

64. *Eco del Sannio*, May 10, 1896, p. 1.

65. Ibid., January 27, 1905, p. 3; Masciotta, *Molise*, vol. 1, p. 345.

66. *Eco del Sannio*, June 10, 1894, p. 2.

67. *Il rinnovamento*, March 29, 1912, p. 3.

68. *Il cittadino agnonese*, September 18, 1901, p. 1.

69. Ibid.

70. Ascenso Marinelli, *I miei racconti*, p. 224.

71. Josa, "Emigrazione nel Molise," p. 5.

72. Ibid.

73. *Aquilonia*, December 1, 1884, pp. 3–4.

74. Ibid., February 16, 1884, p. 1.

75. Ibid., January 1, 1885, p. 3.

76. Ibid., February 1, 1885, p. 3.

77. Ibid., April 16, 1885, p. 3.

78. Mark Jefferson, *Peopling the Argentine Pampa*, pp. 46–49.

79. Between 1876 and 1895 Argentina received 590,125 Italian immigrants, according to Vicente Vásquez Presedo, *Estadísticas históricas argentinas*, p. 32. In 1895 the population of the nation was only 3,954,911 (ibid., p. 20).

80. James R. Scobie, *Argentina*, pp. 118–119.

81. Ibid., p. 118.

82. *Aquilonia*, April 17, 1884, pp. 1–2.

83. Ibid., April 1, 1886, p. 4.

84. Ibid., October 5, 1886, p. 1.

85. Ibid., May 22, 1887, p. 4.

86. *Eco del Sannio*, June 10, 1894, p. 4.

87. Ibid., September 10, 1896, p. 1.

88. *Il nuovo risveglio*, December 18, 1895, p. 1.

89. As compiled from the pages of the local newspaper the *Eco del Sannio*, which by then was listing the names and destinations of emigrants in practically every issue.

90. Comune di Agnone, "Elenco delle famiglie e elle persone censite il 10 febbraio, 1901."

91. This figure is derived from the official census book conserved in Agnone municipal archive, which is at variance with the Italian national census. The latter places Agnone's 1901 population at 10,189. ISTAT, *Popolazione residente e presente dei comuni ai censimenti dal 1861 al 1961*, p. 290.

92. *Nuovo risveglio*, March 3, 1897, p. 4.

93. Ibid., July 3, 1897, p. 4.

94. *Eco del Sannio*, April 10, 1898, p. 3.

95. Ibid., November 13, 1901, p. 2.

96. Ibid.

97. Comune di Agnone, "Elenco delle famiglie," passim.

98. *Eco del Sannio*, October 25, 1902, p. 1.

99. Ibid.

100. Ibid., July 28, 1902, p. 2.

101. Ibid., May 28, 1903, p. 1.

102. Ibid., March 25, 1903, p. 2.

103. Ibid., June 25, 1903, pp. 1–2.

104. Ibid., August 11, 1903, p. 1.

105. Ibid., October 28, 1903, p. 1.

106. In Agnone's municipal archive, there is a series of books, "Libri dei passaporti," that, with some gaps, contains the applications for passports made by all of Agnone's "legal" emigrants beginning in 1903. The following estimates of the magnitude of emigration in Agnone from 1903 until World War I are derived primarily from this source. Foerster (*Italian Emigration of Our Times*, p. 11) argues that such statistics are unreliable because some of those who secured passports failed to emigrate. In the Agnone books, however, such cases are indicated by inscribing "annulled" or "denied" across the application. All such entries have been subtracted from the totals. Of course the possibility still remains that not all changes were recorded.

107. "Libro dei passaporti, comune di Agnone," 1903.

108. *Eco del Sannio*, June 12, 1903, p. 3.

109. Camille Lauriente, *The Chronicles of Camille*, passim.

110. *Eco del Sannio*, March 20, 1913, p. 2.

111. Josa, "Emigrazione nel Molise," p. 7.

112. The same total of 576 emigrants in 1896 and in the two-year period 1903–1904 *is* a coincidence and not a typographical error.

113. "Libro dei passaporti," 1903.

114. Josa, "Emigrazione nel Molise," p. 8.
115. Foerster, *Italian Emigration of Our Times*, p. 529.
116. *Eco del Sannio*, February 26, 1903, p. 2.
117. Ibid., April 15, 1909, p. 1.
118. Ibid., October 13, 1909, pp. 1–2.
119. Ibid., September 17, 1910, p. 1.
120. *Rinnovamento*, October 28, 1912, p. 3.
121. *La lotta*, March 10, 1912, p. 2.
122. *Rinnovamento*, February 2, 1913, p. 3.
123. Carl Solberg, *Immigration and Nationalism*.
124. *Eco del Sannio*, June 30, 1914, p. 3.
125. Michele Cervone, *In memoria di Giovanni Tirone*.
126. *Eco del Sannio*, April 10, 1896, p. 2.
127. *Rinnovamento*, May 8, 1912, p. 2.
128. "Libro dei passaporti," 1913.
129. *Aquilonia*, November 16, 1884, p. 3.
130. Ibid., October 1, 1888, p. 1.
131. "Stato di anime, 1882–1885, parrocchia di San Pietrò."
132. This latter category requires qualification because many of the town's earliest peasant and artisan emigrants to Argentina became small-scale merchants there and ultimately came to be listed as such in Agnone records. Thus, if a peasant established a shop in Argentina and sent for his peasant brother to become his clerk, the new emigrant would likely be registered in the Agnone parish census as a "storekeeper."
133. Comune di Agnone, "Elenco delle famiglie," passim.
134. *Lotta*, August 26, 1913, p. 2; *Eco del Sannio*, September 26, 1913, p. 3.
135. *Nuovo risveglio*, November 18, 1896, p. 2.
136. Comune di Agnone, "Elenco delle famiglie," passim.
137. William A. Douglass, "The South Italian Family," pp. 345–347.
138. Further evidence of the strength of ties within the extended-family household.
139. *Eco del Sannio*, November 27, 1913, p. 2.
140. Ibid., April 25, 1900, p. 2.
141. Ibid., December 10, 1905, p. 1.
142. For example, ibid., June 30, 1908, p. 2; November 27, 1913, p. 2.
143. For a graphic treatment of Italian emigration, *see* Gianfausto Rosoli and Oreste Grossi, *L'altra Italia*.
144. *Nuovo risveglio*, November 18, 1896, p. 2.
145. *Eco del Sannio*, August 10 and 25, 1906, p. 4.
146. *La fucina*, February 14, 1972, p. 4.
147. *Aquilonia*, September 10, 1886, p. 4.

148. Ibid., June 16, 1886, p. 4.

149. Masciotta, *Molise*, vol. 1, p. 345.

150. *Eco del Sannio*, September 28, 1907, p. 6.

151. Ibid., January 10, 1900, p. 3.

152. For example, on August 13, 1821 the town council agreed to pay Giuliana Mariani to care for an infant found abandoned in the streets (Campobasso, August 13, 1821).

153. "Atti di nascita, comune di Agnone," 1820–1829, passim.

154. Ibid., 1880–1889, passim.

155. There is, of course, a question regarding the strict comparability of the statistics. As a sensitive subject, illegitimacy was readily a matter for subterfuge. It is likely that in both periods some illegitimate births were reported as legitimate ones. The 1880–1889 figures include only those cases of actual abandonment and do not record "fatherless" children retained by their mothers. Despite the many possible qualifications, however, it seems clear that illegitimacy increased enormously in the wake of transatlantic emigration.

156. *Eco del Sannio*, September 10, 1897, p. 1.

157. Ibid., April 25, 1900, p. 1.

158. Masciotta, *Molise*, vol. 1, p. 342.

159. Ibid., p. 345.

160. Luigi Gamberale, *Interessi agnonesi*, p. 14.

Chapter 6

1. In 1885 the priest Felice Sammartino returned to Agnone after a fifteen-year absence, during which time he had resided in Buenos Aires, Montevideo, Lima, Mexico, and New York (*L'Aquilonia*, July 16, 1885, p. 4). In 1902 he died in Campeche, Mexico (*Eco del Sannio*, November 14, 1902, p. 2). In 1894 Michelangelo Maddalena was reported leaving Krebs, Indian Territory (Oklahoma) for Mexico (*Eco del Sannio*, December 25, 1894, p. 4).

2. Charles Tilly, "Migration in Modern European History," p. 53. Students of Italian immigration in Australia have also emphasized the chain-migration effect; see Charles A. Price, *Southern Europeans in Australia*, pp. 107–139; John S. MacDonald and Leatrice D. MacDonald, "Chain Migration, Ethnic Neighborhood Formation and Social Networks"; Rina Huber, *From Pasta to Pavlova*.

3. *La lotta*, August 26, 1913, p. 2.

4. *Aquilonia*, October 11, 1888, p. 1.

5. *Eco del Sannio*, January 4, 1934, p. 8.

6. Ibid., June 10, 1938, p. 1.

7. Ibid., January 4, 1934, p. 8.

8. Ibid.

9. *Aquilonia*, January 24, 1886, p. 3.

10. Ibid., January 16, 1885, p. 3; January 24, 1886, p. 3.

11. *Eco del Sannio*, November 10, 1895, p. 3.

12. Ibid., December 10, 1897, p. 3.

13. An underdeveloped theme in the migration literature is the extent to which the emigration process itself fomented Italian national consciousness. Since Robert F. Foerster's work (*The Italian Emigration of Our Times*, pp. 398–399), there has been a tendency, when discussing the issue at all, to note political apathy among the emigrant population. Emigrant political apathy is a relative matter, however, in the comparative context of regional rivalries and political apathy in Italy itself. The reverse side of the chain migration coin, which replicated Old World differences in New World settings, was the creation of an ethnic group coexisting among many with a collective ethnic interest to manifest and defend. In places like southern South America, North America, and Australia, Sicilians, Calabrians, Abruzzesi, and north Italians were ascribed an "Italian" identity by much of the wider population whether they liked it or not.

14. Samuel L. Baily, "Chain Migration of Italians to Argentina," pp. 78, 80.

15. Ibid., p. 79.

16. Ibid., p. 78.

17. *Il nuovo risveglio*, January 3, 1896, p. 4.

18. Ibid., August 18, 1897, p. 4.

19. *Eco del Sannio*, December 31, 1910, pp. 1–2.

20. *Nuovo risveglio*, May 3, 1897, p. 2.

21. *Eco del Sannio*, December 31, 1910, pp. 1–2.

22. Ibid., July 16, 1913, p. 2.

23. *Il rinnovamento*, February 17, 1912, p. 2.

24. *Eco del Sannio*, November 27, 1913, p. 2.

25. *Rinnovamento*, December 17, 1911, p. 3.

26. *Eco del Sannio*, September 30, 1908, p. 5.

27. Ibid.

28. Ibid., November 30, 1911, p. 3.

29. *Rinnovamento*, August 28, 1912, p. 2.

30. Ibid.

31. *Eco del Sannio*, May 27, 1913, p. 3.

32. Ibid., January 30, 1909, p. 3.

33. Ibid., December 31, 1910, p. 2.

34. Ibid., November 10, 1899, p. 3.

35. Ibid., January 30, 1909, p. 3.

36. Ibid., December 31, 1906, p. 1.

37. *Aquilonia*, June 4, 1884, p. 3.

38. Ibid., November 24, 1885, p. 4.
39. *Eco del Sannio*, March 28, 1906, p. 3.
40. *Nuovo risveglio*, May 3, 1897, p. 2.
41. *Eco del Sannio*, September 12, 1903, p. 2.
42. Ibid., April 5, 1911, p. 3.
43. Ibid., February 12, 1912, p. 3.
44. Ibid., March 28, 1906, p. 3.
45. *Aquilonia*, June 1, 1888, p. 4.
46. *Eco del Sannio*, May 27, 1906, p. 3.
47. Ibid., May 15, 1908, p. 3.
48. Ibid., April 22, 1913, p. 1.
49. Ibid., January 25, 1898, p. 4.
50. Ibid., August 28, 1905, p. 3; February 29, 1908, p. 2.
51. *Il cittadino agnonese*, June 3, 1900, p. 3.
52. *Nuovo risveglio*, May 3, 1897, p. 2.
53. *Eco del Sannio*, September 28, 1907, p. 4.
54. Ibid., July 26, 1913, p. 2.
55. Ibid., March 4, 1913, p. 5.
56. Ibid., March 19, 1910, p. 2.
57. Ibid., August 3, 1911, p. 2.
58. Ibid., May 12, 1904, p. 3.
59. *Eco del Sannio*, April 12, 1906, p. 2.
60. Ibid., May 30, 1908, p. 2.
61. *Il risveglio*, February 17, 1912, p. 2.
62. *Eco del Sannio*, February 12, 1912, p. 3.
63. Ibid., September 30, 1908, p. 5.
64. *Risveglio*, July 19, 1889, p. 3.
65. *Aquilonia*, February 16, 1884, p. 2.
66. Ibid., December 17, 1884, p. 3.
67. Ibid., June 16, 1886, p. 3.
68. Ibid., January 1, 1887, p. 3.
69. Ibid., May 1, 1888, p. 1.
70. *Risveglio*, February 10, 1889, pp. 2–3.
71. *Nuovo risveglio*, December 3, 1895, p. 3.
72. *Aquilonia*, April 18, 1889, pp. 1–2.
73. *Cittadino agnonese*, February 3, 1901, p. 3.
74. *Aquilonia*, January 1, 1887, p. 4.
75. Ibid.
76. Ibid., May 22, 1887, p. 3.
77. Ibid., July 30, 1887, p. 4.
78. Ibid., October 1, 1888, p. 4.
79. *Risveglio*, May 20, 1911, p. 8.

80. *Eco del Sannio*, May 12, 1905, pp. 2–3.
81. Ibid.
82. *Nuovo risveglio*, February 18, 1896, p. 2.
83. *Eco del Sannio*, July 10, 1896, pp. 2, 4.
84. *Nuovo risveglio*, March 3, 1897, p. 4.
85. *Risveglio*, October 5, 1889, p. 2.
86. Ibid., June 11, 1890, p. 3.
87. *Eco del Sannio*, December 10, 1900, p. 2.
88. Ibid., November 29, 1906, p. 2; December 13, 1906, p. 1.
89. Ibid., March 25, 1901, p. 2.
90. Ibid., September 25, 1894, p. 4.
91. Ibid., March 10, 1896, p. 4.
92. *Cittadino agnonese*, May 7, 1904, p. 4.
93. *Eco del Sannio*, September 13, 1905, p. 4.
94. Ibid.
95. Ibid.
96. Ibid., March 25, 1900, p. 1.
97. Ibid., December 10, 1900, p. 2.
98. Ibid., January 12, 1906, p. 3.
99. Ibid., May 12, 1905, pp. 2–3.
100. Ibid., February 15, 1907, p. 3.
101. Ibid., May 20, 1911.
102. Ibid., pp. 1–2.
103. *Rinnovamento*, October 18, 1912, p. 4.
104. Ibid., June 8, 1913, p. 2.
105. *Eco del Sannio*, May 12, 1905, pp. 2–3.
106. *Cittadino agnonese*, April 13, 1900, p. 3.
107. *Aquilonia*, August 18, 1885, p. 1.
108. *Eco del Sannio*, March 10, 1899, p. 2.
109. Foerster, *Italian Emigration of Our Times*, p. 457.
110. *Eco del Sannio*, June 30, 1908, p. 2; September 13, 1908, p. 2.
111. Foerster notes, "Sometimes, as in a number of communes of the Abruzzi and Molise, there are entire quarters that have grown up with the new abodes of the Americans" (*Italian Emigration of Our Times*, p. 457).
112. *Aquilonia*, September 10, 1886, p. 4; March 20, 1886, p. 3; *Nuovo risveglio*, September 3, 1896, p. 2; *Aquilonia*, September 10, 1886, p. 4; *Nuovo risveglio*, April 3, 1896, p. 4; April 18, 1897, p. 4.
113. *Eco del Sannio*, July 28, 1908, p. 1.
114. Ibid., November 8, 1909, p. 5.
115. Ibid., September 28, 1913, p. 4.
116. Ibid., February 13, 1906, p. 1; May 7, 1914, p. 2.
117. Ibid., February 13, 1906, p. 1.

118. Banca Operaia Cooperativa di Agnone, *Resoconto e bilancio per l'anno 1900*, p. 27.

119. Ibid., p. 26.

120. La Sannitica Banca Popolare Cooperativa di Agnone, *Assemblea generale ordinaria dei soci*, 1902, p. 6.

121. Banca Operaia Cooperativa di Agnone, *Resoconto e bilancio per l'anno 1910*, p. 7.

122. La Sannitica Banca Popolare Cooperativa di Agnone, *Assemblea generale ordinaria dei soci*, 1911, p. 11.

123. Banca Operaia Cooperativa di Agnone, *Resoconto e bilancio per l'anno 1928*, p. 9.

124. *Atto costitutivo e statuto per la società anonima per azioni della ferrovia Agnone-Pietrabbondante-Pescolanciano*, p. 8.

125. *Eco del Sannio*, March 27, 1911, p. 1.

126. Ibid., April 13, 1910, p. 10.

127. Ibid., April 22, 1913, p. 2.

128. *Nuovo risveglio*, February 18, 1896, p. 3.

129. *Aquilonia*, February 16, 1884, p. 4.

130. Ibid., June 20, 1884, p. 3.

131. *Eco del Sannio*, August 10, 1897, p. 1.

132. *Nuovo risveglio*, August 18, 1897, p. 2.

133. *Aquilonia*, May 16, 1885, p. 3.

134. *Eco del Sannio*, May 25, 1901, p. 2.

135. *Nuovo risveglio*, August 18, 1897, p. 1.

136. *Eco del Sannio*, September 10, 1906, p. 1.

137. Ibid., April 14, 1907, p. 1.

138. Ibid., September 30, 1908, p. 2.

139. Ibid., January 15, 1909, p. 2.

140. Ibid., July 22, 1909, p. 1.

141. *Atto costitutivo*.

142. *Eco del Sannio*, February 18, 1910, p. 1.

143. Custode Carlomagno, *Agnone dalle origini ai nostri giorni*, p. 286.

144. *Provincia di Molise anno 1814*.

145. Comune di Agnone, "Elenco delle famiglie e delle persone censite il 10 febbraio, 1901," passim.

146. *Risveglio*, October 5, 1889, p. 3.

147. *Il risveglio sannitico*, December 3, 1900, p. 3.

148. *Aquilonia*, July 16, 1885, p. 4.

149. Ibid., January 1, 1888, p. 4.

150. Ibid., January 1, 1888, p. 3.

151. Ibid., August 1, 1888, p. 2.

152. *Eco del Sannio*, September 25, 1895, p. 5.

153. Ibid., September 25, 1896, p. 4.

154. The Agnonesi of Buenos Aires organized their own *festa* in that city to honor the occasion (*Nuovo risveglio*, August 18, 1897, p. 4).

155. *In memoria del VI centenario di Maria Santissimo del Carmelo celebrato in Agnone*, pp. 3–17.

156. Ibid.

157. *Eco del Sannio*, July 10, 1898, p. 3.

158. Ibid., June 25, 1898, p. 3.

159. It may well be that this particular *festa* was actually initiated by an emigrant. In 1885 *Aquilonia* reported that "sig. Alfonso de Paola, our cocitizen living in Buenos Aires, has sponsored on August 23 in the church of Carmine a splendid *festa* in honor of M^a SS^a della Mercede" (September 2, 1885, p. 1).

160. *Eco del Sannio*, October 25, 1898, p. 3.

161. Ibid., October 10, 1899, p. 3.

162. Ibid., October 25, 1901, p. 2.

163. Ibid., April 10, 1903, p. 2.

164. Ibid., July 12, 1904, p. 3.

165. Ibid., September 30, 1904, p. 3.

166. Ibid., September 13, 1905, p. 4.

167. Ibid., August 27, 1905, p. 3.

168. Ibid., October 12, 1905, p. 3.

169. Ibid.

170. Of interest was the fact that the fund raisers in the Americas were also, in their zeal, soliciting money from donors who had no personal tie with Agnone. Of the 65 Denver donors, 3 were from Bari and 4 were Anglo-Americans (ibid.). Thus Agnone was receiving financial support from what might be regarded as extraneous New World sources as well.

171. Ibid., November 18, 1905, pp. 3–4.

172. Ibid., December 27, 1905, p. 3.

173. Ibid., August 13, 1904, p. 3.

174. Ibid., August 27, 1905, p. 3.

175. Ibid., August 31, 1909, p. 5.

176. Ibid., September 28, 1907, p. 7.

177. Ibid., October 31, 1907, p. 3.

178. Ibid., December 31, 1910, pp. 4–5.

179. Ibid., July 16, 1913, p. 3; November 7, 1913, p. 5; November 27, 1913, p. 4; December 16, 1913, p. 3.

180. Ibid., September 28, 1907, p. 7.

181. Ibid., September 29, 1903, p. 3.

182. Giambattista Masciotta, *Il Molise dalle origini ai nostri giorni*, vol 1, p. 350.

183. *Eco del Sannio*, September 13, 1905, p. 2.

184. Ibid., October 28, 1912, p. 5.

185. Ibid., April 22, 1913, p. 3.

186. Ibid., December 13, 1906, p. 2.

187. Ibid., September 25, 1895, pp. 1–3.

188. *Nuovo risveglio*, June 3, 1896, p. 1; June 18, 1896, p. 2.

189. *Aquilonia*, October 16, 1884, p. 1.

190. Ibid., June 17, 1885, p. 4.

191. *Eco del Sannio*, September 25, 1895, pp. 1–3, 5.

192. Ibid., July 14, 1910, p. 3.

193. Ibid., June 16, 1913, p. 2.

194. *Cittadino agnonese*, January 18, 1900, p. 3; April 18, 1900, p. 1.

195. *Aquilonia*, September 20, 1885, p. 4.

196. Ibid., October 5, 1886, p. 3.

197. Ibid., January 1, 1888, p. 3.

198. *Eco del Sannio*, March 12, 1904, p. 2.

199. Ibid., October 12, 1905, p. 1.

200. Ibid.

201. Ibid., March 28, 1906, p. 2.

202. Ibid., October 12, 1906, p. 2.

203. Ibid., December 31, 1906, p. 2.

204. Ibid., January 30, 1907, p. 2.

205. Ibid., July 28, 1908, p. 2.

206. Ibid., August 3, 1911, p. 2.

207. *Rinnovamento*, July 20, 1912, p. 3.

208. Onorato Jacapraro, *L'amministrazione comunale di Agnone e il partito dell'opposizione*. . . , p. 11.

209. *Aquilonia*, August 18, 1885, p. 3.

210. Ibid., January 24, 1886, p. 1.

211. Ibid., January 1, 1889, p. 4.

212. *Risveglio*, May 3, 1890, p. 3.

213. *Per la congrega di carità di Agnone contro 1° Paolo ed altri Sabelli 2° e Maria Paradiso*.

214. Enrico Morpurgo, "Un orologiaio italiano a Neuchatel," p. 3.

215. Ibid.

216. Ibid., p. 4.

217. *Aquilonia*, November 1, 1884, p. 2.

218. *Eco del Sannio*, June 25, 1897, p. 2.

219. Morpurgo, "Orologiaio italiano a Neuchatel," p. 4.

220. *Eco del Sannio*, May 28, 1903, p. 2.

221. Ibid., October 14, 1913, p. 3.

222. Ibid., January 12, 1904, p. 3.

223. Ibid., November 29, 1906, p. 1.

224. Ibid., December 31, 1906, p. 1.
225. Ibid., January 16, 1907, p. 1.
226. Ibid., October 31, 1907, p. 1.
227. *Rinnovamento*, November 11, 1911, p. 2.
228. Morpurgo, "Orologiaio italiano a Neuchatel," p. 4.

Chapter 7

1. Rudolph M. Bell, *Fate and Honor, Family and Village*, pp. 178–180.
2. Francesco d'Ovidio, *Rimpianti vecchi e nuovi*, p. 105.
3. Giovanni Zarrilli, *Il Molise dal 1860 al 1900*, pp. 137–138.
4. Ibid., p. 137.
5. Nicola Marinelli, *Agnone e la conciliazione fra la S. Sede e Italia*, pp. 9–10.
6. Baldassare La Banca, *Ricordi autobiografici*, pp. 27–28; Giambattista Masciotta, *Il Molise dalle origini ai nostri giorni*, vol. 3, p. 71.
7. *Il sindaco e il consiglio comunale di Agnone nei giorni 4 e 17 novembre 1867*, p. 4.
8. He was subsequently denied the sacraments by his confessor for collaborating with the government (*Eco del Sannio*, March 14, 1929, p. 4).
9. Luigi Gamberale, *Il mio libro paesano*, p. 58.
10. *Sindaco e il consiglio comunale*, p. 13.
11. Ibid., pp. 31–32.
12. Ibid., p. 32.
13. Ascenso Marinelli, *Il buon esempio nel proprio paese*, p. 106.
14. Ibid., p. 113.
15. Baldasare La Banca, *Il mio testamento*, p. 83.
16. Ibid., p. 82.
17. *Sindaco e il consiglio comunale*, pp. 38–39.
18. Ascenso Marinelli, *La mia relazione dopo essere messo a riposo*, p. 12.
19. *Aquilonia*, March 1, 1885, p. 1.
20. Ibid., January 24, 1886, p. 3.
21. *Eco del Sannio*, July 25, 1895, p. 2.
22. *Il rinnovamento*, October 28, 1912, p. 2.
23. *Eco del Sannio*, January 12, 1904, p. 1.
24. *Aquilonia*, January 1, 1884, p. 2.
25. Ibid., April 17, 1884, p. 3.
26. Ibid.
27. Ibid., June 4, 1884, p. 4.
28. Ibid., November 16, 1888, p. 4.
29. Ibid., January 16, 1885, p. 3.

30. Ibid., November 16, 1888, p. 4.

31. *Eco del Sannio*, January 30, 1908, p. 2.

32. Ibid., December 3, 1908, p. 2.

33. Ruggiero Apollonio, *L'amministrazione municipale di Agnone innanzi agli elettori nel 1878*, p. 64.

34. *Aquilonia*, September 2, 1884, p. 4.

35. Ibid.

36. *Eco del Sannio*, October 25, 1894, p. 1.

37. Ibid., July 28, 1905, p. 2.

38. *Il risveglio sannitico*, October 10, 1900, p. 3.

39. *Eco del Sannio*, April 25, 1903, p. 3.

40. Apollonio, *Amministrazione municipale di Agnone*, p. 66.

41. *Foglio periodico della prefattura di Campobasso*, pp. 36–37.

42. *Eco del Sannio*, January 30, 1908, p. 2.

43. Ibid., August 10, 1927, p. 1.

44. Ibid.

45. Ibid.

46. Ibid.

47. *Aquilonia*, February 16, 1886, p. 1.

48. Ibid., January 24, 1886, p. 3.

49. Ibid., May 2, 1885, p. 3.

50. *Eco del Sannio*, April 25, 1897, p. 2.

51. Ibid., February 25, 1896, p. 2.

52. *Aquilonia*, January 16, 1884, p. 2.

53. John W. Briggs, *An Italian Passage*, pp. 15–36.

54. In his treatment, Briggs discounts the importance of a socially activist priest in the formation of Workers' Mutual Benefit Societies in Calabria (*Italian Passage*, p. 32). I would not be so prone to do so, given the Agnone data.

55. *Aquilonia*, March 10, 1886, p. 3.

56. *Eco del Sannio*, April 10, 1895, p. 5.

57. *Il nuovo risveglio*, October 3, 1896, p. 1.

58. *Risveglio sannitico*, July 10, 1900, p. 1.

59. *Aquilonia*, May 16, 1885, p. 2.

60. Men from the region of Mantova were famed as itinerant agricultural laborers.

61. *Aquilonia*, November 1, 1886, p. 3.

62. *Eco del Sannio*, March 25, 1895, p. 2.

63. *Risveglio sannitico*, November 20, 1900, p. 3.

64. Ibid., April 30, 1901, p. 2.

65. Luigi Gamberale, *Interessi agnonesi*, p. 15.

66. *Eco del Sannio*, January 13, 1905, p. 1.

67. Ibid., April 30, 1907, p. 2. Nor was the situation restricted to Agnone.

A parliamentary inquiry concluded that, throughout the Molise, "the peasant converted into a small-scale proprietor by employing his savings accumulated from abroad . . . now makes it clear to the landowner who calls upon him to work for wages that he is conceding a *favor;* while the landowners remember a not-too-distant time in which the peasant . . . begged for a piece of ground to cultivate" (emphasis his): Cesare Jarach, *Inchiesta parlamentare sulle condizione dei contadini nelle provincie meridionali e nella Sicilia,* p. 94.

68. Un Gruppo di Agnonesi, "Ai nostri sfruttatori."

69. *Eco del Sannio,* June 15, 1908, p. 3.

70. Ibid., December 24, 1908, p. 1.

71. Ibid., February 25, 1898, p. 3.

72. *Rinnovamento,* December 25, 1911, p. 2.

73. *Eco del Sannio,* February 15, 1911, p. 2.

74. Jarach, *Inchiesta parlamentare,* pp. 86–87.

75. An extreme example of the social implications of such transfers is seen in the fact that recently in Agnone a successful building contractor purchased vineyards from a local prominent family at a price that was considerably below the offer made by a peasant-emigrant. The rationale given by the seller was that, if possible, "the land should remain in the same social class."

76. Gamberale, *Interessi agnonesi,* p. 12.

77. Ibid.

78. *Eco del Sannio,* September 28, 1913, p. 3.

79. *La lotta,* January 10, 1912, p. 3.

80. Ibid., January 27, 1912, p. 3.

81. *Eco del Sannio,* July 14, 1910, p. 2.

82. Ibid., September 15, 1911, p. 2.

83. Ibid., August 3, 1911, p. 1.

84. For example, *Eco del Sannio,* April 26, 1904, p. 3.

85. Ibid., November 28, 1903.

86. Ibid., November 27, 1904, p. 1.

87. Ibid., March 13, 1906, p. 1.

88. Ibid.

89. Ibid., May 12, 1905, p. 1.

90. Masciotta, *Molise,* vol. 3, p. 52.

91. *Eco del Sannio,* May 15, 1908, pp. 1–2.

92. Ibid.

93. Salvatore Pannunzio, *Le nostre miserie!*

94. Ibid., pp. 2, 13.

95. Ibid., p. 5.

96. Ibid., p. 7.

97. Ibid., pp. 4, 19–20.

98. Ibid., p. 16.

99. *Eco del Sannio*, July 31, 1907, pp. 1–2.

100. Ibid., September 30, 1908, p. 3.

101. Ibid.

102. Ibid., December 12, 1908, p. 2.

103. Ibid., May 17, 1909, p. 2.

104. Ibid., June 10, 1909, p. 3.

105. *Lotta*, February 25, 1912, p. 1.

106. Ibid., January 10, 1912, p. 3.

107. Ibid., June 25, 1912, p. 3.

108. Ibid., November 10, 1912, p. 5.

109. *Rinnovamento*, April 11, 1913, p. 1.

110. Ibid.; ibid., July 20, 1913, p. 1.

111. Ibid., September 19, 1912, p. 1; April 11, 1913, p. 1.

112. Ibid., April 11, 1913, p. 1.

113. Ibid., July 20, 1912, p. 1.

114. Ibid., July 24, 1913, p. 1.

115. *Lotta*, November 11, 1913, p. 2.

116. *Eco del Sannio*, September 28, 1912, p. 1.

117. Ibid., November 7, 1913, pp. 1–2.

118. *Rinnovamento*, January 19, 1913, p. 2.

119. *Eco del Sannio*, September 28, 1913, pp. 2, 4; October 14, 1913, p. 2.

120. Ibid., January 31, 1914, p. 2.

121. *Lotta*, January 26, 1914, p. 3; March 11, 1914, p. 2; March 28, 1914, p. 2. The paper urged the citizenry to back the civic improvements proposed by a councilman who was a relative of *La lotta*'s editor. Shortly thereafter, the newspaper ceased publication, quite possibly because it had alienated its natural constituency.

122. *Eco del Sannio*, March 5, 1914, p. 1.

123. Ibid., March 31, 1914, p. 1.

124. Agnone's income from timber sales, a major source of revenue during the nineteenth century, had all but evaporated by the time of the investigation. Scapinelli noted the allegations of usurpation of large tracts of commons by *galantuomini*. By the end of the nineteenth century, several important families in Agnone were in legal difficulties over the matter (for example, *Relazione sui danni nel bosco Poste*; Scipione Marracino, *Per il signor Costantino La Banca control l'amministrazione comunale di Agnone*; Donato Foschini and Gaetano Foschini, *Memoria in difesa di Costantino La Banca contro comune di Agnone*). It is therefore not surprising that the *galantuomini*-controlled town council was treating the issue with benign neglect.

125. *Contradeduzioni del consiglio comunale di Agnone alla relazione Scapinelli*, pp. 49–79.

126. *Eco del Sannio*, June 16, 1913, p. 2.

127. Ibid., May 7, 1914, p. 3.

128. Ibid., June 11, 1914, p. 2.

129. Ibid., pp. 1, 2.

130. *Il grido del popolo*, July 22, 1914, p. 4.

131. *Eco del Sannio*, July 25, 1914, p. 1.

132. Every male thirty years of age and older with permanent residence received the vote, as did every twenty-one-year-old permanent resident who had (1) passed the elementary school examination, (2) paid a minimum of 19.80 liras annually in taxes, and (3) completed at least ten months of military service (*Eco del Sannio*, September 12, 1912, p. 2).

133. Ibid., July 25, 1914, p. 1.

Chapter 8

1. *Eco del Sannio*, June 2, 1915, p. 2.

2. Ibid., March 30, 1917, p. 3.

3. Ibid., June 30, 1917, pp. 2–3.

4. Ibid., February 28, 1917, p. 2.

5. Ibid., p. 1.

6. Ibid., June 30, 1917, p. 3.

7. Ibid., May 4, 1918, p. 2.

8. Ibid., December 14, 1918, p. 1.

9. Ibid., September 5, 1933, pp. 3–4.

10. Ibid., January 31, 1919, p. 3.

11. Ninetta Tucker, *Italy*, p. 67.

12. Ibid., pp. 68–73.

13. Ibid., pp. 76–77.

14. *Eco del Sannio*, July 31, 1917, p. 2.

15. Ibid., January 31, 1919, p. 3.

16. Ibid., May 3, 1919, p. 1.

17. Ibid., p. 2.

18. Ibid., July 14, 1919, p. 2.

19. Ibid., p. 1.

20. Ibid., July 3, 1920, p. 1.

21. Ibid., p. 2.

22. Ibid., September 4, 1920, p. 1.

23. Ibid., October 5, 1920, p. 1.

24. Ibid., February 3, 1920, p. 1.

25. Ibid.

26. Ibid., November 12, 1920, pp. 1–2.

27. Ibid., p. 2.

28. Ibid., p. 1
29. Ibid., January 25, 1921, p. 1;; February 27, 1921, p. 1.
30. Ibid., January 25, 1921, p. 3.
31. Ibid., pp. 3–4.
32. Ibid., p. 4.
33. Ibid., March 26, 1921, p. 2.
34. Ibid., April 23, 1921, p. 3.
35. Ibid., May 13, 1921, pp. 1–2.
36. Ibid., p. 4.
37. Ibid.
38. Ibid., July 29, 1921, p. 2.
39. Ibid., August 4, 1922, p. 2.
40. Ibid., February 5, 1922, p. 3.
41. Ibid., June 4, 1922, p. 2.
42. Ibid., December 31, 1922, p. 2.
43. Ibid., June 4, 1922, p. 1.
44. Ibid., September 11, 1922, p. 3.
45. Ibid., April 1, 1927, p. 1.
46. Ibid., November 5, 1922, p. 1.
47. Ibid., December 31, 1922, p. 3.
48. Ibid.
49. Ibid., February 4, 1923, pp. 2–3.
50. Ibid, p. 3.
51. Ibid., March 8, 1923, p. 2.
52. Ibid.
53. Ibid., May 13, 1923, p. 1.
54. Ibid., p. 2.
55. Ibid., July 6, 1923, p. 1.
56. Ibid., October 31, 1923, p. 1.
57. Ibid., November 30, 1923, p. 1.
58. "Al dottor Michele Cervone, ex-fascista d'occasione."
59. "Per la moralità."
60. *Eco del Sannio*, December 30, 1923, p. 1.
61. Ibid., January 30, 1924, p. 4.
62. Ibid., p. 2.
63. Ibid., April 5, 1924, p. 1.
64. Ibid., October 7, 1923, p. 1.
65. Ibid., December 31, 1924, p. 2.
66. Ibid., March 5, 1925, p. 2.
67. Ibid., August 3, 1925, p. 2.
68. Ibid., March 17, 1926, p. 1.
69. Ibid., May 15, 1926, p. 2.

70. Ibid., March 7, 1927, p. 2.

71. Ibid., May 8, 1927, p. 2.

72. Ibid.

73. Ibid., June 13, 1927, p. 2.

74. Ibid., p. 3.

75. Ibid., October 11, 1927, p. 3.

76. Ibid., June 10, 1928, p. 2.

77. Ibid., April 29, 1929, p. 1.

78. Ibid., July 29, 1921, p. 2.

79. Ibid., May 30, 1924, p. 2.

80. Ibid., June 30, 1924, p. 1.

81. *La città di Agnone*, p. 22.

82. A. di Pasquo, *Natale di Roma*, p. 10.

83. *Eco del Sannio*, September 8, 1925, pp. 1–2; March 7, 1927, p. 2.

84. Ibid., April 15, 1926, p. 2.

85. Ibid., May 15, 1926, p. 3; May 8, 1927, p. 4; January 6, 1932, p. 4.

86. Ibid., June 7, 1927, p. 2.

87. Ibid., June 10, 1920, p. 3.

88. Nicola Marinelli, *Agnone e la conciliazione fra la S. Sede e Italia*.

89. *Eco del Sannio*, May 7, 1931, p. 2.

90. Ibid., June 25, 1934, p. 3.

91. Ibid., February 13, 1929, p. 5; July 19, 1937, p. 1.

92. For example, ibid., September 17, 1931, p. 3; February 14, 1935, p. 2.

93. Ibid., January 16, 1936, p. 3.

94. Ibid., May 1, 1925, p. 2; May 15, 1926, p. 2; October 14, 1933, p. 3; March 10, 1936, p. 5.

95. Ibid., February 2, 1926, p. 1.

96. Ibid., November 16, 1928, p. 1.

97. Ibid., December 15, 1928, p. 2.

98. Ibid., May 23, 1934, p. 4.

99. Ibid., April 27, 1930, p. 1.

100. Ibid., April 25, 1933, p. 4; August 14, 1935, p. 1.

101. Jack F. Bernard, *Italy*, p. 452.

102. ISTAT, *Catasto agrario, 1929*, p. 106. The statistic includes Belmonte del Sannio, which for a brief period was incorporated administratively into Agnone.

103. ISTAT, *Secondo censimento generale dell'agricoltura*, This figure is derived by summing all lands in *seminative* for *both* Agnone and Belmonte del Sannio in order to effect comparison with the 1929 totals.

104. ISTAT, *Catasto agrario, 1929*, p. 106.

105. *Eco del Sannio*, October 6, 1934, p. 1.

106. Ibid., April 30, 1935, p. 2.

107. Ibid., March 10, 1936, p. 3.

108. Ibid., February 6, 1938, p. 3.

109. Ibid., November 27, 1937, p. 3.

110. Ibid., January 7, 1927, p. 3.

111. Ibid., March 14, 1929, p. 2.

112. Ibid., September 15, 1929, p. 2.

113. Ibid., February 25, 1930, p. 3.

114. Ibid., June 16, 1929, p. 4.

115. Ibid., May 31, 1930, p. 3.

116. Ibid., November 6, 1934, p. 3.

117. Ibid., January 17, 1933, p. 1.

118. Ibid., January 6, 1938, p. 4.

119. Ibid., December 6, 1924, p. 3.

120. Ibid., October 12, 1926, p. 2.

121. Ibid., March 7, 1927, p. 1.

122. Ibid.

123. Ibid., August 18, 1929, p. 1.

124. Ibid., February 6, 1931, p. 2.

125. "Reclamo operai Agnone avverso il ruolo tassa artigianati."

126. Agnone, November 1, 1931.

127. *Eco del Sannio*, August 4, 1922, p. 1.

128. Ibid., July 6, 1923, p. 1.

129. Ibid., October 31, 1923, p. 1.

130. Ibid., December 31, 1924, p. 1.

131. Ibid., April 7, 1923, p. 1.

132. Ibid., January 30, 1924, pp. 1–2.

133. Ibid., April 12, 1928, pp. 1–2.

134. Ibid., March 10, 1931, p. 2.

135. Ibid., April 30, 1935, p. 1.

136. Ibid., December 15, 1936, p. 1.

137. Ibid., April 10, 1931, p. 1.

138. Ibid., August 18, 1929, p. 1.

139. Ibid., April 15, 1932, p. 3.

140. Ibid., November 8, 1932, p. 5.

141. Ibid., December 15, 1936, p. 4.

142. Ibid., October 27, 1937, p. 3.

143. Ibid., March 10, 1938, pp. 1–2; August 18, 1938, p. 1; July 19, 1937, p. 1; September 27, 1937, pp. 1–2; August 22, 1937, p. 1.

144. Ibid., March 10, 1938, p. 3.

145. Ibid., April 10, 1938, p. 1.

146. Ibid., April 1, 1927, p. 1.

147. Ibid., May 30, 1924, p. 1.

148. Salvatore Pannunzio, *Discorso pronunziato il 18 marzo 1945 nella grande manifestizione pro partigiani*, p. 3.

149. Ibid., p. 4.

150. *La fucina*, June 8, 1968, p. 1.

151. Ibid., November 26, 1950, pp. 2–3.

152. Ibid., December 24, 1950, p. 5.

153. Ibid., June 30, 1951, p. 1.

154. Ibid., May 31, 1951, p. 2.

155. Ibid., December 31, 1951, p. 1.

156. Ibid., March 23, 1952, p. 1.

157. Ibid., May 13, 1952, p. 1.

158. Ibid., June 29, 1950, p. 2.

159. Ibid., March 31, 1953, p. 3.

160. Ibid., July 5, 1953, p. 2; August 5, 1953, p. 4; September 8, 1953, p. 2.

161. Ibid., August 5, 1953, p. 4.

162. Ibid., April 30, 1950, p. 2.

163. Ibid., February 26, 1950, p. 2.

164. Ibid., October 7, 1951, p. 1.

165. Ibid., February 28, 1951, p. 2.

166. Ibid., April 29, 1951, p. 1.

167. Ibid., February 28, 1951, p. 2.

168. Ibid., February 5, 1950, p. 3.

169. Custode Carlomagno, *Agnone dalle origini ai nostri giorni*, p. 294.

170. Ibid.

171. Ibid.

172. The state not only aids Agnone's schools with building and operating funds; it provides them with students. Both the Italian navy and the National Entity for Assistance to Orphans of Italian Workers provide grants-in-aid to allow orphans from elsewhere in Italy to attend Agnone's schools. In the year 1972–1973 approximately half of the 120 boarders in one student boarding house were recipients of such assistance.

173. Michele di Ciero, *Sc-terlambe che se pèrde*, pp. 75–76, 78–81.

174. The process is not unique to Agnone but generic to south Italy. Mario de Luca, "Le conseguenze economiche sui luoghi di provenienza," p. 73.

175. There are still a few people in Agnone who own land that is worked by a sharecropper, though they now possess little leverage in the arrangement. As one man told me, "I know my sharecropper is stealing from me, but if I dare go to the fields at harvest time, he will accuse me of not trusting him and leave. Then instead of a small yield I will have none at all."

176. Enzo Gàzzera and Lucio Selvaggi, *Integrazione agricola e industriale nel Molise*, p. 99.

177. See Corrado Barberis, "La femme dans l'agriculture italienne" and idem, "L'esodo."

178. *Fucina*, February 5, 1950, p. 3.

179. Ibid., May 31, 1950, p. 1; September 15, 1951, pp. 1–4; December 8, 1954, p. 1.

180. Ibid., May 28, 1967, p. 3.

181. Ibid., February 15, 1965, p. 1.

182. Ibid., February 5, 1950, p. 2.

183. Ibid., August 5, 1956, p. 2.

184. Ibid., June 30, 1957, p. 1; July 28, 1961, p. 1.

185. *Turisport*, March 4, 1966, p. 4.

186. Comune di Agnone, "Elenco delle famiglie e delle persone censite il 10 febbraio, passim; "Censimento di Agnone," passim.

187. *Fucina*, April 30, 1950, pp. 1–2.

188. The new importance of the old age pension for the household economy is neatly summed up by the poem of Michele Di Ciero entitled "E' muorte ze cola: R'accise la pensieune," or "Uncle Nicholas Is Dead: The Pension Is Killed," in which it is the loss of the pension that is mourned! See Di Ciero, *Sc-terlambe che se pèrde*, pp. 66–67.

189. M. Carosella, "Tribuna aperta."

190. *Fucina*, September 12, 1970, p. 1.

191. Ibid., December 13, 1970, p. 2.

192. *Operazione terra*.

193. *Fucina*, July 30, 1971, p. 6; September 1, 1971, p. 4.

194. *Piazza del tomolo*, June 1973, p. 2; October 1973, p. 1.

195. Ibid., October 1973, p. 1.

196. *Fucina*, June 29, 1950, p. 1.

197. Ibid., November 6, 1955, p. 4.

198. Ibid., July 10, 1965, p. 3.

Chapter 9

1. "Libro dei passaporti, comune di Agnone," 1914–1918, passim.

2. Eugenio Jannone, "L'emigrazione nel Molise," p. 16.

3. *Eco del Sannio*, February 28, 1924, p. 2.

4. Ibid., December 8, 1925, p. 3.

5. Ibid., February 28, 1917, p. 2.

6. Ibid., August 12, 1924, p. 1.

7. U.S. Department of Labor, *Annual Report of the Commissioner General of Immigration to the Secretary of Labor, Fiscal Year Ended June 30, 1922*, p. 5.

8. U.S. Department of Labor, *Annual Report of the Commissioner General of Immigration to the Secretary of Labor, Fiscal Year Ended June 30, 1925*, p. 6.

9. U.S. Department of Labor, *Annual Report, 1922*, pp. 100–102.

10. Alessandro Ghigi, "Migratorie, correnti,' pp. 255–256.

11. *Eco del Sannio*, January 19, 1915, p. 3.

12. Ibid., July 7, 1915, p. 3.

13. Ibid., January 31, 1917, p. 1; February 28, 1917, p. 3. It is interesting to note that actually there were two committees, differentiated along class lines. The first to act was the workers' committee, which sent 750 liras and a letter that challenged the rich Agnonesi of Argentina to follow their lead. So the budding class confrontation in the town was reflected in the immigrant diaspora as well.

14. Ibid., December 16, 1917, p. 2.

15. Ibid., November 18, 1917, p. 2.

16. Ibid., September 15, 1918, p. 2.

17. Ibid., December 14, 1919, p. 3.

18. Ibid., March 31, 1919, p. 2.

19. Ibid., July 14, 1919, p. 2.

20. Ibid., August 5, 1920, p. 1.

21. Ibid., p. 4.

22. Ibid., February 3, 1920, p. 2.

23. Ibid., April 23, 1921, p. 2; August 2, 1921, pp. 1–2.

24. Ibid., April 23, 1921, p. 3.

25. Ibid., February 4, 1923, p. 2; October 7, 1923, p. 1.

26. Ibid., September 28, 1921, p. 1.

27. Ibid., September 14, 1927, p. 1.

28. *Il rinnovamento*, September 23, 1911, p. 2.

29. *Eco del Sannio*, May 27, 1913, p. 2.

30. Ibid., February 20, 1916, p. 2.

31. Ibid., November 5, 1922, pp. 1–2.

32. Ibid., March 5, 1922, p. 3.

33. Ibid., January 3, 1919, p. 3.

34. La Sannitica Banca Popolare Cooperativa di Agnone, *Assemblea generale ordinaria dei soci*, 1919, p. 9.

35. La Sannitica Banca Popolare Cooperativa di Agnone, *Assemblea generale ordinaria dei soci*, 1925, p. 8.

36. Ibid., p. 9.

37. Banca Operaia Cooperative di Agnone, *Resoconto e bilancio per l'anno 1925*, p. 13.

38. *Eco del Sannio*, September 8, 1925, p. 3.

39. Ibid., July 13, 1927, p. 1.

40. Ibid., August 10, 1927, p. 2.

41. Ibid., November 5, 1925, p. 2.

42. Ibid., June 5, 1925, p. 3.

43. Ibid., September 11, 1922, pp. 3–4.

44. Ibid., October 5, 1924, p. 3.

45. Ibid., July 6, 1923, p. 2; February 2, 1926, p. 1.

46. Ibid., June 16, 1929, p. 2.

47. Ibid., October 5, 1920, p. 5.

48. Ibid., October 6, 1925, p. 4.

49. For example, ibid., September 15, 1929, p. 4; November 24, 1929, p. 4; July 16, 1931, p. 4.

50. Ibid., September 15, 1928, p. 1.

51. Ibid., January 16, 1930, p. 4.

52. Ibid., May 5, 1936, p. 4.

53. Ibid., June 20, 1936, p. 8.

54. Ibid., February 14, 1935, p. 5.

55. Ibid., April 30, 1935, p. 3.

56. Ibid., June 30, 1936, p. 8.

57. Ibid., September 27, 1937, p. 4.

58. Ibid., March 10, 1938, p. 4.

59. Ibid., April 10, 1938, p. 4.

60. Ibid., September 22, 1938, p. 3.

61. Anthony A. Richmond, *Post-war Immigrants in Canada*, pp. 7, 9.

62. ISTAT, *Sommario di statistiche storiche dell'Italia, 1861–1965*, p. 29.

63. José Panettieri, *Inmigración en la Argentina*, pp. 133–136.

64. Richmond, *Post-war Immigrants in Canada*, pp. 9–11.

65. Ibid., p. 5.

66. *La fucina*, April 18, 1973, p. 3.

67. ISTAT, *Sommario*, p. 29.

68. Charles A. Price, *Southern Europeans in Australia*, pp. 9–10.

69. Charles A. Price, *Australian Immigration Research Report No. 2*.

70. Ibid., pp. 34–35.

71. *Fucina*, April 2, 1950, p. 1.

72. Ninetta Tucker, *Italy*, pp. 141–142.

73. F. Alberoni, "Aspects of Internal Migration Related to Other Types of Italian Migration," pp. 292–293.

74. ISTAT, *Sommario* p. 24.

75. Giovanni Blumer, *L'emigrazione italiana in Europa*, pp. 137–138.

76. *Fucina*, February 5, 1950, pp. 3–4.

77. F. Roy Willis, *Italy Chooses Europe*, p. 156.

78. *Piazza del tomolo*, January-February 1974, p. 3.

79. Antonio Arduino, *Agnone*, unpaginated.

80. The number of departures was, of course, considerably greater but was partially offset by returnees.

81. I restrict the analysis to the *cittadina* because during the period there has been little in-migration to Agnone's rural areas. In 1901, 92.48 percent of the *agro* dwellers were born in the town, and the proportion actually increased to 96.26 percent by 1971. In both periods, the majority of the outsiders were peasants from communities contiguous to Agnone who happened to marry an Agnonese *contadino* or *contadina*.

82. Comune di Agnone, "Elenco delle famiglie e delle persone censite il 10 febbraio, 1901," passim; "Censimento di Agnone," 1971, passim.

83. Information is lacking for 82 persons in the 1901 census and 13 persons in the 1971 census.

84. *Turisport*, April 30, 1965, p. 1.

85. Ibid., August 31, 1964, p. 3.

86. *Fucina*, April 2, 1950, p. 4.

87. Ibid., July 30, 1950, p. 4.

88. Ibid., September 30, 1950, p. 2.

89. Ibid., January 31, 1953, p. 2.

90. Ibid., February 28, 1951, p. 3.

91. Ibid., August 27, 1950, p. 4.

92. Ibid., January 31, 1951, p. 1.

93. Ibid., April 30, 1953, p. 2.

94. Ibid., September 25, 1955, p. 4.

95. Ibid., December 10, 1969, p. 4.

96. Ibid., August 10, 1970, p. 3; August 4, 1972, p. 4.

97. Ibid., February 4, 1950, p. 4.

98. Ibid., May 13, 1952, p. 4.

99. Ibid., June 17, 1954, p. 3.

100. *Turisport*, February 28, 1965, p. 4.

101. *Fucina*, May 31, 1972, p. 3.

102. Ibid., April 18, 1973, p. 3.

103. Ibid., June 25, 1973, p. 4.

104. Ibid., June 21, 1967, p. 4.

105. Ibid., November 15, 1968, p. 5.

106. Ibid., December 12, 1967, p. 4.

Chapter 10

1. Peter Benedict, *Ula.*
2. Gideon Sjoberg, *The Preindustrial City.*
3. Benedict, *Ula,* p. 6.
4. Giancarlo Moretti, "Nord-sud"; Giselle Podbielski, *Italy,* pp. 131–144; William A. Douglass, "Migration in Italy."
5. Maria Liguori, "Fenomeni migratori e socilogia."
6. For example, Enrico Capo, "I problemi economici e socio-culturali delle zone di destinazione dell'esodo rurale"; L. Cavalli, *Gli immigrati meridionali e la società ligure*; G. Fofi, *Immigrazione e industria*; G. Fofi, *Immigrazione meridionale a Torino*; Mariano Livolsi, "Integazione dell'immigrato e integrazione comunitaria"; C. Manucci, "Emigrants in the Upper Milanese Area"; Andrea Villani, "Analisis delle conseguenze economiche e finanziarie delle migrazioni interne sulle zone di destinazione."
7. For example, Gianfranco Albertelli and Giuliana Ziliani, "Le condizione alloggiative della popolazione immigrata"; Francesco Compagna, *I terroni in città*; G. Fofi, "Immigrants to Turin"; Giorgio Majorino, "Il tempo libero e gli immigrati."
8. Cavalli, *Gli immigrati meridionali*; Manucci, "Emigrants"; Giovanni Pellicciari, *L'immigrazione nel triangolo industriale.*
9. L. Diena, *Borgata milanese.*
10. Adriano Baglivo and Giovanni Pellicciari, *La tratta dei meridionali.*
11. See Corrado Barberis, *Le migrazioni rurali in Italia*; Antonio Golini, "Le tendenze recenti nelle migrazioni interne"; La Redazione, "Le migrazioni interne italiane oggi"; Eugenia Malfatti, "Le migrazioni meridionali alla luce delle fonti statistiche ufficiali (1951–1975)"; Emilio Reyneri et al., *L'emigrazione meridionale nelle zone d'esodo*; G. B. Sacchetti, "Regioni e migrazione."
12. Corrado Barberis, "Esodo agricolo e strutture fondiarie"; Salvatore Cafiero and Guido de' Rossi, "Lo spopolamento della montagna meridionale"; Innocenzo Gasparini, "Tratti socio-economici dell'emigrazione dalla montagna e dalla collina del Veneto"; Guglielmo Tagliacarne, "Spopolamento montano ed esodo rurale, misura e prospettive."
13. Corrado Barberis, "La femme dans l'agriculture italienne"; idem, "Esodo."
14. Ibid.
15. Mario de Luca, "Le consequenze economiche sui luoghi di provenienza"; Reyneri et al., *Emigrazione meridionale*; Paolo Vicinelli, "Esodo rurale e programmi di sviluppo del mezzogiorno italiano."
16. Baglivo and Pellicciari, *Tratta dei meridionali,* p. 146; Documentazioni," "Recenti immigrati a Torino."
17. Frank Bovenkerk, *The Sociology of Return Migration.*

18. Immanuel Wallerstein, *The Modern World System.*

19. For example, C. R. Boxer, *The Dutch Seaborne Empire, 1600–1800*; idem, *The Portuguese Seaborne Empire*; Pierre Chaunu, *Conquête et exploitation des nouveaux mondes*; E. J. Hobsbawn, *Industry and Empire*; J. H. Parry, *The Spanish Seaborne Empire*; John F. Ramsey, *Spain*; Glyndwr Williams, *The Expansion of Europe in the Eighteenth Century.*

20. For example, Ruth Pike, *Enterprise and Adventure.*

21. María Lourdes Díaz-Trechuelo Spínola, *La real compañía de filipinas*; Roland Dennis Hussey, *The Caracas Company, 1728–1789.*

22. Oscar Handlin, *The Uprooted*; Marcus Lee Hansen, *The Atlantic Migration, 1607–1860.*

23. Francis J. Brown and Joseph Slabey Roucek, *One America*; Maldwyn Allen Jones, *American Immigration.*

24. Paul M. Migus, *Sounds Canadian.*

25. José Panettieri, *Inmigración en la Argentina.*

26. Charles A. Price, *Southern Europeans in Australia.*

27. For example, Charles Tilly, "Migration in Modern European History." For a good discussion of the complexities, see Charlotte Erickson, "Introduction."

28. Caribbeanists have emphasized the importance of the "remittance economy" in their studies of emigration; see Julia G. Crane, *Educated to Emigrate*; David Lowenthal and Lambros Comitas, "Emigration and Depopulation"; Stuart B. Philpott, *West Indian Migration.*

29. Gianfausto Rosoli, "L'emigrazione di ritorno," p. 235.

30. Commissione Nazionale Italiana UNESCO, *L'esodo rurale e lo spopolamento della montagna nella società contemporanea*; Ruth M. Crichton, *Commuters' Village*; S. H. Franklin, *The European Peasantry*; Joseph Lopreato, *Peasants No More*; Eugene Weber, *Peasants into Frenchmen.*

References

Archival Documents without Author or Title, by Date

MUNICIPAL ARCHIVES

Agnone

November 1, 1931. Fondo Archivio Comunale di Agnone.

STATE ARCHIVES

Campobasso

December 29, 1768. Fondo Regia Udienza di Abruzzo Citra, protocollo 126.
December 3, 1809. Fondo Intendenza del Molise, protocollo 1013, fascio 139.
August 3, 1811. Fondo Intendenza del Molise, protocollo 206, fascio 17.
September 21, 1811. Fondo Intendenza del Molise, protocollo 210, fascio 24.
November 12, 1811. Fondo Intendenza del Molise, protocollo 206, fascio 17.
January 31, 1812. Fondo Monasteri Soppressi, protocollo 3, fascio 10.
May 23, 1812. Fondo Monasteri Soppressi, protocollo 3, fascio 10.
June 15, 1812. Fondo Monasteri Soppressi, protocollo 3, fascio 10.
November 12, 1812. Fondo Intendenza del Molise, protocollo 206, fascio 17.
January 18, 1814. Fondo Intendenza del Molise, protocollo 200, fascio 9.
August 1, 1814. Fondo Intendenza del Molise, protocollo 210, fascio 22.
October 27, 1814. Fondo Intendenza del Molise, protocollo 206, fascio 17.
December 27, 1815 (proclamation). Fondo Intendenza del Molise, protocollo 1013, fascio 140.
August 28, 1816. Fondo Intendenza del Molise, protocollo 198, fascio 4.
September 25, 1816. Fondo Intendenza del Molise, protocolo 210, fascio 22.
October 8, 1816. Fondo Intendenza del Molise, protocollo 201, fascio 10.
February 28, 1817. Fondo Intendenza del Molise, protocollo 201, fascio 10.
May 11, 1817. Fondo Intendenza del Molise, protocollo 210, fascio 22.
June 30, 1817. Fondo Intendenza del Molise, protocollo 206, fascio 17.

September 14, 1817. Fondo Intendenza del Molise, protocollo 211, fascio 3.
November 1, 1817. Fondo Intendenza del Molise, protocollo 198, fascio 4.
December 10, 1817. Fondo Intendenza del Molise, protocollo 211, fascio 3.
August 10, 1818. Fondo Monasteri Soppressi, protocollo 3, fascio 10.
August 8, 1820. Fondo Intendenza del Molise, protocollo 198, fascio 5.
July 28, 1821. Fondo Intendenza del Molise, protocollo 195, fascio 1.
August 13, 1821. Fondo Intendenza del Molise, protocollo 207, fascio 18.
August 21, 1821. Fondo Intendenza del Molise, protocollo 209, fascio 21.
August 28, 1821. Fondo Monasteri Soppressi, protocollo 3, fascio 10.
October 2, 1821. Fondo Intendenza del Molise, protocollo 207, fascio 18.
June 8, 1822. Fondo Intendenza del Molise, protocollo 209, fascio 21.
November 15, 1823. Fondo Intendenza del Molise, protocollo 207, fascio 18.
November 8, 1827. Fondo Brigantaggio Processi, protocollo 47.
April 13, 1831. Fondo Intendenza del Molise, protocollo 208, fascio 19.
N.d. (ca. 1833). Fondo Intendenza del Molise, protocollo 210, fascio 22.
N.d. (ca. 1835). Fondo Intendenza del Molise, protocollo 200, fascio 8.
September 26, 1835. Fondo Intendenza del Molise, protocollo 204, fascio 14.
December 17, 1836. Fondo Intendenza del Molise, protocollo 209, fascio 19.
September 2, 1838. Fondo Monasteri Soppressi, protocollo 3, fascio 10.
December 31, 1839. Fondo Intendenza del Molise, protocollo 211, fascio 1.
June 15, 1850. Fondo Intendenza del Molise, protocollo 209, fascio 21.
May 1, 1860. Fondo Brigantaggio Processi, protocollo 93.
October 1, 1860. Fondo Brigantaggio Processi, protocollo 92.
December 3, 1860. Fondo Brigantaggio Processi, protocollo 90.
January 13, 1862. Fondo Brigantaggio Processi, protocollo 142.
May 31, 1862. Fondo Brigantaggio Processi, protocollo 193.
July 29, 1862. Fondo Brigantaggio Processi, protocollo 224.
March 13, 1863. Fondo Brigantaggio Processi, protocollo 142.
March 22, 1863. Fondo Brigantaggio Processi, protocollo 241.
December 22, 1869. Fondo Brigantaggio Processi, protocollo 93.

Chieti

July 13, 1760. Fondo Regia Udienza di Abruzzo Citra, protocollo 101.
July 4, 1761. Fondo Regia Udienza di Abruzzo Citra, protocollo 101.
July 5, 1761. Fondo Regio Udienza di Abruzzo Citra, protocollo 101.
July 19, 1777. Fondo Regio Udienza di Abruzzo Citra, protocollo 173.
August 4, 1777. Fondo Regia Udienza di Abruzzo Citra, protocollo 173.
August 8, 1781. Fondo Regia Udienza di Abruzzo Citra, protocollo 197.
August 9, 1781. Fondo Regia Udienza di Abruzzo Citra, protocollo 197.
June 23, 1788. Fondo Regia Udienza di Abruzzo Citra, protocollo 276.
January 7, 1789. Fondo Regia Udienza di Abruzzo Citra, protocollo 93.

References

Naples

March 13, 1782. Fondo Sezzione Politico-amminstrativa Intestazioni Feudali, vol. 118, no. 2040.

March 16, 1782. Fondo Sezzione Politico-amministrativa Intestazioni Feudali, vol. 118, no. 1040.

February 16, 1810 (decree). Fondo Ministero dell'Interno, inventario no. 2, fascio 548, item 12.

January 1, 1812. Fondo Ministero dell'Interno, inventario no. 2, fascio 547, item 6.

N.d. (ca. 1834). Fondo Ministero dell'Interno, inventario no. 2, fascio 4213.

Archival Documents with Author or Title, and Published Works

Alberoni, F. "Aspects of Internal Migration Related to Other Types of Italian Migration." In *Readings in the Sociology of Migration*, ed. Clifford J. Jansen, pp. 285–316. Oxford: Pergamon, 1970.

Albertelli, Gianfranco, and Giuliana Ziliani. "Le condizione alloggiative della popolazione immigrata." In *L'immigrazione nel triangolo industriale*, ed. Giovanni Pellicciari, pp. 283–303. Milan: Angeli, 1970.

Aldimari, Biagio. *Historia genealogica della familia Carafa*, vol. 1. Naples, 1691.

"Al dottor Michele Cervone ex-fascista d'occasione," October 12, 1923. Handbill. Archivio Comunale di Agnone.

Aloi, Vincenzo. *Memoria da presentarsi al supremo tribunale della regal camera di S. Chiara per lo regio patronato dell'arcipretura di S. Marco in Agnone centro all'illustre Principe di S. Buono e D. Emilio Pannunzio*. Naples, 1786.

Alsina, Juan A. *La inmigración europea en la República Argentina*. Buenos Aires, 1898.

Amoroso, Gaetano. *Il Molise in una circoscrizione regionale*. Campobasso, 1946.

Antinori, A. Ludovico. *Raccolta di memorie istoriche delle tre provincie degli Abbruzzi*, vol. 4. Naples, 1783.

———."Corografia, parte 2ª," vol. 25, n.d. Biblioteca Provinciale di Aquila.

Apollonio, Ruggiero. *L'amministrazione municipale di Agnone innanzi agli elettori nel 1878*. Naples, 1878.

L'Aquilonia. Newspaper published in Agnone. Biblioteca La Banca.

Arduino, Antonio. *Agnone, paese di suoni antichi*. Pescopennataro, 1979.

Atti del consiglio provinciale di Molise: Sessione ordinaria dell'anno 1861. Naples, 1863.

259

References

"Atti di morte, comune di Agnone, 1820–1829; 1885–1892." Archivio Comunale di Agnone.

"Atti di nascita, comune di Agnone," 1809–1972. Archivio Comunale di Agnone.

"Atti per la vendita del grano, granone, vino mosto di ragione di queste chiese pel corrente anno 1852." Biblioteca La Banca.

Atto costitutivo e statuto per la società anonima per azioni della ferrovia Agnone-Pietrabbondante-Pescolanciano. Agnone, 1909.

Baglivo, Adriano, and Giovanni Pellicciari. *La tratta dei meridionali*. Milan: Sapere, 1973.

Baily, Samuel L. "Chain Migration of Italians to Argentina: Case Studies of the Agnonesi and Sirolesi." *Studi emigrazione* 19, no. 65(1982):73–91.

Banca Operaia Cooperativa di Agnone. *Resoconto e bilancio per l'anno 1900.* Agnone, 1901.

———. *Resoconto e bilancio per l'anno 1910.* Agnone, 1911.

———. *Resoconto e bilancio per l'anno 1925.* Agnone, 1926.

———. *Resoconto e bilancio per l'anno 1928.* Agnone, 1929.

Banfield, Edward C. *The Moral Basis of a Backward Society.* Glencoe, Ill.: Free Press, 1958.

Barberis, Corrado. *Le migrazione rurali in Italia.* Milan: Feltrinelli, 1960.

———. "La femme dans l'agriculture italienne." *Etudes rurales* 10 (1963): 50–67.

———. "Esodo agricolo e strutture fondiarie: Con particolare riferimento ai comprensori montani." In *L'esodo rurale e lo spopolamento della montagna nella società contemporanea*, Commissione Nazionale Italiana UNESCO, pp. 41–69. Milan: Società Editrice Vita e Pensiero, 1966.

———. "L'esodo: Conseguenze demografiche e sociali." In *L'esodo rurale e lo spopolamento della montagna nella società contemporanea*, Commissione Nazionale Italiana UNESCO, pp. 25–40. Milan: Società Editrice Vita e Pensiero, 1966.

Barbieri, Carlo. "Riposte su de' quesiti statistici fatti da S. E. il sig' ministro dell'interno," n.d., 1817. Fondo Intendenza del Molise, protocollo 1011, fascio 133. Archivio di Stato di Campobasso.

Barton, Josef J. *Peasants and Strangers: Italians, Rumanians and Slovaks in an American City, 1890–1950.* Cambridge: Harvard University Press, 1975.

Bell, Rudolph M. *Fate and Honor, Family and Village: Demographic and Cultural Change in Rural Italy since 1800.* Chicago: University of Chicago Press, 1979.

Benedict, Peter. *Ula: An Anatolian Town.* Leiden: Brill, 1974.

Bernard, Jack F. *Italy: An Historical Survey.* Devon: David and Charles, 1971.

Biondo Flavio. *Italia illustrata.* Venezia, 1510.

Blok, Anton. *The Mafia of a Sicilian Village, 1860–1960: A Study of Violent*

Peasant Entrepreneurs. Oxford: Basil Blackwell, 1974.

Blumer, Giovanni. *L'emigrazione italiana in Europa*. Milano: Feltrinelli, 1970.

Bovenkerk, Frank. *The Sociology of Return Migration: A Bibliographic Essay*. The Hague: Nijhoff, 1974.

Boxer, C. R. *The Dutch Seaborne Empire, 1600–1800*. London: Hutchinson, 1965.

————. *The Portuguese Seaborne Empire*. London: Hutchinson, 1969.

Boyd, Catherine E. *Tithes and Parishes in Medieval Italy: The Historical Roots of a Modern Problem*. Ithaca, N.Y.: Cornell Univerity Press, 1952.

Briggs, John W. *An Italian Passage: Immigrants to Three American Cities, 1890–1930*. New Haven, Conn.: Yale University Press, 1978.

Brown, Francis J., and Joseph Slabey Roucek, eds. *One America: The History, Contributions, and Present Problems of Our Racial and National Minorities*. New York: Prentice-Hall, 1945.

Cafiero, Salvatore, and Guido de' Rossi. "Lo spopolamento della montagna meridionale." In *L'esodo rurale e lo spopolamento della montagna nella società contemporanea*, Commissione Nazionale Italiana UNESCO, pp. 79–92. Milan: Società Editrice Vita e Pensiero, 1966.

Cantalupo, D. Benedetto. *Stato economico-morale del contado del Molise*. Campobasso, 1834.

Capo, Enrico. "I problemi economici e socio-culturali delle zone di destinazione dell'esodo rurale." In *L'esodo rurale e lo spopolamento della montagna nella società contemporanea*, Commissione Nazionale Italiana UNESCO, pp. 121–131. Milan: Società Editrice Vita e Pensiero, 1966.

Carlomagno, Custode. *Agnone dalle origini ai nostri giorni*. Campobasso, 1965.

Carosella, M. "Tribuna aperta." *Il Carroccio del Poverello* 1, no. 1(1973):10.

"Catasto vecchio di Agnone," n.d., but earliest entry is from the year 1815. Uffizio Distrettuale delle Imposte Dirette di Agnone.

Cavalli, L. *Gli immigrati meridionale e la società ligure*. Milan: Angeli, 1964.

Censimento degli italiani all'estero 31 dic. 1871: Statistica generale del regno d'Italia. Rome, 1874.

"Censimento di Agnone," 1971. Archivio Comunale di Agnone.

Cervone, Michele. "In memoria di Giovanni Tirone: discorso funebre." Naples, 1887.

Chaunu, Pierre, *Conquête et exploitation des nouveaux mondes (XVIe siècle)*. Paris: Presses Universitaires de France, 1969.

Ciani, Odoardo. *La città di Agnone e la sua cronistoria*. Agnone, 1888.

Ciarlanti, G. Vincenzo. *Memorie historiche del Sannio*. Isernia, 1644.

"Città di 'Agnone,' i demani comunali: Il loro stato e la loro sistemazione. Relazione sugli atti all'ill^{mo} Signor R. Commissario Regionale per la liquidazione degli usi civici in Napoli, 1926. Fondo Demani Comunali, protocollo 5. Archivio di Stato di Campobasso.

References

La città di Agnone: Stazione climatica estiva. Forlì: Società Editrice Annuari Guide Regionali Italiane, 1928.

Il cittadino agnonese. Newspaper published in Agnone. Biblioteca La Banca.

Il Comitato della Provincia. *La provincia di Molise nelle nuove circoscrizioni amministrative*. Campobasso, 1867.

Commissione Nazionale Italiana UNESCO. *L'esodo rurale e lo spopolamento della montagna nella società contemporanea*. Milan: Società Editrice Vita e Pensiero, 1966.

Compagna, Francesco. *I terroni in città*. Bari: Laterza, 1959.

"Comune di Agnone, censimento-notizie statistiche, 1838." Fondo Intendenza del Molise, protocolo 1012, fascio 137. Archivio di Stato di Campobasso.

Comune di Agnone. "Elenco delle famiglie e delle persone censite il 10 febbraio, 1901." Archivio Comunale di Agnone.

Contradeduzioni del consiglio comunale di Agnone alla relazione Scapinelli. Agnone, 1914.

Crane, Julia G. *Educated to Emigrate: The Social Organization of Saba*. Assen: Gorcum, 1971.

Cremonese, Domenico. *Congetture sulla tavola osca di Agnone*. Agnone, 1875.

Crichton, Ruth M. *Commuters' Village: A Study of Community and Commuters in a Berkshire Village of Stratfield Mortimer*. Dawlish: David and Charles, 1964.

Cronin, Constance. *The Sting of Change: Sicilians in Sicily and Australia*. Chicago: University of Chicago Press, 1970.

Crosby, Alfred W., Jr. *The Columbian Exchange: Biosocial and Cultural Consequences of 1492*. Westport, Conn.: Greenwood, 1972.

Dandolo, V. "Discorso su i danni della soverchia divisione de' fondi." *Giornale economico rustico del Sannio* 2(1820):58–65.

Davis, John. "Town and Country." *Anthropological Quarterly* 42(1969): 171–185.

————. *Land and Family in Pisticci*. London School of Economics Monographs on Social Anthropology, no. 48. London: Athlone, 1973.

de Ciocchis, Remo Nicola. *Agnone: La cittadina e il suo agro*. Rome, 1966.

del Re, Giuseppe. *Descrizione generale della provincia del Molise* [1836]. Edited by Pasquale Albino. Campobasso, 1876.

de Luca, Mario. "Le conseguenze economiche sui luoghi di provenienza." In *L'esodo rurale e lo spopolamento della montagna nella società contemporanea*, Commissione Nazionale Italiana UNESCO, pp. 70–78. Milan: Società Editrice Vita e Pensiero, 1966.

de Luca, Nicola. *Condizioni economiche ed industriali della provincia di Molise nel 1844*. Campobasso, 1845.

de Viti de Marco, Antonio. "Gli effetti del protezionismo." In *Il sud nella storia d'Italia*, vol. 1, ed. Rosario Villari, pp. 199–206. Bari: Laterza, 1971.

References

Díaz-Trechuelo Spínola, María Lourdes. *La real compañía de filipinas*. Seville: Escuela de Estudios Hispano-Americanos de Sevilla, 1965.

di Ciero, Michele. *Sc-terlambe che se pèrde: Poesie in dialetto molisano*. Pompei, 1972.

Diena, L. *Borgata milanese*. Milan: Angeli, 1963.

di Pasquo, A. *Natale di Roma*. Agnone, 1926.

"Di stato d'introito ed esito del monastero di S. Chiara di Agnone," n.d. Biblioteca Emidiana.

"Documentazioni." "Recenti immigrati a Torino: Un indagine sui terremotati." *Studi emigrazione* 6, no. 15(1969):204–218.

Douglass, William A. "Peasant Emigrants: Reactors or Actors?" In *Migration and Anthropology*, Proceedings of the Annual Spring Meeting of the American Ethnological Society, ed. Leonard Kasden, pp. 21–35. Seattle: University of Washington Press, 1970.

————. *Echalar and Murelaga: Opportunity and Rural Exodus in Two Spanish Basque Villages*. London: Hurst, 1975.

————. "The South Italian Family: A Critique." *Journal of Family History* 5(1980):338–359.

————. "Migration in Italy." In *Urban Life in Mediterranean Europe: Anthropological Perspectives*, ed. Michael Kenny and David Kertzer, pp. 162–202. Urbana, Ill.: University of Illinois Press, 1983.

d'Ovidio, Francesco. *Nel primo centenario della provincia di Molise*. Campobasso, 1911.

————. *Rimpianti vecchi e nuovi*. Caserta, 1930.

Eco del Sannio. Newspaper published in Agnone. Biblioteca La Banca.

Enciclopedia italiana, vol. 21. Rome, 1934.

Erickson, Charlotte. "Introduction." In *Emigration from Europe, 1815–1914: Select Documents*, ed. Charlotte Erickson. London: Black, 1976.

"Esercizio 1827, ruolo per transazione pel dazio pel macinato descritto nell'art° dello stato." Fondo Intendenza del Molise, protocolo 199, fascio 7. Archivio di Stato di Campobasso.

Finley, M. I. "Anthropology and the Classics." In *The Use and Abuse of History*, ed. M. I. Finley, pp. 102–119. London: Chatto and Windus, 1975.

Florenzano, Giovanni. *Della emigrazione italiana in America comparata alle altre emigrazioni europee*. Naples, 1874.

Foerster, Robert F. *The Italian Emigration of Our Times*. Cambridge: Harvard University Press, 1924.

Fofi, G. *Immigrazione e industria*. Milan: Comunità, 1962.

————. *Immigrazione meridionale a Torino*. Milan: Feltrinelli, 1964.

————. "Immigrants to Turin." In *Readings in the Sociology of Migration*, ed. Clifford J. Jansen, pp. 269–284. Oxford: Pergamon, 1970.

Foglio periodico della prefattura di Campobasso 1(Campobasso, 1886).

Fortunato, Giustino. "Il problema demaniale." In *Il sud nella storia d'Italia*, vol. 1, ed. Rosario Villari, pp. 161–170. Bari: Laterza, 1971.

———. "L'emigrazione e le classi dirigenti." In *Il sud nella storia d'Italia*, vol. 1, ed. Rosario Villari, pp. 171–179. Bari: Laterza, 1971.

Foschini, Donato, and Gaetano Foschini. *Memoria in difesa di Costantino La Banca contro comune di Agnone*. Naples, 1894.

Franchetti, Leopoldo. *Condizione economiche ed amministrative delle provincie napoletane, Abruzzi e Molise—Calabria e Basilicata*. Firenze, 1875.

Franklin, S. H. *The European Peasantry: The Final Phase*. London: Methuen, 1969.

Friedmann, F. G. "The World of *La Miseria*." *Community Development Review* 7(1962):91–100.

La fucina. Newspaper published in Agnone. Biblioteca La Banca.

Galanti, Giuseppe M^a. *Descrizione del contado del Molise*, vol. 1. Naples, 1781.

———. *Della descrizione geografica e politica delle Sicilie*, vols. 1–2. Naples: Edizione Scientifiche Italiane, 1969. (First published in 1793–1794.)

Gamberale, Luigi. *Notizie sui fatti di Agnone nel 1799*. Campobasso, 1900.

———. *Interessi agnonesi: Conferenza letta nella sala del consiglio comunale il 9 marzo, 1902*. Agnone, 1902.

———. *Il mio libro paesano: Ricordi di maestri e scuole agnonesi*. Agnone, 1915.

Gans, Herbert J. *The Urban Villagers: Group and Class in the Life of Italian-Americans*. New York: Free Press, 1962.

Gasparini, Innocenzo. "Tratti socio-economici dell'emigrazione dalla montagna e dalla collina del Veneto." In *L'esodo rurale e lo spopolamento della montagna nella società contemporanea*, Commissione Nazionale Italiana UNESCO, pp. 150–176. Milan: Società Editrice Vita e Pensiero, 1966.

Gàzzera, Enzo, and Lucio Selvaggi. *Integrazione agricola e industriale nel Molise*. Campobasso: Camera di Commercio, Industria e Agricoltura di Campobasso, 1953.

Genovesi, Antonio. "Il problema della terra." In *Il sud nella storia d'Italia*, vol. 1, ed. Rosario Villari, pp. 3–11. Bari: Laterza, 1971.

Ghigi, Alessandro. "Migratorie, correnti." *Enciclopedia italiana*, 23(1934): 249–261.

Il giornale d'intendenza della provincia di Molise, anno 1838. Campobasso.

Giustiniani, Lorenzo. *Dizionario geografico ragionato del regno di Napoli*, vol. 1. Naples, 1797.

Golini, Antonio. "Le tendenze recenti nelle migrazioni interne." *Studi emigrazione* 15, 51(1978):401–403.

Goody, Jack; Joan Thirsk; and E. P. Thompson, eds. *Family and Inheritance:*

References

Rural Society in Western Europe, 1200–1800. Cambridge: Cambridge University Press, 1976.

Il grido del Popolo. Newspaper published in Agnone. Biblioteca La Banca.

Un Gruppo di Agnonesi. "Ai nostri sfruttatori: Voce d'oltre oceano," Philadelphia, 1907. Biblioteca La Banca.

Halpern, Joel M., and Barbara Kerewsky Halpern. *A Serbian Village in Historical Perspective*. Case Studies in Cultural Anthropology. New York: Holt, Rinehart and Winston, 1972.

Handlin, Oscar. *The Uprooted*. Boston: Little, Brown, 1951.

Hansen, Marcus Lee. *The Atlantic Migration, 1607–1860*. New York: Harper and Row, Torchbooks, 1961.

Hobsbawn, E. J. *Industry and Empire*. The Pelican History of Britain. Bungay, Suffolk: Penguin, Pelican, 1969.

Horwitz, Richard P. *Anthropology toward History: Culture and Work in a Nineteenth Century Maine Town*. Middletown, Conn.: Wesleyan University Press, 1978.

Huber, Rina. *From Pasta to Pavlova: A Comparative Study of Italian Settlers in Sydney and Griffith*. St. Lucia: University of Queensland Press, 1977.

Hussey, Roland Dennis. *The Caracas Company, 1728–1789: A Study in the History of Spanish Monopolistic Trade*. Cambridge: Harvard University Press, 1934.

In memoria del VI centenario di Maria Santissimo del Carmelo celebrato in Agnone. Castel di Sangro, 1898.

"Inter universitatem civitatis anglonis et I⁸1em Pnpēm Stⁱ Boni," vol. 1, n.d. Biblioteca Emidiana.

ISTAT, Istituto Centrale di Statistica. *Catasto agrario, 1929*. Vol. 8, *Compartimento degli Abruzzi e Molise, provincia di Campobasso*, fascicolo 63. Rome, 1935.

———. *Annuario statistico dei comuni italiani*. Rome, 1958.

———. *Popolazione residente e presente dei comuni ai censimenti dal 1861 al 1961*. Rome, 1967.

———. *Sommario di statistiche storiche dell'Italia, 1861–1965*. Rome, 1968.

———. *Primi risultati provinciali e comunali sulla popolazione e sulle abitazioni, dati provvisori*. Vol. 1, *11° censimento generale della popolazione*. Rome, 1972.

———. *Secondo censimento generale dell'agricoltura*. Vol. 2, *Dati sulle caratteristiche strutturali delle aziende, provincia di Isernia*, fascicolo 66. Rome, 1972.

———. *Popolazione e movimento anagrafico dei comuni*, vol. 24. Rome, 1980.

Jacapraro, Onorato. *L'amministrazione comunale di Agnone e il partito dell'opposizione ovvero poche parole di risposta all'opuscolo pubblicato dal Sig*.

References

Ruggiero Apollonio. Agnone, 1878.

Jamison, Evelyn. "The Administration of the County of the Molise in the Twelfth and Thirteenth Centuries, Part 2." *English Historical Review* 55 (1930):1–34.

Jannone, Eugenio. "L'emigrazione nel Molise." *Molise* 1, no. 1(1923):16–17.

Jarach, Cesare. *Inchiesta parlamentare sulle condizione dei contadini nelle provincie meridionali e nella Sicilia*. Vol. 2, *Abruzzi e Molise*. Rome, 1909.

Jefferson, Mark, *Peopling the Argentine Pampa*. New York: American Geographical Society, 1926.

Jones, Maldwyn Allen. *American Immigration*. Chicago: University of Chicago Press, 1960.

Josa, Guglielmo. "L'emigrazione nel Molise." Extract from *Bollettino dell'emigrazione* 10(1907), 22 pages.

————. "Il caseificio nomade nell'Italia meridionale." Extract from *L'industria lattiera e zootecnica*, no vol., n.d.

Klein, Julius. *The Mesta: A Study in Spanish Economic History, 1273–1836*. Cambridge: Harvard University Press, 1920.

La Banca, Baldassare. *Il mio testamento: Raccolta di pensieri pratici*. Agnone, 1913.

————. *Ricordi autobiografici*. Agnone, 1913.

Ladurie, Emmanuel le Roy. *The Peasants of Languedoc*. Urbana: University of Illinois Press, 1974.

————. *Montaillou: Village occitan de 1294 à 1324*. Paris: Gallimard, 1975.

La Gamba, Filippo. *Statuti e capitoli della terra di Agnone*. Naples, 1972.

Laslett, Peter, and Richard Wall, eds. *Household and Family in Past Time*. Cambridge: Cambridge University Press, 1972.

Lauriente, Camille. *The Chronicles of Camille*. New York: Pageant, 1953.

Lewis, I. M. "Introduction." In *History and Social Anthropology*, ASA Monographs, no. 7, ed. I. M. Lewis, pp. ix–xxviii. London: Tavistock, 1968.

"Lib. I. S. Visita 1615–1675: visitationis totius dioc. annibis." Curia Vescovile di Trivento.

"Libro de' conti del pbte monastero di Santa Chiara di questa città di Agnone, diocesi di Trivento, in dove si registrano gl'introiti ed esiti, regolati giusta lo stato discusso, e real decreto del di ventisette del mese di decembre dell'anno 1815. Biblioteca Emidiana.

"Libro dei passaporti, comune di Agnone," 1903–1945. Archivio Comunale di Agnone.

Liguori, Maria. "Fenomeni migratori e sociologia: La letteratura sociologica sulle migrazioni interne nel triangolo industriale (1958–1968)." *Rassegna italiana di sociologia* 20, no. 1(1979):109–146.

"Lista degli eligibili del comune di Agnone redatta a seconda del circolare del

Sig^e Intend^{te} della provincia, anno 1821. Fondo Intendenza del Molise, protocolo 195, fascio 1. Archivio di Stato di Campobasso.

Livolsi, Mariano. "Integrazione dell'immigrato e integrazione comunitaria." *Studi emigrazione* 5(1966):124–151.

Longano, Abate. *Viaggio dell'abate Longano per lo contado del Molise*. Naples, 1788.

Lopreato, Joseph. "How Would You Like to Be a Peasant?" *Human Organization* 24(1965):298–307.

———. *Peasants No More: Social Class and Social Change in an Underdeveloped Society*. San Francisco: Chandler, 1967.

———. *Perchè emigrano i contadini*. Extract from *Quaderni calabresi* 4(1968), 23 pages.

Lopreato, Joseph, and Janet E. Saltzman. "Descriptive Models of Peasant Society: A Reconciliation from Southern Italy." *Human Organization* 27 (1968):132–141.

La lotta. Newspaper published in Agnone. Biblioteca La Banca.

Lowenthal, David, and Lambros Comitas. "Emigration and Depopulation: Some Neglected Aspects of Population Geography." *Geographical Review* 52 (1962):195–210.

MacDonald, John S. "Italy's Rural Social Structure and Emigration." *Occidente* 12, no. 5(1956):437–456.

———. "Some Socio-economic Emigration Differentials in Rural Italy, 1902–1913." *Economic Development and Cultural Change* 7, no. 1(1958):55–72.

———. "Agricultural Organization, Migration and Labour Militancy in Rural Italy." *Economic History Review*, 2d ser. 16(1963):61–75.

MacDonald, John S., and Leatrice D. MacDonald. "Chain Migration, Ethnic Neighborhood Formation and Social Networks." *Milbank Memorial Fund Quarterly* 13, no. 42(1964):82–95.

Macfarlane, Alan. *The Family Life of Ralph Josselin, an Eighteenth Century Clergyman: An Essay in Historical Anthropology*. Cambridge: Cambridge University Press, 1970.

Macfarlane, Alan; Sarah Harrison; and Charles Jardine. *Reconstructing Historical Communities*. Cambridge: Cambridge University Press, 1977.

Majorino, Giorgio. "Il tempo libero e gli immigrati: I rapporti tra i vari gruppi." In *L'immigrazione nel triangolo industriale*, ed. Giovanni Pellicciari, pp. 304–323. Milan: Angeli, 1970.

Malfatti, Eugenia. "Le migrazioni meridionali alla luce delle fonti statistiche ufficiali (1951–1975)." *Studi emigrazione* 13, no. 42(1976):148–158.

Mancinelli, Ascanio. *Floridum opusculum hic inde a tot pomariis a recollectum de morsu canis rabidi ejusque curatione*. Venetiis, 1587.

Manucci, C. "Emigrants in the Upper Milanese Area." In *Readings in the Sociology of Migration*, ed. Clifford J. Jansen, pp. 257–267. Oxford: Pergamon, 1970.

Marinelli, Ascenso. *Il buon esempio nel proprio paese*. Naples, 1882.

———. *Alcune biografie di uomini illustri agnonesi*. Naples, 1886.

———. *Memorie patrie con alcune biografie di uomini illustri agnonesi*. Agnone, 1888.

———. *I miei racconti*. Agnone, 1890.

———. *La mia relazione dopo essere messo a riposo*. Agnone, 1898.

Marinelli, Nicola. *La Chiesa e l'ex-convento di Maiella in Agnone*. Agnone, 1923.

———. *Agnone e la conciliazione fra la S. Sede e Italia*. Agnone, 1929.

Marinelli, Nicolino. *Luigi Gamberale (1840–1929)*. Agnone, 1956.

Marracino, Scipione. *Per il signor Costantino La Banca contro l'amministrazione comunale di Agnone*. Isernia, 1893.

Masciotta, Giambattista. *Il Molise dalle origini ai nostri giorni*, vol. 1, Naples, 1914; vol. 3, Cava de' Tirreni, 1952.

"Memoria senza autore e senza titolo riguardante il principe di Santo Buono ed il duca di Castel di Sangro," n.d. Archivio della Società Napoletana di Storia Patria.

Migus, Paul M., ed. *Sounds Canadian: Languages and Cultures in a Multiethnic Society*. Toronto: Martin, 1975.

Il Molise altissimo e i suoi problemi. Edizioni dell'Associazione del Comuni Molisani, no. 2. Rome, n.d.

Moretti, Giancarlo. *"Nord-sud: Squilibri che tendono a persistere." In L'immigrazione nel triangolo industriale*, ed. Giovanni Pellicciari, pp. 49–184. Milan: Angeli, 1970.

Morpurgo, Enrico. "Un orologiaio italiano a Neuchâtel: Pasquale Mario." *La clessidra* (1954).

Moss, Leonard W., and Stephan C. Cappannari. "Estate and Class in a South Italian Hill Village." *American Anthropologist* 64(1962):287–300.

Nelli, Humbert S. *Italians in Chicago, 1880–1930: A Study in Ethnic Mobility*. New York: Oxford University Press, 1970.

Il nuovo risveglio. Newspaper published in Agnone. Biblioteca La Banca.

"Onciario dell'università della città di Agnone," 1753. Biblioteca La Banca.

Operazione terra, no. 2. Special issue of *Nuova frontiera*. Agnone, 1971.

Orlandi, Cesare. *Delle città d'Italia e sue isole adjacenti*, vol. 1. Perugia, 1770.

Panettieri, José. *Inmigración en la Argentina*. Buenos Aires: Macchi, 1970.

Pannunzio, Salvatore. *Le nostre miserie! Cause e rimedi*. Agnone, 1909.

———. *Discorso pronunziato il 18 marzo 1945 nella grande manifestazione pro partigiani*. Agnone, 1945.

Parry, J. H. *The Spanish Seaborne Empire*. London: Hutchinson, 1966.

Pellicciari, Giovanni, ed. *L'immigrazione nel triangolo industriale*. Milan: Angeli, 1970.

Per la congrega di carità di Agnone contro 1° Paolo ed altri Sabelli 2° e Maria Paradiso. Naples, 1891.

"Per la moralità," October 12, 1923. Handbill. Archivio Comunale di Agnone.

"Per li fratelli di Nicola, e D. Aloisio Fioriti della città di Agnone contro l'università della città sudetta," Naples, August 20, 1791. Biblioteca Emidiana.

Philpott, Stuart B. *West Indian Migration: The Montserrat Case*. London: Athlone, 1973.

Piazza del tomolo. Newspaper published in Agnone. Biblioteca La Banca.

Pike, Ruth. *Enterprise and Adventure: The Genoese in Seville and the Opening of the New World*. Ithaca, N.Y.: Cornell University Press, 1966.

Podbielski, Giselle. *Italy: Development and Crisis in the Post-war Economy*. Oxford: Clarendon, 1974.

Popolazione presente ed assente per comuni, centri e frazioni di comune: Statistica generale del regno d'Italia, vol. 1. Rome, 1874.

Price, Charles A. *Southern Europeans in Australia*. Melbourne: Oxford University Press, 1963.

———. *Australian Immigration Research Report No. 2: National Population Inquiry*. Canberra, 1975.

"Processo relativo alla cospirazione ed attentata avenuti per oggetti di distruggere e cambiare il governo, da 7 a 14 ottobre 1860." Fondo Brigantaggio Processi, protocollo 90. Archivio di Stato di Campobasso.

"Provincia di Molise anno 1813: Mappa IV, contenente i nati legittimi, ed illegittimi, i nuovi domiciliati, i morti, e gli emigrati." Fondo Ministero dell'Interno, inventario no. 1, fascio 2282. Archivio di Stato di Napoli.

"Provincia di Molise anno 1814: Statistica-popolazione, mappe I, III." Fondo Ministero dell'Interno, inventario no. 1, fascio 2282. Archivio di Stato di Napoli.

"Provincia di Molise, distretto d'Isernia: Supplemento alla statistica elementare, 1816." Fondo Intendenza del Molise, protocolo 1011, fascio 136. Archivio di Stato di Campobasso.

"Provincia di Molise, statistica-popolazione anno 1845." Fondo Ministero dell'Interno, inventario no. 1, fascio 2282. Archivio di Stato di Napoli.

"Ragioni per il regio fisco coll'ill: Principe di S. Buono intorno alla devoluzione della terra d'Agnone," n.d. Biblioteca della Società Napoletana di Storia Patria.

"Ragioni per l'università della città d'Agnone con li magnifici fratelli Fioriti," Naples, February 28, 1743. Biblioteca Provinciale di Campobasso.

Ramsey, John F. *Spain: The Rise of the First World Power*. University: University of Alabama Press, 1973.

"Reclamo operai Agnone avverso il ruolo tassa artigianati," March 2, 1929.

Archivio Comunale di Agnone.

La Redazione. "Le migrazioni interne italiane oggi." *Studi emigrazione* 6, no. 16(1969):225–272.

Relazione sui danni nel bosco Poste. Agnone, 1892.

Reyneri, Emilio, et al. *L'emigrazione meridionale nelle zone d'esodo*. Vol. 3, *Sintesi e conclusioni operative*. Catania: Facoltà di Scienze Politiche dell' Università di Catania, 1976.

Richmond, Anthony H. *Post-war Immigrants in Canada*. Toronto: University of Toronto Press, 1967.

Il rinnovamento. Newspaper published in Agnone. Biblioteca La Banca.

Il risveglio. Newspaper published in Agnone. Biblioteca La Banca.

Il risveglio sannitico. Newspaper published in Agnone. Biblioteca La Banca.

Romano, Ruggiero. *Prezzi, salari e servizi a Napoli nel secolo XVIII (1734–1806)*. Milan, 1965.

Rosen, Lawrence. "Language, History and the Logic of Inquiry in Lévi-Strauss and Sartre." *History and Theory* 10(1971):269–294.

Rosoli, Gianfausto. "L'emigrazione di ritorno: Alla ricerca di una impostazione." *Studi emigrazione* 14, no. 47(1977):235–244.

Rosoli, Gianfausto, and Oreste Grossi. *L'altra Italia: Storia fotografica della grande emigrazione italiana nelle Americhe (1880–1915)*. Rome: Centro Studi Emigrazione, n.d.

Sacchetti, G. B. "Regioni e migrazioni." *Studi emigrazione* 14, no. 47(1977): 235–244.

Sacco, Francesco. *Dizionario geografico-istorico-fisico del regno di Napoli*. Naples, 1795.

Salmon, E. T. *Samnium and the Samnites*. Cambridge: Cambridge University Press, 1967.

La Sannitica Banca Popolare Cooperativa di Agnone. *Assemblea generale ordinaria dei soci*. Agnone, 1902.

———. *Assemblea generale ordinaria dei soci*. Agnone, 1911.

———. *Assemblea generale ordinaria dei soci*. Castel di Sangro, 1919.

———. *Assemblea generale ordinaria dei soci*. Agnone, 1925.

Savastano, Guiseppantonio. *La forza educativa pensieri pratici*. Agnone, 1888.

Scobie, James R. *Argentina: A City and a Nation*. New York: Oxford University Press, 1964.

Serafini, Alessandro. *Sul colera del 1837 in Agnone*. Naples, 1896.

Silverman, Sydel. *Three Bells of Civilization: The Life of an Italian Hill Town*. New York: Columbia University Press, 1975.

Simoncelli, Ricciarda. *Il Molise: Le condizioni geografiche di una economia regionale*. Rome, 1969.

Il sindaco e il consiglio comunale di Agnone nei giorni 4 e 17 novembre 1867. Naples, 1868.

Sjoberg, Gideon. *The Preindustrial City: Past and Present*. New York: Free Press, 1960.

Solberg, Carl. *Immigration and Nationalism: Argentina and Chile, 1890–1914*. Austin: University of Texas Press, 1970.

Sonnino, Sidney. "La crisi agraria." In *Il sud nella storia d'Italia*, vol. 1, ed. Rosario Villari, pp. 183–198. Bari: Laterza, 1971.

"Specchio della istruzione della provincia di Molise, che si ha dalle scuole primarie, secondarie, private, dai seminarii, e dal Collegio Sannitico." December 3, 1835. Fondo Ministero dell'Interno, inventario no. 2, fascio 4213. Archivio di Stato di Napoli.

"Squarciafoglie pecore, anno 1597–1598." Fondo Dogana delle Pecore, fascio 752. Archivio di Stato di Foggia.

"Statistica-popolazione, provincia di Molise, anno 1814." Mappa III. Fondo Ministero dell'Interno, inventario no. 1, fascio 2282. Archivio di Stato di Napoli.

"Statistica stato di popolazione, provincia di Molise, 1830." Fondo Ministero dell'Interno, inventario no. 1, fascio 2282. Archivio di Stato di Napoli.

"Stato conforme si ritrova l'università di Agnone prov^a di Apruzzo Citra iuxta la relat^e inviata sotto li 4 di giugno 1627." Biblioteca La Banca.

"Stato de' maestri e maestre primarie, maestri secondari e privati, n^o degli alunni, seminarii essistenti nella detta provincia," December 3, 1835. Fondo Ministero dell'Interno, inventario no. 2, fascio 4213. Archivio di Stato di Napoli.

"Stato delle anime della chiesa parrocchiale di S. Emidio di questa città di Agnone, riformato sotto la cura di me parroco Giuseppe Nicola Lemme nel 1841." Biblioteca Emidiana di Agnone.

"Stato delle condanne forestale compilato nell'anno 1863," Archivio Comunale di Agnone.

"Stato delle pecore del 1834." Fondo Intendenza del Molise, protocolo 200, fascio 8. Archivio di Stato di Campobasso.

"Stato di anime, 1882–1885, parrocchia di San Pietro." Archivio della Chiesa di San Pietro.

Summonte, Giovanni Antonio. *Historia della città e regno di Napoli*, vols. 1–2. Naples, 1675, 1693.

Tagliacarne, Gugliemo. "Spopolamento montano ed esodo rurale, misura e prospettive." In *L'esodo rurale e lo spopolamento della montagna nella società contemporanea*, Commissione Nazionale Italiana UNESCO, pp. 3–14. Milan: Società Editrice Vita e Pensiero, 1966.

Tilly, Charles. "Migration in Modern European History." In *Human Migration: Patterns and Policies*, ed. William H. McNeill and Ruth S. Adams, pp. 48–72. Bloomington: Indiana University Press, 1978.

Tirabasso, Angelo. *Breve dizionario biografico del Molise*. Oratino, 1932.

References

Tucker, Ninetta. *Italy*. London: Thames and Hudson, 1970.

Turisport. Newspaper published in Agnone. Biblioteca La Banca.

U.S. Department of Labor, Bureau of Immigration. *Annual Report of the Commissioner General of Immigration to the Secretary of Labor, Fiscal Year Ended June 30, 1922*. Washington, D.C., 1922.

————. *Annual Report of the Commissioner General of Immigration to the Secretary of Labor, Fiscal Year Ended June 30, 1925*. Washington, D.C., 1925.

Vásquez Presedo, Vicente. *Estadísticas históricas argentinas: Primera parte, 1875–1914*. Buenos Aires: Macchi, 1971.

Velez de Guevara, Indigo. *Nova situazione de pagamenti fiscali delli carlini 42 a foco delle provincie del regno di Napoli, et adohi de baroni, e feudatarii*. Naples, 1652.

Vicinelli, Paolo. "Esodo rurale e programmi di sviluppo del mezzogiorno italiano." In *L'esodo rurale e lo spopolamento della montagna nella società contemporanea*, Commissione Nazionale Italiana UNESCO, pp. 132–149. Milan: Società Editrice Vita e Pensiero, 1966.

Villani, Andrea. "Analisi delle conseguenze economiche e finanziarie delle migrazioni interne sulle zone di destinazione." In *L'esodo rurale e lo spopolamento della montagna nella società contemporanea*, Commissione Nazionale Italiana UNESCO, pp. 93–120. Milan: Società Editrice Vita e Pensiero, 1966.

Viti, Il conte. *Discorso sulla inaugurazione del monte de' pegni di Agnone*. Naples, 1854.

Wachter, Kenneth W.; Eugene A. Hammel; and Peter Laslett. *Statistical Studies of Historical Social Structure*. New York: Academic, 1978.

Wallerstein, Immanuel. *The Modern World System: Capitalist Agriculture and the Origins of the European World-Economy in the Sixteenth Century*. New York: Academic, 1974.

Weber, Eugene. *Peasants into Frenchmen: The Modernization of Rural France, 1870–1914*. Stanford, Calif.: Stanford University Press, 1976.

Williams, Glyndwr. *The Expansion of Europe in the Eighteenth Century: Overseas Rivalry, Discovery and Exploitation*. London: Blandford, 1966.

Willis, F. Roy. *Italy Chooses Europe*. New York: Oxford University Press, 1971.

Zarrilli, Giovanni. *Il Molise nel declino del regno borbonico*. Extract from *Samnium* 35, nos. 3–4(1962).

————. *Il Molise dal 1789 al 1860: Dagli albori del risorgimento all'Italia unita*. Campobasso, n.d.

————. *Il Molise dal 1860 al 1900*. Campobasso, n.d.

Index

Abbandonati (abandoned children), 106–107

Abruzzo (region), 9, 10

Address (formal speech), 13, 14, 21

Africa, 99, 169, 170, 189

Age: of Agnone residents, 211, 214; of Agnonese society, 24, 25; of emigrants, 102, 201

Agents (emigration), 116–120

Agnone: *baroni* and, 19, 34–35; brigands in, 89; civil accomplishments and, 45–47; as concept, 2; demographic analysis and, 67–71; disaffected social class in, 71–74; ecological zones of, 4–6; education and, 74–77; effects of emigration in, 3; feudalism and, 3, 31–34, 37–39; 47–48; the *galantuomini* and, 52–55, 65–67; geographical location of 1–2; intellectual portrait of, 77–79; landownership and, 38–39, 62–63; liberalism and, 55–58, 79–80; liberalism and social balance in, 59–65; litigation in, 35–36; political factionalism in, 21–23; population of, 9, 16, 23–24, 67–68; revolt of 1860 in, 88–89; riot of 1860 in, 87–88; Rome and, 29–31; seasonality and, 27; settlement pattern and, 6–9; situational factors and, 9–12; social hierarchy in,

12–21, 42–45. *See also* Alto Molise; Molise

Agricultural Society, 53, 54

Agriculture: Agnone's ecological setting and, 5–6; Barbieri (Mayor, 1817) and, 58; class conflict and, 145–149; drop in exports of, 90; family structure and, 6; fascism and, 169–170; feudal, 40–41, 43; liberals and, 53–55, 64; location and, 9; population increase and, 68–69; post-WWII failure of, 178–179; restriction on exports of, 159; seasonality and, 27

Air travel, 206, 207

Alcoholism, 72

Alfonso of Aragon, 33–34, 37

Alto Molise, 33, 96, 179, 201; brigandage problem and, 21; feudal isolation of, 43; highways in, 10; outmigration and, 9; tourism and, 183. *See also* Agnone; Molise

Amicarelli, Biaše, 58

Amicarelli, Donato, 64

Amicarelli, Ippolito, 76, 77, 138, 139

Amicarelli, Michele, 118

Amicarelli family, 111

Animal husbandry. *See* Livestock

Antonelli, Domenico, 150

Apollonio, Adolfo, 131